The Palestinian-Arab Minority in Israel, 1948–2000

A Political Study

As'ad Ghanem

State University of New York Press

Cover photo: PhotoDisc

Published by
STATE UNIVERSITY OF NEW YORK PRESS
ALBANY

© 2001 State University of New York

All rights reserved

Printed in the United States of America

For information address State University of New York Press,
90 State Street, Suite 700, Albany, NY 12246

Production by Judith Block
Marketing by Anne M. Valentine

Library of Congress Cataloging-in-Publication Data

Ganim, As'ad
The Palestinian-Arab minority in Israel, 1948–2000 : a political study / As'ad Ghanem.
p. cm — (SUNY series in Israeli studies)
Includes bibliographical references (p.) and index.
ISBN 0-7914-4997-1 (alk. paper) — ISBN 0-7914-4998-X (pbk. : alk. paper)
1. Palestinian Arabs—Israel—history. 2. Israel—Ethnic relations. I. Title. II. Series.

DS113.7.G38 2001
956.94'0049274—dc21
00-058826
Rev.

10 9 8 7 6 5 4 3 2 1

To Ahlam, Lina, and Hala

Contents

Tables

Preface

In this book, the fruit of long and diversified research, I have attempted to summarize my findings and impressions since I began studying Palestinian-Arab society in Israel some eight years ago. During this period I have focused on the aspects that interest me as a political scientist—namely, politics and its interaction with other sides of life—the social, economic, educational, religious, and so on.

This summary is not the outcome of work based exclusively on findings gathered using pure scientific tools. Indeed, the research findings are analyzed without denying a basic fact, which is that in all the past years, since I began to be involved in what is taking place in my own society, I have played a certain role in influencing political and social developments, whether as an independent actor or as part of the change processes implemented by voluntary organizations and public associations. Taking into account that the researcher's personal opinions inevitably influence his perspective on the situation and how he interprets it, I have endeavored to isolate my personal stance and offer readers a summary of the situation to the best of my understanding as a scholar.

The book consists of three parts. The first comprises the general introduction and chapter 1, which presents the historical background and surveys those factors that influenced the development of the Palestinian minority in Israel. The second part, begins with chapter 2, which presents the general framework of the second part of the book and presents a classification of the ideological and political currents among the Palestinian minority in Israel. Chapter 3 presents the Israeli-Arab stream within the Palestinian minority in Israel, including the major aspects on which I have chosen to focus: organization, positions, and profile. Chapter 4 through 6 deal in similar fashions with the Communists, the nationalist stream, and the Islamic stream respectively. Chapter 7 surveys the political scene on the local and municipal level.

In part 3 of the book, chapter 8 analyzes the political distress of Palestinian-Arab politics in Israel. Chapter 9, the last, expands on the

Arabs' distress in other realms and proposes a way out of it in the form of the inclusion of the Palestinians in Israel within a binational, Palestinian-Israeli solution that would include Israel, the West Bank, and the Gaza Strip. It offers an optimum solution to all the issues on the agenda of a conflict that has been going on since the late nineteenth century.

Most of the data was gathered from the archives of the Arabic-language newspaper *al Ittihad,* the information center of the Institute for Peace Research at Givat Haviva, and the Israeli Arab section of the Jewish-Arab Center at the University of Haifa. I would like to express my gratitude to those in charge of these places. I would also like to thank the many persons who gave of their precious time and allowed me to interview them. Their names appear in the relevant chapters of this book.

Many of my colleagues, in the academic world and outside it, have helped me in my research and influenced my conclusions. I would like to thank all of them. Deserving special mention and gratitude are Prof. Nadim Rouhana, Prof. Oren Yiftachel, Prof. Majid al-Haj, Prof. Sammy Smooha, Dr. Sarah Ozacky-Lazar, Dr. Ilan Saban, the late Mr. Saliba Khamais, Mr. Alouph Hareven, Dr. Elie Rekhess, Mr. Khaled Abu Asba, Mr. Elias Eady, and Mr. Taha Ashkar.

Over the years, many students helped me gather my data and classify it. I should like to thank all of them, especially Rami Abbas and Anwar Abu Alhijja, and my students at the University of Haifa who helped me clarify some of the issues presented in this book. I would also like to thank Mr. Lenn Schramm, who edited my draft.

I have no doubt that this book is part of an ongoing research project starting in the past, continuing in the present, and moving toward the future. Many have contributed and continue to contribute to our understanding of the fundamental issues concerning the situation of the Palestinians in Israel, especially in light of the fact that this section of the Middle East and Palestinian-Israeli conflict, the internal conflict in Israel between Jews and Palestinians, is not addressed within the context of the peace agreements between the PLO (Palestine Liberation Organization) and Israel. Hence sooner or later the situation of the Palestinians in Israel will rise as a key issue that the Palestinian national movement and Israel will have to deal with, each on its own and both of them together.

Part One

Introduction and Historical Background

INTRODUCTION

On the eve of the 1948 war and the establishment of the state of Israel, nearly two million persons lived within the borders of Mandatory Palestine, two-thirds of them Palestinian Arabs and one-third Jews. The vast majority of the Palestinians (almost 940,000) and almost all the Jews lived in the areas that became Israel. As a result of expulsions and mass flight, by the end of the war only about 150,000 Arabs—10 percent of all Palestinians—remained in the territory under Israeli control. The difficult situation of these Arabs was a direct result of the war and subsequent events. After the war they were distinguished from other Palestinians by the fact that they had stayed on their land and become citizens of Israel. In the intervening five decades, the Arab citizens of Israel have known many vagaries in their political, social, cultural, and economic development. In what follows I will enumerate some of the conspicuous hallmarks of the Arabs in Israel fifty years after they became a minority.

DEMOGRAPHY

There has been a significant demographic evolution and modifications in the physical structure of Arab towns and villages. At the end of 1998, there were about 900,000 Arabs living within the Green Line—roughly 17 percent of the total population. The demographic growth created large Arab settlements, some of them distinctly urbanized. Of the 112 locales in Israel with 5,000 residents or more, 41 are Arab; 15 of the latter have more than 10,000 residents. A continuous belt of Arab settlements has emerged in several strips; in some areas the Arabs constitute an overwhelming majority (Sakhnin, Wadi Ara, Majd al-Kurum). This is in addition to the Arabs who live in the mixed cities (CBS 1999).

1

The growth in the Arab population and the changes in the physical structure of the villages, including infrastructure development from the early 1970s on, have reinforced the Arabs' self-confidence and provided a basis for the emergence of cultural life, separate political organizations, and greater weight in joint Arab-Jewish organizations, as well as attempts to forge a separate Arab economy.

With regard to age structure, the Arabs of Israel are much younger than the Jews. Whereas about 46 percent of the Arabs are younger than seventeen, only 31 percent of the Jews fall into this category. Accordingly, even though Arabs constitute only about 16 percent of the Israeli population, they account for about 25 percent of the under-seventeen population. This age structure indicates a large potential for development if the state provides assistance to improve the level of education and physical development (CBS 1999).

GEOGRAPHIC DISTRIBUTION AND RELIGIOUS STRUCTURE

The Arabs of Israel are concentrated in three parts of the country. Most of them (about 60 percent) live in the Galilee, (a region that includes all of northern Israel from the Lebanese border down to a line drawn between Haifa and Beesan). About 20 percent live in the Triangle, (a region abutting the Green Line and running parallel to the coast between Haifa and Tel Aviv). Another 10 percent of the Arabs live in the southern region Al-Naqab. Finally, the remaining 10 percent live in the mixed cities of the coastal plain, such as Acre, Haifa, Leda, Ramle, and Yaffa (Ghanem 1992).

With regard to religious affiliation, the Arabs fall into three distinct groups: Muslims, who live in Arab communities all over the country, account for about 75 percent of them. Christians—almost all of them in the Galilee—account for about 14 percent. They are divided into many denominations: Catholic, Orthodox, Maronite, Protestant, and Armenian. The Druze, who live exclusively in the Galilee, account for the remaining 11 percent (Ghanem 1992).

MODERNIZATION

After the establishment of Israel, a process accompanied by the expulsion and mass flight of the Palestinian population, about 150,000 Palestinians remained in the country. This confused remnant of the Palestinian community was characterized by the absence of even a minimal level of organization, the predominance of traditional values and norms, and an economic, social, and cultural life typical of a traditional society at the very beginning of modernization, including an extremely low level of education.

Under the impact of contact with the Jews and the influence of population streams copied from western Europe and the United States, this group entered upon a process of modernization. This was manifested in a slow and hesitant change of sociocultural values, an increase in the importance of the nuclear family, a slow change in the status of women, a steady drop in the fertility rate, an improvement in housing conditions and medical services, the development of municipal government and establishment of political and social organizations, and, especially, a consistent rise in the average educational level of Arabs in Israel, including a consistent upward trend in the number of those with a university education (Ghanem 1996).

The number and level of educated Arabs grew apace. In 1961, about 49 percent had had no schooling whatsoever, and only one percent had a postsecondary education. By 1996, the percentage of those with no formal schooling had plummeted to 8.3 percent, and that of those who had studied in a postsecondary institution had risen to about 7 percent. This reflects the improvement in the level of education, an increased awareness of the importance of advanced studies, and a greater willingness to invest in one's children and provide them with a higher level of education, where and when possible.

ECONOMIC SITUATION AND STANDARD OF LIVING

There has also been slow economic progress in the Arab community. It had lost its agricultural basis as the result of a series of expropriations of land that was turned over to the Jewish sector. In parallel, the state did not encourage and did not initiate the development of an industrial base in the Arab sector. As a result, many Arab laborers commute daily to work in the Jewish cities. Surveys conducted of economic development in recent years show that although there has been some progress here, the large gap between the two sectors continues to expand. The economic problem is fed by the absence of an internal agricultural or industrial base and the consequent absolute dependence on the Jewish sector (Rouhana and Ghanem 1998).

The Arabs' standard of living has risen consistently over the years, but the gap between the Arab and Jewish sectors remains large and has not contracted. Average Arab family income in 1980 was 77 percent that of a Jewish family. In 1985 the figure had dropped to about 70 percent; by 1993 it had risen again slightly, to 72 percent. The percentage of Arab families living beneath the poverty line in 1993 was 2.26

times that of Jewish families. The fact that Arab families were more than twice as large as Jewish families, on average, exacerbates this disparity.

These characteristics of the Arab population of Israel, as well as others not mentioned above, constitute the basic infrastructure for a presentation of the "normal development approach," which is the theoretical and empirical model most often employed to describe the Arabs' condition and development. After that I will consider the alternate model on which this book is based.

STUDIES OF THE POLITICAL DEVELOPMENT OF THE ARABS IN ISRAEL

In recent years, scholars interested in multiethnic societies have turned their attention to political development in such countries. Some of their studies have focused on clarifying the political and social questions that influence the political evolution of these countries in general and of its various constituent groups. Israel is deeply riven by the existence of ethnic, religious, and national groups that compete for control of the various systems that make up the state. Scholars tend to present a division based on ethnic-national affiliation—Palestinian Arabs versus Jews; to further subdivide the Jews into ethnic communities—Ashkenazim versus Sephardim; and to add several other classifications of greater or lesser importance.

Here I will focus on trying to understand the political evolution of the Palestinians who became Israeli citizens in 1948 when the state was established. Recent years have seen a significant increase in the number of scholars and studies dealing with the political development of the Arabs in Israel (see Yiftachel 1993b). The research problem is rooted in the attempt to come up with an original but acceptable way to understand the political development of the Palestinian-Arab minority. Studies of the Arabs in Israel present a number of alternate models and approaches for understanding their status and political development. In principle, these can all be arranged under two headings: the normal development model and the distress model.

THE NORMAL DEVELOPMENT MODEL

According to the normal development model, as the Arabs endeavored to adopt the living standard and norms of the majority, they went through significant changes in the social, cultural, economic, and political arenas, which have been documented in dozens of original and secondary studies (for a review of the literature, see Smooha 1984; Smooha and Cibulski 1987; Yiftachel 1993b). For all the significant variation among scholars when it comes to disciplines and research specialties, reliance on general theories, and presentation of models, the literature about the Arabs in Israel tends to describe their development as being similar to that of minorities in Western democracies (Ghanem 1996a; 1996b; Rouhana and Ghanem 1998). It asserts that the following are the typical lines of the Arabs' development:

1. The Arabs of Israel went through a process of becoming aware of their status as a minority that wishes to perpetuate that status and does not aspire for self-determination or for secession and annexation by another country. This means that the future political orientation of the Arabs in Israel is fairly clear and includes recognition of what exists and the aspiration to improve it within the Israeli context (see, for example, Smooha 1989a; 1992; Rekhess 1993).

2. Since 1948, the Arab minority has gone through the process of clarifying the various strands within its identity, and notably parallel processes of Palestinization and Israelization. In the Palestinian dimension, it has arrived at a clear definition of itself as part of the Palestinian people while recognizing its unique status within the Palestinian national movement because it is also Israeli and part of the Israeli milieu (see, for example, Smooha 1989a; 1992; Rekhess 1993; Landau 1993). This identity expresses and serves the dual affiliation of the Arabs in Israel.

3. The Arab minority in Israel is experiencing an accelerated process of modernization, chiefly as a result of its special link with Israeli society. This process encompasses every segment and stratum of Arab society in Israel. It is manifested, inter alia, in the adoption of Western norms, values, and lifestyles, under the influence of Israeli society. These are "progressive" values, as compared to those held by the Arabs in Israel in the past. They are very different from the values of Arab societies elsewhere in the Arab world (see, for example, Smooha 1989a; 1992; Rekhess 1993; Landau 1993). Ultimately this process will modernize the Arabs in Israel and help them integrate into the Israeli context.

4. The Arabs in Israel have experienced advanced processes of political organization that involved the rapid but controlled emergence of political pluralism, as parliamentary and extraparliamentary parties and movements arose and consolidated their positions since the early 1970s. In addition to the Communist Party, which was the central and just about the only political force and dominated the Arab scheme for many years, the Sons of the Village,

the Islamic Movement, the Progressive Movement, and the Democratic Arab Party have all been established since the early 1970s. Many other lesser known and for the most part local organizations have sprung up. At the same time, the Jewish-Zionist parties moved from reliance on satellite lists to accepting Arab members on an equal footing with Jews, at least formally. In general, the various parties and movements offer the Arabs different hues of ideology and political thinking, reflected in their platforms. These incorporate various answers and solutions for extricating the Arabs from their problems—internally or externally (see, for example, Reiter and Aharoni 1992). This development has permitted adequate representation for all the political, social, and ideological streams among the Arabs of Israel.

5. During the 1970s and 1980s, the Arabs in Israel established representative bodies that bring together all the political streams in the Arab sector. Various committees were set up during the 1970s, including the Committee of Heads of Arab Local Authorities (1974) and the Land Defense Committee (1975). The Supreme Monitoring Committee for Israeli Arab Affairs was set up in the 1980s, along with subcommittees for education, health care, sports, and welfare. These bodies garnered recognition as representative organizations. The Monitoring Committee even functioned as a collective leadership of the Arab minority and was recognized as such by the Arabs, by the Israeli government, and by the Palestinian leadership in the West Bank and Gaza Strip and the Diaspora (see, for example, Rouhana 1989; Al-Haj 1988b). This development testifies to internal consolidation as the result of a process of normal development.

6. As part of their development, the Arabs in Israel built up institutions of local government and grappled effectively with the local problems of Arab communities. These institutions also waged successful campaigns against the central government to obtain adequate levels of funding (see, for example, Al-Haj and Rosenfeld 1990a).

7. Because of its contact with Jewish-sector institutions, the Arab minority in Israel is developing as a political, democratic, and pluralistic community, with multiple political parties and movements and social streams. It is adopting democratic norms and values and democratic modes of conduct on most levels, such as the nuclear family, the clan, the attitude to other people, respect for the law, and so on. This development promotes its integration

into the national political and social system. This model, which is found in most of the research literature written and published to date, seems to assume, consciously or otherwise, a number of elements that can buttress the main contention: the Arabs in Israel are experiencing a process of natural development and normalization. This involves the ongoing processes of construction and consolidation that are turning it into a society with all the characteristics of a modern well-ordered society.

THE DISTRESS MODEL

The distress model sees the development of the Arabs in Israel in light of the ethnic character of the country. The normal development model would be applicable if Israel were a state with a democratic system that guarantees full equality for all its citizens. In the normal condition of a country that practices the standard democratic system and grants equal rights to all its citizens, as individuals and as members of groups, by virtue of their citizenship, groups can attain or realize equality on both levels, or at least on one of them, depending on the nature of the democratic system (Lijphart 1977). In a liberal democracy of the type epitomized by the United States, for example, competition for determining the "general good" is conducted not between groups but between equal citizens, whatever their national or ethnic affiliation. In a consociational democracy, of the sort that existed in Lebanon until the mid-seventies and still exists there formally, the competition to determine the general good is not among citizens by virtue of their citizenship but by virtue of their affiliation with a particular ethnic group or confession. Hence it is the groups that compete to determine the public arrangements and divide up power and rewards (see Smooha 1990a; Ghanem 1998a).

In the case at hand—that of a national minority group in an ethnic state—even though the state is democratic on the procedural level, in its relations with the minority it lapses into an ethnic state that practices systematic discrimination at all levels against the minority. In such a state, democracy can be no more than semidemocracy, because the state is identified with one group only; that is, it offers a national home to only one of the ethnic groups within its society (see Maynes 1993) and offers only partial equality to members of other groups. In such a state, the majority controls the various organs of authority and permits minorities to enjoy only limited individual and collective equality (for details on the limitations of Israeli democracy because it is an ethnic state, see Smooha 1990a; 1998; Ghanem 1998a; Rouhana 1997; Yiftachel 1997a; 1997b; Ghanem, Rouhana, and Yiftachel 1998).

In an ethnic state in which the majority rules over a minority, intentional policy, both overt and covert, shunts the development of the minority into pressured conditions. If appropriate means are not adopted to deal with this situation, these conditions create a distress that can grow into a serious crisis in the minority's relations with its surroundings, including the majority group and the state, as well as in its own internal structure. There are ample examples of the crises that have beset minorities in nondemocratic ethnic states—the Kurds in Iraq, the blacks in South Africa under apartheid—as well as in democratic states—the Catholics in Northern Ireland, the Chinese in Malaysia, the Kurds in Turkey, and the Hungarians in Romania (Horowitz 1985). In all these cases, the minorities suffered an external and internal crisis that eventually attained crisis proportions, leading to an eruption of tension and a degeneration of the political system into violence that could have been prevented had the system accorded parity to the minority.

The distress model has evolved as a reaction to the normal development model. It maintains that the latter is flawed by a fundamental misperception of the situation of the Arabs (Ghanem 1996a; 1996b; 1998a; Rouhana and Ghanem 1998). The Palestinian-Arab community in Israel is in fact in distress on the verge of deteriorating to a crisis on two levels, tactical and strategic. The community's options in its relations with the state and with the Palestinian people are limited and do not permit it to develop normally. On the one hand, Israel is an ethnic state that restricts the development of the Arab minority. On the other hand, the Arab minority isolation from their own people and from the Arab nation has impinged upon their internal development.

A minority in an ethnic state is confronted by uncomfortable political and existential situations that stem from the ethnic structure of the state. An ethnic state by definition excludes national-ethnic collectives other than the dominant group from the national objectives and affords the dominant group a preferential treatment anchored in the legal system. The discrimination against the minority group stems from the strategic refusal of the state to accept its demands for equality, participation, and equity within the apparatus of the state. Any ethnic group that wishes to be part of the state system will demand, as a matter of course, equality, security, and identity. These are basic and nonnegotiable human needs that cannot be ignored or repressed permanently (Burton 1990).

At every appropriate level of political awareness and group consciousness, any national or ethnic minority will demand equal opportunities and equal access to resources and power (Gurr 1993). It is in this spirit that the Arab minority demands equality within Israel. But because of the ethnic mission of the state, which anchors the impossibility of genuine equality in basic laws (Kretzmer 1990; Ghanem 1998a), Israel relies on two policy elements in its dealings with its Arab citizens—a maximum ethnic component and a limited democratic one. The ethnic policy emphasizes the superiority of the Jews in all spheres. The democratic policy incorporates the Arabs to a limited extent and produces an erroneous sense of normal development, even among members of the minority group, when in fact it exacerbates the distressing situation in which they find themselves.

The combination of limited democracy and ethnic orientation, which guides policy toward the minority, harms the minority rather than helping it. It creates a sense of progress and involvement in the life of the state and a deceptive aura of normal development. In fact, the options available do not help the minority attain equality and actually create a confused developmental situation that erodes the existing structure of the minority while not permitting it to integrate into the state. Ultimately the minority forfeits its traditional way of life, and political and social structure, but cannot adopt a different path. This leads to the existential stress and crisis situations that beset the minority. Because of the ethnic policy, the minority faces a grave existential threat that permeates its collective life in many areas. This distress involves various dimensions of the development of the Arab minority and applies to its relations with both the state and the Palestinian people (see Ghanem 1996a; 1996b; 1998a; Rouhana and Ghanem 1998).

This book describes a central axis of the life and development of the Arabs in Israel—their political world. I will be considering the specific implications of the distress model for the political life of the Arab citizens of Israel. My basic thesis is that in the context of distressed development, their political development suffers from a distress manifested in a severe restriction of their political development. In my opinion, their political development in the organizational and ideological spheres and their political participation suffer from the severe restrictions that stem first and foremost from the ethnic character of the state of Israel and their isolation from the Palestinian people and Arab nation.

1

The Palestinian-Arab Minority in Israel

Historical Background

The dispersal of the Palestinians disrupted and impeded social and political processes that had been at work among them before the 1948 war. Many villages were destroyed, totally or partially. Their inhabitants fled the country or moved elsewhere in Israel, where they became "internal refugees" (al-Haj 1986; 1988). Numerous families were split in two, with some members in Israel and others in neighboring Arab states. The incipient industry that had begun to appear in Arab communities, as well as voluntary and social organizations, were wiped out. Worst of all, processes that should have produced greater cohesion among all Palestinians and could have led to the emergence of a Palestinian political entity were disrupted or halted in their tracks.

In addition to the disruption and delay in these processes, the various segments of the Palestinian people, who lived under different regimes, suffered problems that were both similar and different, but common to all was that they were the result of the 1948 war and together generated the hard core of what has since been called the "Palestinian problem." In 1952 there were about 1.6 million Palestinians, of whom only 11 percent lived in Israel; 18 percent lived in the Gaza Strip, and 47 percent in the West Bank. The balance, some 21 percent, lived in neighboring countries, and 3 percent elsewhere.

The problems and condition of the Arabs in Israel, immediately after the 1948 war, were a direct outcome of the hostilities and their aftermath. The essential difference between them and other Palestinians lay in the fact that they had remained on their land and become Israeli citizens. This important fact did not help them much, however, because as far as the Israeli authorities and security services were concerned, they were deemed in many respects to be part of the Arab and Palestinian "enemy" and subjected to various measures to deter or repress

11

subversive activity. The Arabs living in Israel after 1948 lived in a state of shock engendered by their unexpected defeat by the Jewish forces. They were weak, divided, and devoid of a countrywide political leadership to guide them. The Arabs, too, saw this situation as part of the development and evolution of the broader Palestinian problem.

In this chapter I will sketch a general picture of the history of the Palestinian national movement through 1948 and the birth of Israel, of the subsequent history of the Arabs in Israel, and of the major factors that have affected their development.

THE PALESTINIAN NATIONAL MOVEMENT BEFORE 1948

The first steps in the development of the Palestinian national movement were taken in the early twentieth century and were strongly influenced by the Zionist movement and the Jews' aspirations to establish a state. They emerged from Feisal's abortive attempt to establish a state of "Greater Syria" and the subsequent institution of the British mandate over Palestine, as provided for by the Sykes-Picot agreement that allocated Syria and Lebanon to France and "Southern Syria" (Jordan and Palestine) to Great Britain. This political separation helped reinforce the Palestinian national consciousness at the expense of the pan-Syrian trend. During the twenties and thirties real attempts were made to establish national institutions and develop organizational structures for the movement.

Special efforts were invested in founding Moslem-Christian societies in the larger cities, and, somewhat later, national societies that were considered to be "more "advanced forms of organization than the communal societies. Various bodies were established to represent all or most of the Palestinian population. The first of these was the Palestinian Arab Executive Committee, in 1920, soon followed by the Palestinian Higher Committee, headed by Haj Amin al-Husseini. These organizations made a serious contribution toward crystalizing the early ideological lines of the Palestinian national movement and its arguments for the existence of a Palestinian people with a right to a Palestinian homeland (Porat 1976, 223–250).

Violent disturbances against the Jews and the Zionist movement, as well as against the Mandate, broke out in 1929. The first serious steps were taken toward the formation of Palestinian political parties. These parties, with the exception of the Independence Party (Hizb al-Istiqlal), reflected the clan structure of contemporary Palestinian society: the Husseini family and its allies versus the Nashashibi family and its supporters (Abd al-Jawed 1990, 479–495; Porat 1978, 69–104). During the thirties, because of events in Europe and the rise of the Nazis in

Germany, there was massive Jewish immigration to Mandatory Palestine. The pressures created by this immigration and by the British Mandatory government led to the outbreak of the 1936–1939 revolt, which included extended strikes and demonstrations. These events were a further step toward the appearance of the Palestinian national movement. In a number of senses, however, the results of these events were disappointing from the Palestinian point of view, especially after the massive intervention by Arab leaders from some neighboring countries to end the strike and disturbances. This intervention, which widened in subsequent years, marked in a certain sense the beginning of the "Arabization" of the Palestinian problem, which subsequently had a significant impact on the course of the Palestinian problem and the evolution of political activity among the Palestinians.

The disappointing results of the 1936–1939 revolt and later events caused the political strength of the Palestinian national movement to wane. A considerable part of its leadership went into exile. Haj Amin al-Husseini moved to Beirut and then to Baghdad, from where he did his best to frustrate all attempts to establish an alternative leadership within the country. The Zionist movement became stronger economically, politically, and militarily. Immediately after World War II it realized that, given the changes in the international balance of power, it had to move its focus of activities from London to Washington, and win the support of the Soviet Union as well (Abd Al-Jawed 1990, 486–492).

All this culminated in the adoption of General Assembly Resolution 181, which called for the partition of Mandatory Palestine into two states, one Jewish and the other Arab, and set the stage for the establishment of the state of Israel.

The Palestinians' natural political development until 1948, similar to that in the other Arab countries and of many Third World peoples, was disrupted by the outcome of the war and the establishment of the state of Israel. There were a number of aspects to this.

DISPERSION

On the eve of Israel's establishment, close to two million persons were living in Mandatory Palestine—two-thirds of them Arabs and one-third of them Jews. A majority of the Arabs (close to 940,000) and almost all the Jews lived in the region that became the state of Israel. As the result of mass expulsions and flight, only 150,000 Palestinians (10 percent of the total) remained there when the fighting ended. Nearly 780,000 became refugees in the West Bank, the Gaza Strip, and the neighboring Arab countries (Cayman 1984, 5). In 1952 there were about 1.6 million Palestinians, of whom only 11 percent (179,300) lived in Israel; 18 percent (about 300,000) lived in the Gaza Strip, and 47 percent (about

742,300) in the West Bank. The balance, some 380,000, lived in neighboring countries: 114,000 (seven percent) in Lebanon, 83,000 (five percent) in Syria, 150,000 (nine percent) in the East Bank, and three percent elsewhere. The dispersion of the Palestinian population disrupted political and social processes that had been at work in the Palestinian community before the war. Many communities had been completely destroyed; others had been partially demolished, and some residents had left the country or moved elsewhere within Israel. Many families were divided across hostile borders. Incipient industries and social organization in Arab communities were also devastated. Worst of all, the processes that should have led to the formation of a Palestinian political entity were disrupted or halted in their tracks.

DISPERSION OF THE LEADERSHIP THAT HAD BEEN EMERGING AFTER THE 1936–1939 REVOLT

One result of the dispersal of the Palestinian population was the concomitant dispersal of the leadership that could have provided the center for the formation of a Palestinian entity, which had only just begun to recover from the blow it had suffered in the 1936–1939 revolt.

In the absence of an agreed-upon Palestinian leadership, the Arab countries decided to send the prime minister of Syria, Jamil Mardam, to Palestine to attempt to put together a Palestinian delegation to participate in the Arab countries' discussion of the Palestine question in Alexandria in October 1944. Mardam's attempt to constitute a consensus delegation of the Husseinis and the heads of the Independence (Istiqlal) Party failed. Instead, he nominated Mussa al-Alami, who was an official of the British Mandate, as the Palestinian representative (Smith 1984, 82). Mardam's failure testifies to the intensity of the differences among the Palestinians and the Husseinis' refusal to cooperate in matters that were not subject to their full control.

Alami failed as the Palestinian representative because of the opposition to his activities by both the Independence Party and the Husseinis. Trying again, in November 1945, Mardam set up the "second" Arab Higher Committee (the "first" committee had been established in 1920, but gradually lost its status as a result of the of 1936–1939 events). This attempt, too, did not yield a joint Palestinian leadership because of the Husseinis' domination of the committee and their exclusion from it of Alami and the representatives of the Independence Party. When the British allowed Jamal al-Husseini to return from exile in Rhodesia in 1946, he established the "third" Arab Higher Committee. But this committee, too, encountered problems in its attempt to represent all Palestinians, especially after the founding of the rival Supreme Arab Front by the Independence Party and representatives of other parties, in cooperation with the National Liberation Front *(Asbat al-Tahrir al-Watani)* and the Arab Workers Union, two organizations that were controlled by the Arab Communists.

Only after June 1946, as a result of massive intervention by the Arab League, founded in 1945, was the "fourth" Arab Higher Committee, sometimes called the Higher Arab Executive Committee, established. This body was composed of representatives of the Husseini-controlled Arab Higher Committee and the Higher Arab Front. Jamal al-Husseini was elected deputy chairman; the position of chairman was reserved for Haj Amin al-Husseini, who was still in exile in Cairo and Beirut, and barred from the country by the British authorities. In the course of time representatives of other bodies were added, including the National Arab Fund, the Reform Party *(Hizb al-Eslah)*, and several other groups—additions that reinforced the Husseinis' hold on the Arab Committee and Haj Amin's leadership (Smith 1984, 83–84).

The British declaration, in February 1947, that they intended to surrender their mandate over Palestine and refer a decision on the country's future to the United Nations, intensified the preparations by both the Arab League and the Arab Committee to frustrate any attempt to establish a Jewish state in part of Mandatory Palestine. In October 1947, the Arab League decided to set up an army, under the command of Ismail Safwat, to assume offensive positions along the borders of Palestine. In December of that year, almost a month after the passage of the UN partition resolution, the Arab League resolved to establish the Liberation Army *(Jaish al-Enqad)*, composed of volunteers, which would be stationed inside the country in order to prevent the establishment of the Jewish state. Two months later, the league decided to establish a joint command of the armies of Egypt, Transjordan, Iraq, and Lebanon, headed by an Iraqi officer, Nur ed-Din Mahmud, to be dispatched to Palestine. Later, the Emir Abdallah became the supreme commander of the Arab armies that entered the country.

The league's measures were opposed by Haj Amin, who feared for his position and the future of the country in the wake of such massive Arab intervention. Independently of the Arab League's measures, he decided to establish the Army of the Sacred Jihad *(Jaish al-Jihad al-Muqadas)*, made up of Palestinian volunteers. There was not even minimal coordination between the Liberation Army and the regular Arab armies, on the one side, and the Jihad force, on the other. Later this made it easier for the Jewish army to occupy broad areas of the country, including regions that were supposed to be part of the Palestinian state under the partition plan. Elsewhere in the country, the combined Jordanian-Iraqi forces occupied "Central Palestine," later known as the West Bank, including eastern Jerusalem. The Egyptian army occupied the

Gaza Strip. The army established by Haj Amin collapsed and the heads of the Arab Higher Committee fled for their lives.

When he reached Gaza, Ahmad Hilmi Pasha, the treasurer of the committee, immediately convened a Palestinian National Council of Palestinian representatives. This assembly met in Gaza, declared an independent state of Palestine in all the territory of Mandatory Palestine, and established an "All-Palestine" government *(Hukumat Umum Falastin)*. Hilmi was elected prime minister of this state; Haj Amin was named its president. Abdallah, who was interested in annexing the West Bank to his kingdom, prevented this government from operating in the West Bank and Gaza Strip under his control, thereby denying it all contact with a considerable proportion of its putative citizens (about 47 percent of all Palestinians). Israel, of course, prevented any contact between this government and the Palestinians who remained in the West Bank and Gaza Strip held by the Jewish army (about 10 percent of all Palestinians). This Palestinian government's activities were thus limited to the Gaza Strip. In 1959, its offices in the Gaza Strip were closed by order of the president of Egypt, Jamal Abd al-Nasser (Smith 1984, 84–87).

Local leadership, which was to a great extent linked to the national leadership, although it had come into being earlier and constituted the seedbed from which the national leadership developed, began to emerge in the form of clans, especially in the larger cities. In the mid-forties, most towns and their hinterlands were dominated by one or two clans, who made extensive use of social, economic, and religious instruments to guarantee their control (Morris 1989). The members of these extremely well-to-do families, drawing on their financial resources and family ties in neighboring countries, began leaving the country immediately after the adoption of the UN partition resolution, apprehensive of coming to grief at the hands of both the Jewish army and the Arab volunteers. The departure of so many members of the moneyed class— most of them principals and teachers, physicians, lawyers, and the like— paralyzed public life in the cities. This situation, which created tremendous pressures on the middle and lower classes, who feared that they would be left alone to face the "Zionist enemy" after the British left, facilitated the mass departure and flight of April–June 1948 (Morris 1989).

The dispersal of the Palestinians, absence of a national and local leadership, and the sense of impotence and loss of the initiative all combined to create a situation that permitted the Arabization of the Palestinian question in the 1950s and 1960s. This helped Israel take steps and apply various policies vis-à-vis the Palestinians who remained in its territory, the subject of this study. These factors, which will be explained below, frustrated the possibility of any normal political development for the Arabs in Israel.

TWO DISTINCT PERIODS IN THE HISTORY OF THE PALESTINIAN-ARAB MINORITY IN ISRAEL

In general, the history of the Arab minority in Israel can be divided into two distinct periods, each with its own characteristics.

THE LOST YEARS: 1948–1966

During the first periods, which lasted from 1948 until the abolition of the military government in 1966, the Arab citizens of Israel were the victim of severe discrimination in every sphere. Nevertheless, consciousness of this discrimination was not strongly crystalized or well developed; the demand for equality was voiced hesitantly and in limited terms, and there was no demand whatsoever for collective equality, including recognition of the Arabs as a national minority. All the attempts to set up countrywide Arab political organizations failed. This situation produced diffident political participation and deterred the presentation of ideological alternatives that posed a challenge to the authorities. A number of factors contributed to this quiescence.

The Arabization of the Palestinian Problem after 1948. One of the processes that overtook the Palestinian problem in the wake of the 1936–1939 revolt was Arabization, which made it into a pan-Arab problem. The status and role of the Palestinians themselves in the efforts to find a solution to it became marginal, while the Arab states, especially those bordering on Mandatory Palestine—Syria, Lebanon, Egypt, and Transjordan—took the lead. This process was spurred by the conviction of many Palestinians and of the Arabs in general that the struggle to prevent the Zionists and Jews from establishing a Jewish homeland in Palestine required a joint effort on the part of all Arabs. What is more, the Arabs and the Palestinians believed that Great Britain, as the mandatory power, favored the pan-Arab approach. For the Arabs, this legitimized joint treatment of the Palestinian problem and turned it into "their problem" (Ben-Dor 1981, 163).

After 1948 and the defeat, the Arab League, organized only in 1945, went into high gear in its handling of the Palestinian problem. Ahmad Shukeiry, in his maiden speech as the Palestinian representative to the Arab League, noted that since the league's inception it had adopted 589 resolutions on the Arab-Israeli conflict (Harkaby 1975, 13), a number that testified to an attempt to be actively involved in the problem. The annexation of the West Bank by Jordan, the Free Officers' coup in Egypt, and the repeated coups in Syria and Iraq, which brought military officers to power, intensified these countries' involvement with the Palestinian problem. The various juntas sought to use the Palestinian problem and their calls for a total military solution as an instrument to enhance the legitimacy of their regimes. During the fifties and sixties they issued thousands of declarations in favor of a war against Zionism and the establishment of a Palestinian entity. Although many Palestinians were included as partners to these efforts, in most cases they served only as fig leaves whose roles in events and decision-making were marginal.

The trend toward Arabization began to weaken and give way to Palestinization, in which the Palestinians play the decisive role in their own cause, only after the founding of the PLO (Palestine Liberation Organization) in 1964. Although the initiative for this came from the Arab League, Fatah's growing strength and the defeat of the Arab armies in 1967 gave the trend added momentum (see further below). For our present subject, the Arabization of the Palestinian problem was one of the factors that neutralized the Palestinians and left them in an inferior position vis-à-vis the Arab countries in dealing with the problem. Since their role in events was only marginal, there was no need for them to be actively involved and no decisive significance to the consolidation of the national movement and its institutions. As we shall see, these received greater importance and weight only after 1967.

Israeli Rule over Its Palestinian Minority, 1948–1967.   After the 1948 war, Israel found itself with close to 150,000 Palestinian residents—10 percent of the Palestinian people—who were still in a state of shock at the Arabs' utter defeat by the Jews, weak, fragmented, and lacking a countrywide leadership. For its part, the new state was not prepared to deal with the situation that had been created. Before independence, Zionism and the various Jewish movements had not invested great efforts in defining the policies of the state-to-be toward an Arab minority (Rekhess 1988, 33–37; Lustick 1980, 43). The Jewish politicians and authorities had to adopt temporary and ad hoc policies to deal with the "problem."

The Israeli authorities' policies toward the Palestinian minority were guided by three main considerations. The first was the "security" consideration—viewing the Arabs a security threat, immediate or potential, to the state of Israel because they were part of the Palestinian people and the Arab nation surrounding Israel and liable to join the military effort against Israel in the event of an Arab attack (Benziman and Mansour 1992, 11–32). The second was the "Jewish-Zionist" consideration—viewing the state as first and foremost a "Jewish-Zionist" state and even "the state of the Jewish people," whose raison d'être and mission were to serve the Jewish people. Discrimination against Arabs, land expropriation, and other measures were considered "legitimate" if intended to serve these goals (Lustick 1980; Smooha 1980a; Jeryis 1966). The third consideration was the "democratic-liberal" one—viewing Israel as a democratic state that must see to the welfare of its citizens, including the Arabs, with full equality and without discrimination (Rekhess 1988, 33–37; Smooha 1980a, 1980b). In the period under surveillance here (1948–1967), the security and Jewish-Zionist considerations received greatest weight, whereas the democratic-liberal factor played only a very minor role. This was reflected in the military government imposed on areas of Arab population concentration in the Galilee, the Triangle, and the Al-Naqab between 1948 and 1966.

The suspicion of the Arabs, who were perceived as liable to constitute a substantive security risk and the need to provide maximum welfare for the waves of Jewish immigrants, who needed land for houses and farming, and the need to provide them with employment in other economic branches, led the authorities to adopt various techniques to control the Arabs. The most important of these, in the pre-1967 period, are enumerated below.

POLITICAL SUPERVISION OF THE ARABS.   To prevent the formation of any political or other force among the Arabs that might threaten the state's stability or create domestic conflicts, the authorities systematically endeavored to control the Arabs. They adopted measures and techniques to neutralize any such threats.

With the aid of the security services and civilian officials, and relying upon the Emergency (Defense) Regulations introduced by the Mandatory authorities in 1945, the military government kept a close watch on the Palestinian minority, frustrating all attempts at subversive organization or to assist cross-border infiltrators in the 1950s. There was extremely tight supervision of Arab municipal, education, social, and religious institutions, in order to prevent the emergence of independent centers of power. Organizations and institutions that tried to disseminate general Arab or Palestinian nationalism or attempted to consolidate a national Arab force were banned or suspected of subversion. Some of their leaders were arrested or banished to other parts of the country (Lustick 1980, 130–135; Smooha 1980b, 19).

There were three attempts at Arab national organization during this period. In 1955, Elias Khoussa attempted to set up an Arab party. In 1958, the Arab Popular Front was established, under the leadership of Yani Yani, the head of the Kafr Yassif municipal council. In 1961, Nasserists founded the Al-Ard movement. All three attempts aroused the suspicion of the authorities, who moved successfully to keep the organizations from gaining strength and thereby prevented the emergence of an Arab national leadership in the country.

The authorities preferred to deal with the Arabs as ethnic groups or as families and clans. After the establishment of the state, the first advisor to the prime minister on Arab affairs, Yehoshua Palmon, suggested that the Palestinian minority be viewed as religious communities and dealt with through the ministry of religions—a solution that seemed desirable and quite reasonable (Ozacky-Lazor 1990, 15). This approach continued to guide policy toward the Palestinian minority throughout the period under discussion, even though it totally ignored the fact that all the Palestinians in Israel are members of the same people and share a common nationality.

During the years of the military government severe restrictions were placed on the Arabs' freedom of movement and expression. Travel from one place to another required a permit from the military governor (Lustick 1980, 130–132). Most of the Mandate-era newspapers were closed; only al-Ittihad and the governmental al-Yawm continued to appear. Circulation of the Communist Party daily al-Ittihad, considered to be an opposition paper, was allowed in some regions and banned in others (Cayman 1984, 63–67).

Those considered to be moderates were "bribed" and co-opted. Travel permits were issued them more generously, abandoned parcels of land in destroyed villages were placed in their custody, and jobs and other benefits were distributed to them generously. They generally served as intermediaries between the authorities and the Arab minority (Cayman 1984, 67–68; Lustick 1980, 200–232).

These and other techniques employed by the authorities hindered attempts at political organization. They deterred many Israeli Palestinians citizens from political activity, prevented the consolidation of a national leadership, and encouraged "conciliatory" elements among the Arabs. In this way the authorities' active intervention prevented any "natural" political development among the Palestinian minority during the 1948–1967 years.

ECONOMIC DEPENDENCE ON THE ISRAELI AUTHORITIES AND THE JEWISH MAJORITY: The economic policies applied to the Arabs in Israel were guided by security concerns and Jewish-Zionist interests. They were designed to eliminate any possibility that the Arabs would amass economic power or capital that could help them achieve political liberation. Potential Arab profits, it was thought, should accrue to Jews instead, and be directed to benefit new immigrants. Thus in several senses the economic policies were conducted according to the rules of a zero-sum game: what was good for the Arabs was deemed bad for the Jews, and vice versa. Equal wages and benefits for Jews and Arabs might help the latter establish their own separate economic, political, and cultural center. Consequently, a systematic disparity in economic rewards was maintained to the Jews' advantage (Benziman and Mansour 1992, 127–178). Restrictions were imposed on starting new enterprises in Arab communities or reopening those that had been closed during the 1948 war. There were also severe problems with the supply of basic food commodities in Arab communities, and the authorities sought to control the marketing of the Palestinians' agriculture produce (Cayman 1984, 53–57).

There were restrictions on agricultural production during this period. The Arab communities were poor and lacked the industry and municipal development that could have absorbed some of the Arab labor force. In addition, much Arab-owned land was expropriated by the authorities. As a result, tens of thousands of Arab workers became dependent on the developing Jewish economy and had to commute to nearby or distant Jewish communities to find work of one sort or another. Those who found civil service jobs in their own communities, as clerks or teachers, had to pass strict security checks and prove their unwavering loyalty to the authorities and even to the dominant Mapai Party. Teachers were sometimes dismissed, for example, for expressing sympathy with the Communist Party (Lustick 1980, 155–199). As part of the policy of co-opting the elites, the authorities helped the notables and their intimates find jobs and leased them the lands of destroyed villages. These circles repaid the authorities by keeping a close eye on their neighbors (Lustick 1980, 200–232).

These economic policies helped the authorities control the Arabs in Israel and forced most of them to focus on finding work and feeding their families. There was no time for political activity. This economic dependence also deterred potential political activists, who were afraid they might lose their jobs and their families' livelihood.

THE YEARS OF AWAKENING: 1967 TO THE PRESENT

Since the mid–1960s (the "second period") a major change took place in the nature, level, and scope of political activity by the Arabs of Israel, including political institution-building and participation and a willingness to put forward ideologies and positions that challenge the regime and the Jewish majority. This was sparked by increased awareness of the issue of equality and of resolving the Palestinian problem and the willingness to make some active contribution on these fronts and be a sharp increase in self-confidence.

Demands for Equality and Resolution of the Palestinian Problem. Most studies about the Arabs of Israel since the early 1970s have found that they developed a broad consensus on the question of attaining civic equality with the Jewish majority on both the individual and collective planes and crystalized their demand for the establishment of an independent Palestinian state alongside Israel (in the Gaza Strip, the West Bank, and Jerusalem) as a possible and appropriate resolution of the Israeli occupation of those West Bank and Gaza Strip and for the aspirations and demands of the Palestinian people. A number of factors made this consensus possible.

INCREASED SELF-CONFIDENCE. The changes in the nature and form of the control applied to the Arabs of Israel and the changes in the Israeli political constellation reinforced their self-confidence. This was manifested in a readiness to develop patterns of thought and action unacceptable to the Israeli authorities and Jewish majority. The prime reasons for this increased self-confidence and its manifestations can be summarized as follows:

1. The demographic growth of the Arabs in Israel and the changes in the community's physical structure are important issues in this respect. In late 1998, there were 900,000 Palestinian-Arab citizens living within the Green Line—nearly 17 percent of the state citizens. The changes in the size of the Arab population and in the physical structure of the village, including the development of Arab settlements since the early 1970s, reinforced the Arabs' self-confidence, and provided an infrastructure for the flowering of cultural life, separate Arab political organizations, and a greater weight in joint Arab-Jewish organizations, as well as attempts to develop an autonomous economy in Arab communities.

2. The balance of forces in the Israeli political system between left and right: Starting in the mid-seventies, a balance began to emerge between support for the two main blocs in Israeli politics—the right, led by the Likud, and the left, headed by the Labor. This situation increased Arab self-confidence in two ways. First, it meant that the two blocs needed Arab votes to tip the scales in their favor and win power. The large blocs also needed the support of Arab representatives on various bodies, including the Knesset, the Histadrut executive committee, and the local councils of the mixed cities. The competition for Arab votes, whether direct or by vying for the support of their representatives, spawned awareness among Arabs of their rising importance and increased their self-confidence. Even though this power was frequently an illusion, and in other cases not exploited as it could have been, in principle it gave them a sense that they were being courted for their support and could have an influence—that is, of a group that was needed and appreciated rather than rejected and unwanted.

Second, in 1977 the balance tipped so far as to produce the first change of regime in the country. After twenty-nine years of coalitions dominated by Mapai and its partners on the left, supported by the religious parties, the Likud and its allies on the right came to power. This change was a clear sign of an opening in the Israeli political system and an omen for further change.

For the Arabs in Israel, the end of the period of Mapai domination also marked the end of a difficult period, during which the Mapai-led governments imposed direct and close control over them and used various methods to win their votes and keep them quiet. The end of this period was a potent sign of a change in the nature of the regime. It created the conditions for greater freedom and opened new options for the Arabs in Israel with regard to genuine and sincere expression of their attitude toward the state, its character, and the Palestinian problem.

3. The growing strength of the Palestinian national movement as represented by the PLO. Throughout the 1950s and to some extent the 1960s, the Arabs in Israel, whose problems and condition are a result of 1948 war, were beset by confusion and the absence of a clear direction on the Palestinian-national axis. The tragic results of that war for the Palestinian people were reflected in the absence of strong and recognized institutions within the Palestinian national movement. The incipient organization of the 1950s, which produced Fatah, founded in Kuwait, the Popular Front, and El-Ard, which began among the Arabs in Israel, as well as other less familiar bodies, was too weak. These movements lacked adequate recognition of their importance to constitute a foundation for the institutions of the Palestinian national movement. Serious organization of the Palestinian national movement actually began in the Diaspora and not within Mandatory Palestine, which was ruled by Israel, Egypt, and Jordan.

In 1964, the Palestine Liberation Organization was established to serve as an umbrella organization for the various political groupings among Diaspora Palestinians. The PLO gained momentum with the election of Yasser Arafat, the head of Fatah, as its chairman. His election symbolized the beginning of a new period in the history of the Palestinian national movement, during which the PLO began a major offensive on two fronts: military, against Israeli targets, and political, to consolidate international awareness of the Palestinian people and recognition of the PLO as its representative. This assault succeeded reasonably well from the perspective of the PLO, which won increasing recognition as the "sole representative of the Palestinian people." The process culminated in Arafat's address to the United Nations General Assembly in 1974.

The rise in the prestige of the PLO enhanced self-confidence among all segments of the Palestinian people, including those who had remained in Israel and become citizens there. They too evinced a gradual increase in support for the PLO as the representative of the Palestinian people (Ghanem 1990). Slowly they began to openly express the fact that they were part of the Palestinian people and launched a campaign in support of the establishment of the Palestinian state alongside Israel in the West Bank and Gaza Strip occupied by Israel in 1967. In addition, this development strengthened the internal solidarity of the Arabs in Israel and their willingness to confront the authorities in pursuit of their individual and collective rights.

4. Modernization and improved education. After the establishment of Israel, a process accompanied by the expulsion and mass flight of the Palestinian population, about 150,000 Palestinians remained in the country. This confused remnant of the Palestinian community was characterized by the absence of even a minimal level of organization, the predominance of traditional values and norms, and an economic, social, and cultural life typical of a traditional society at the very beginning of modernization, including an extremely low level of education.

Under the impact of contact with the Jews and the influence of the waves of modernity imported from the West, this group entered upon a process of modernization that was manifested in a slow and hesitant change of sociocultural values—an increase in the importance of the nuclear family, a slow change in the status of women, a steady drop in the fertility rate, an improvement in housing conditions and medical services, the development of municipal government, the establishment of political and social organizations, and, especially, a consistent rise in the average educational level of the Arabs in Israel, including an upward trend in the number of those with a university education.

5. Politicization and a rise in political awareness. The situation faced by the Arabs in Israel when they became a minority in the state, which ruled over them and was engaged in a violent confrontation with other segments of the Palestinian people and the other Arab countries, led to a gradual rise in their political awareness and willingness to act to alter their condition and the situation of their people, and even to substantive action in this direction. This process of the politicization of the Arabs in Israel has many elements (see Smooha 1989b).

Discrimination against the Arabs in Israel. The Palestinian citizens of Israel have always suffered discrimination in almost every sphere of life, as documented in numerous studies. Benziman and Mansour (1992) documented state policies toward them and the discrimination in various fields. Al-Haj and Rosenfeld (1990a, 1990b) dealt with the situation of Arab local governments and their problems, as well as the unequal allocation of resources to Arab and Jewish local authorities. Al-Haj (1995b, 1996b) and Haider (1985) documented the discrimination in education. Haider (1991a) and Khalidi (1988) studied the laggard economic development of Arab communities. Haider (1991b) surveyed the situation of the welfare services in the Arab sector. Kretzmer (1990) documented the discrimination in law between Jews and Arabs in Israel. Many more studies have described and documented discrimination against the Arabs and the disparities between them and the Jews. Despite the changes for the better in recent years, up-to-date comparisons between the two sectors reveal that the discrimination-related gaps persist (Ghanem 1996c) and seem likely to accompany the Arab citizens of Israel for many years to come.

In addition, we can add the fact that the Arab and Palestinian culture and heritage do not receive adequate attention and encouragement in Israel, even in curricula intended for Arab pupils (Al-Haj 1996b). The Arabic language, whose status is officially on a par with that of Hebrew, in practice does not receive equal treatment and its official status is not respected. This situation disturbs the Arabs and in several respects can be described as genuine distress.

In addition to the daily discrimination in allocations and jobs, the Arabs are also discriminated against with regard to the dominant symbols and values of the state and its institutions. Whereas the Jews relate to the symbols, values, and institutions of the state as their own, identify with them, and derive them all from their own heritage, the Arabs are estranged from them, do not identify with them, and are painfully aware that they are drawn exclusively from the heritage of the majority (Kretzmer 1990).

The ongoing discrimination takes on even greater significance because most of the attention to the problems and situation of the Arabs over the years has been channeled through special institutions, whether confidential (e.g., the general security service) or overt (e.g., the prime minister's advisor for Arab affairs, the minister for Arab affairs, and special committees and functionaries), whose perspective on the Arabs was frequently derived from a security-oriented view that sees the Arabs as a potential security threat who must be watched over closely and kept under control by internal forces (Lustick 1980).

The ongoing discrimination, which has not been dealt with properly, contributed to the consolidation of a strong demand for individual and collective equality in the state. It was one of the factors that encouraged the Arabs in Israel to use various methods of participation in order to alter the situation of discrimination.

FACTORS THAT INFLUENCE THE POLITICAL DEVELOPMENT OF THE PALESTINIAN-ARAB MINORITY IN ISRAEL

In principle one can point to or sketch out three circles of factors that influence the political development of the Arabs in Israel. Although these circles are interlocking, for the purposes of analysis I shall try to isolate them.

THE INTERNAL CIRCLE

This circle encompasses the various factors associated with the internal development taking place among the Arabs, such as processes of internal democratization and mutual tolerance, the status of the clan, the family, and women, interconfessional relations, level of development, processes of modernization, and so on.

Traditional Arab society is closed and rigid; in many senses its is intolerant, both inwardly and outwardly. It discriminates against some of its members, particularly women, and rests on clan and confessional affiliations that leave individuals in an inferior position vis-à-vis the collective. The Arabs in Israel, who after the birth of the country found themselves in an inferior position, as a group and as individuals, experienced significant changes in these arenas under the influence of the majority and the modernization processes that influenced their political behavior. In particular, there was a process of internal democratization, and to a large extent an internalization of democratic norms and values. There was a change in the status of women, who went out to work and study in increasing numbers as the years passed. For example, in Knesset elections Arab voting patterns are influenced less and less by clan considerations, unlike municipal elections, where clannish voting has actually gained strength in recent years (Rouhana and Ghanem 1993).

THE PALESTINIAN CIRCLE

This circle includes everything relevant to the Palestinian problem and its influence on the political development of the Arabs in Israel, including attempts by some of the Palestinian leadership in the occupied West Bank and Gaza Strip and Diaspora to influence this development.

For example, in their election campaigns, lists that compete for Arab votes now emphasize the need to solve the Palestinian problem. This emphasis is a result of their estimation that the Arabs in Israel are very much interested in solving the Palestinian problem and in particular in the establishment of an independent Palestinian state alongside Israel. This is one point of the consensus among the Arabs in Israel. Accordingly the political development of the Arabs in Israel is influenced by developments in the Palestinian arena.

THE ISRAELI CIRCLE

This circle takes in all the factors of the relations between Israel and its Arab citizens. Specifically this circle relates to Israeli policy toward Arab citizens and the Arabs' position vis-à-vis the state and its Jewish-Zionist character.

Since its founding, Israel has conducted a discriminatory policy against its Arab citizens (see: Falah 1990; Ghanem 1998a; al-Haj and Rosenfeld 1990a, 1990b; Benziman and Mansour 1992). The state, established as the state of the Jewish people, was concerned first and foremost with realizing the yearnings of the Jews and serving their interests. The Arabs, who became its citizens after 1948, were subjected to a regime directed against them by the state. Even today they occupy an inferior position when it comes to the government's scale of priorities. The political development of the Arabs in Israel can be explained in the context of the mutual influence and relations between this minority and the state, and the Jewish majority that dominates it.

Part Two

Palestinian-Arabs in Israel: Different Manifestations of Politics

2

Political and Ideological Streams among the Palestinian-Arab Minority in Israel

This book traces the political activity of the Arab citizens of Israel. This activity, which is concentrated on two levels, the national and the local, was conducted by both countrywide and local forces within the Arab community itself. Many factors have influenced it. Activists dealt with a broad spectrum of topics deemed vital for the situation and future of the Arabs in Israel. Here I shall treat both levels of political activity. First I will consider national politics and present the main ideological and political streams among the Arabs and the positions they espouse on key questions. After that I will consider local politics and its evolution, including the factors that have shaped it.

Ideology is a term used to define a system of ideas in which the world (or life) can be realized and analyzed. It also gives standards and norms for the group or the individuals for their thoughts and life activities. Ideology could also improve personal feelings of belonging and national identity, which can help in the creation of group solidarity that leads to political action. The formation and development of the basic components of ideology is the responsibility of the elite and the political leadership mainly (Friedrich 1963: 81, 89–90; Seligar 1976: 14). The "ideological stream" is a group of people who use the same ideology for explaining their activities and beliefs, depending on the common thinking that leads to a similar way of behavior.

CLASSIFICATION OF THE IDEOLOGICAL AND POLITICAL STREAMS AMONG THE ARABS IN ISRAEL

The research literature that deals with ideological and political streams among the Arabs in Israel presents three ways of classifying it by ideological and political streams:

a. as a dichotomy;

b. a three-part classification;

c. a categorization into four streams.

Here I shall consider these three approaches.

DICHOTOMY

The advocates of a dichotomous classification, especially Reiter (1989), assert that there are only two ideological and political streams among the Palestinian minority. The first comprises the moderate camp and encompasses people who are affiliated with Jewish-Zionist parties. They have developed an ideology that is shaped by a central idea—namely, acceptance by the Arabs of Israel of their status as an ethnic and cultural minority within a Jewish state (Reiter 1989, 345).

The second stream is the "radical national" camp, which encompasses various political groups, including the Communist Party, the Progressive List, El Ard, and the Sons of the Village movement. What is common to all these groups, according to Reiter, is their fundamental nonacceptance of the political realities of the region. The range of ideologies advocated atop this common platform is vast—ranging from active opposition to the very existence of the state of Israel (El Ard and the Sons of the Village movement) through rejection of its Zionist character only (the Communist Party and Progressive List) (Reiter 1989, 347).

THREE-PART CLASSIFICATION

The proponents of a three-part classification maintain that there are three ideological and political streams among Arabs in Israel. Rekhess (1986) enumerates three camps, as defined by their political organization. The "moderate" camp is represented by the Arabs who are active in the Jewish-Zionist parties or their satellite lists. This second is the "national-Communist" camp, which includes Arabs who identify with the Israel Communist Party and the Progressive List. The third camp is the nationals—those aligned with El Ard and, since the early 1970s, with the Sons of the Village (Rekhess 1986, 1–2).

These camps expanded after the June 1967 war and grew even stronger after the October war of 1973, thanks to the enhanced stature of the PLO. In practice there was a rapprochement between these camps and the Palestinian leadership on the West Bank and the PLO in general, with a clear trend to radicalization in their positions (Rekhess 1989a, 1989b).

This organizational division is the basis for the classification of the Arabs into three ideological streams: the moderates, who have accepted the existence of Israel; the national-Communist stream, which accepts the existence of Israel but insists that its Zionist-Jewish character must be abolished; and the national stream, which rejects the very existence of Israel and demands the establishment of a Palestinian state in the entire territory of Mandatory Palestine.

FOUR-FOLD CLASSIFICATION

Sammy Smooha (1987, 1989a) opts for a four-fold classification. In his view, it emerges from the process of politicization taking place among the Arabs in Israel.

The "Accommodationists." These are Arabs who accept the existing Israeli political system and work in the context of the Jewish-Zionist parties. On the ideological level, this means agreeing with the Jewish consensus; in other words, assent to the perpetuation of the Jewish-Zionist character of the state and its Jewish majority. On the pragmatic level, it means partnership with the Jewish-Zionist parties within the existing Israeli political system, in order to further topics that are important to the Arabs in Israel (Smooha 1987, 86).

Those affiliated with the stream reject the use of violence in the struggle to improve the lot of the Arabs in Israel, support the peace treaty between Israel and Egypt, and ignore the question of the return of Palestinian refugees to their homes within the 1948 borders. In addition to Arabs who are members of the Jewish-Zionist parties, this stream included members and supporters of the satellite lists of those parties. The separate existence of the satellite lists is explained usually as a tactic that was intended to capture as many Arab votes as possible. Their leaders faithfully supported the Jewish parties to which their lists were attached.

The "Reservationists." This stream includes those Arabs located between the Zionist establishment and the "illegitimate" opposition, such as the Democratic Front for Peace and Equality (DFPE or Hadash). Although this group is not fully coalesced on the ideological level, it prefers organization on an Arab national basis, even when it does not reject the Jewish-Zionist character of the state. This stream also rejects the use of violence by Arabs in Israel as a means for improving their status and aspires to have Arabs included in Knesset coalitions and sit at the government table (Smooha 1987, 86). Those who are identified with this stream believe that organization on an Arab national basis can highlight the electoral potential of the Arabs in Israel and give them greater and more effective influence to promote their interests. This tendency makes it difficult to locate this stream among the others, because its support for participation in government coalitions and its leaders' past as members or intimates of the Zionist parties cause it to adopt positions that are not very far from those of the supporters, if measured by their challenge to the existing order in the country and the region.

This stream long lacked any organizational identity and was represented by individual public figures, council heads, intellectuals, and journalists who were close to the Zionist establishment but not part of it. Some of them criticized it from the inside. It was only in 1988 that this stream took on an organizational expression, with the establishment of the Democratic Arab Party headed by MK (Member of Knesset-Israeli Parliament) Abdulwahab Darawshe.

The "Oppositionists." This stream accepts the existence of Israel but wants to make radical changes in its character. Its vehicles are non-Zionist or anti-Zionist parties such as the DFPE, the Israel Communist Party, and the Progressive List for Peace, which support the mainstream of the PLO.

From the ideological perspective this stream rejects the Jewish-Zionist character of the state and considers Zionism to be racist. It supports demonstrations and general strikes as a legitimate means of conducting the struggle of the Arabs in Israel, opposes the peace treaty between Egypt and Israel, and advocates the return of the Palestinian refugees to their homes inside the 1948 borders (Smooha 1987, 86–88).

Based on their analysis of the situation in the country, the "opponents" see anti-Zionist political organization with parity between Jews and Arabs as the way to promote the interests of the Arabs in Israel. They accept as a matter of principle the existing order in Israel. But they forcefully challenge the Jewish-Zionist character of the state and employ a more aggressive tone to highlight their demands and the need for peace and equality in the Middle East and within the state.

The "Rejectionists." This stream is represented by the Sons of the Village and draws its ideology from rejectionist Palestinian organizations like the PFLP and DFLP. Its ideology rejects the very existence of the state in Israel, supports illegal demonstrations, and does not renounce the use of violence to promote the interests of the Arabs in Israel. Above everything else, this stream calls for the establishment of a democratic secular state on the entire territory of Mandatory Palestine (Smooha 1987, 87).

The rejectionists are organized on an Arab national basis. Those who identify with this stream employ extremely vehement rhetoric to underscore their demands. They see peace, as they understand it, and their Palestinian identity as basic values. Their Palestinian identity is extremely prominent and dictates the type of peace they favor.

In my opinion, all these classifications are seriously flawed by the criteria used to define them. These scholars apply the index of proximity to or distance from the state and its Jewish majority as the basis for their schemes. This influences their terminology of (national) moderation and extremism as well as the division itself, so that Arabs who are close to the Jews and the authorities are "moderate" or "supportive," those who are slightly at odds with the Jewish majority and the authorities are "demurrers" or "opponents" or "national Communists," and those who stand farthest from the Jewish majority and the authorities are "radical nationals" and "rejectionists." Drawing on proximity to the positions of the Jewish majority and state authorities as a component of ideology is essential, but it is not the master index to use for classifying the streams. As I shall show below, there is a better basis for classification, based on a broader set of criteria.

CRITERIA FOR CHARACTERIZING THE IDEOLOGICAL STREAMS AMONG THE ARABS IN ISRAEL

The most important criteria for characterizing the ideological streams among Arabs in Israel are as follows:

Broad Ideology: This criterion involves the existence of a broad international or regional ideology from which the local stream derives its justification. Is a local ideological stream associated with or derived from Communism, Islam, Arab and Palestinian nationalism, and so on, or does it rest on acquiescence with the existence of Israel and a willingness to adopt "Israeliness" as its overarching ideology?

Organizational Basis: This criterion has to do with the stream's preferred organizational structure: Does it organize on an Arab-national basis, or on an equal Jewish-Arab basis, or as a junior element within a Jewish-Zionist party? Each stream, of course, justifies it chosen form of organization.

Degree of Radicalism and Extent of Change Advocated: This criterion refers to the declared position on the moderation-extremism scale: Does the stream challenge or accept the existing order? Does it accept or reject the existence of the state of Israel? Does it accept or reject the Jewish-Zionist character of the state? Does it see the PLO as the representative of the Palestinian minority? Does it advocate a non-Israeli Palestinian identity or an Israeli-Palestinian identity? Does it view legal forms of struggle, including demonstrations and propaganda, or illegal means and violence, as the appropriate mode for the Palestinian minority to achieve their aims and realize their interests?

Tone: This criterion to rhetorical style and the types of arguments advanced to ground demands for change. An ideological stream is characterized by the extent to which it uses alienating and threatening terms like "repression" and "racism" to describe discrimination against the Palestinian minority and "colonial movement" to refer to Zionism, or softer phrases.

Key Motifs and Internal Logic: This refers to the existence of key ideological values and the degree of coherence between these values and broader ideologies, such as Palestinian nationalism, Communism, Islam, Israeliness, pragmatism, democracy, and so on.

Our fundamental assumption is that there is an inherent link between these criteria and the total overall of each stream. It stands to reason, then, that a stream that advocates organization as a junior associate within the Zionist parties will make less radical demands for changes in the status of Arabs in Israel. It will use a softer tone and milder rhetoric to voice these demands, avoiding the loaded terms that alienate the Jewish majority from the Arab minority. Its central ideological tenets will relate chiefly to the status of Arabs within the state and equality with the Jewish majority. We may also expect it to display a clear affinity for democracy and pragmatism.

On the other hand, an ideological stream that advocates organization on a Palestinian-national or Islamic basis is more likely to call into question the existing order in the country and the region. Such a stream will not acquiesce in the existence of Israel as a Jewish state and will not avoid the use of extremely provocative terms to describe the state of Israel, discrimination against Arabs, and the distress of the Palestinian people as a result of the protracted occupation. The central themes fostered by this stream are likely to be, first and foremost, the identity of the Arabs in Israel as an organic part of the Palestinian people and of the Arab and Islamic nation, and an aspiration to link their destiny to that of the Palestinian people. The broad ideologies drawn on by this stream will be chiefly Palestinian nationalism and Islamism, which reject the control of a foreign people—the Jews—over Muslims.

POLITICAL AND IDEOLOGICAL STREAMS
AMONG THE ARABS IN ISRAEL

Our basic hypothesis is that, with regard to politics and ideology, the Arabs of Israel fall into four groups, based on a consolidated set of values, positions, and modes of organization.

THE ISRAELI-ARAB STREAM

This group accepts the status of the Arabs as a minority, does not raise unambiguous demands for recognition of the Arabs as a Palestinian-Arab national minority, preaches rapprochement and integration in Jewish parties or government coalitions, and accepts its junior rank in these settings. In addition, it emphasizes the Israeli component of the Arabs' identity without demanding that the state modify its character and objectives in order to facilitate their acceptance of Israeliness. It integrates into the existing order without seeking essential changes in it. This stream is represented by Arabs who are close to the Jewish parties, including members of the satellite lists until the beginning of the 1980s, as well as by the Democratic Arab Party founded by Abdulwahab Darawshe in 1988. This stream has changed significantly since the 1970s. Its tone and demands are becoming more strident as it moves closer to the other Arab streams and to the Arab consensus.

THE COMMUNISTS

This stream derives its basic ideas from Communist-Marxist ideology and insists on an exclusively binational organization, as a matter of both strategy and principle. It rejects the stream character of the state and supports the introduction of far-reaching changes in its nature and goals, including converting it into a secular democratic state. It emphasizes that the identity of the Arabs of Israel is "Palestinian Israeli" or "Israeli Palestinian." This stream has always been represented by Arabs affiliated with the Communist Party.

NATIONALS

This group takes its ideological fundamentals from the Arab National movement in general and the Palestinian National movement in particular. It organizes on an Arab-national basis, although it does not rule out joint Jewish-Arab organization as a tactical maneuver. It does not accept the status quo: in practice its position varies from nonrecognition of the state to recognition accompanied by a demand for autonomy for the Arabs in Israel as the foundation for a binational solution in the country. This stream emphasizes the Palestinian and Arab elements in the identity of the Arabs in Israel.

Its adherents first organized in the 1950s and 1960s in the Arab Front and the el-Ard movement. Later they found their home in the Sons of the Village movement and the Progressive List. As a stream they are concentrated in the National Democratic Alliance (NDA)—the thirtieth of March Movement.

THE ISLAMISTS

This stream bases itself on the values and principles of Islam, calls for organization on an Islamic religious basis, taking into account the stream situation in Israel, and highlights the Islamic-religious component of the identity of the Arabs in Israel.

In what follows, an attempt will be made to delve into the basic worldview of each of these streams and the distinctions among them. I shall also trace their historical development, where appropriate.

3

The Israeli-Arab Stream

Before Israel gained its independence, various elements of the Palestinian community formed alliances with the nascent Jewish society and developed ties with the Jewish leadership that was working, both openly and behind the scenes, to establish a Jewish national home. The founding of Israel provided a significant push to these elements and reinforced them with tens of thousands of additional activists who found a place in Jewish parties as political agents to mobilize Arab voters. Arab affiliation with Jewish parties was hesitant at first but gained momentum over the years. Today there is a visible grouping of Arabs who are members of, vote for, or merely support the positions advocated by Jewish parties.

ORGANIZATION AND PUBLIC SUPPORT

Historically, the Israeli-Arab stream was represented chiefly by Arabs active in the Jewish-Zionist parties, especially Mapai and Mapam, and later Labor, as well as by members of the satellite lists that Jewish-Zionist parties set up to capture Arab votes (a phenomenon that lasted from the first Knesset elections in 1949 until 1981, when the last of the satellite lists disappeared from the Israeli political scene). In 1988, however, MK Abdulwahab Darawshe quit the Labor Party against the background of the *intifada* and set up the all-Arab Democratic Arab Party (DAP) (Ozacky-Lazar and Ghanem 1990). The DAP continued to advocate the positions advocated by Darawshe when he was a member of the Labor Party, but it expressed its demands more stridently and insisted on organization on an Arab national basis to mobilize the Arabs. The organizational plank, however, does not seem to be enough to classify the DAP as a separate stream, as I did some years ago (Ghanem 1990).

ARABS IN ZIONIST PARTIES

The new situation created in the wake of the 1948 war was extremely difficult for the Arabs who remained in Israel. They were in shock at the Arab rout, were forced to accept Israeli citizenship, and subjected to a military government. Political activity among them was extremely limited and manifested itself chiefly in activity by the Israel Communist Party and the first feelers put out by the Zionist parties. The first Zionist party that took a clear position on the matter was Mapam (the United Workers Party), which as early as 1954 opened its ranks to Arabs on an equal footing with its Jewish members. Since then it has maintained a network of workers to conduct vigorous activity among the Palestinian minority—youth and adults. It always insisted on having Arab representation on its Knesset list; it has had Arab MKs ever since the elections to the second Knesset in 1951 (Landau 1971, 98; Ozacky-Lazor 1996, 138–140).

Unlike Mapam, Mapai (the Eretz Israel Workers' Party), which in the 1950s was led by David Ben-Gurion, rejected the idea of opening its ranks to Arab members and continued to work in the Arab sector through satellite lists (see below) or through the traditional leadership that safeguarded the party's interests without being members. The change in the position of the Labor Party, the heir of Mapai, began in 1970, when it agreed to accept Arabs "who serve in the security forces" as members. Later, in 1973, it dropped this condition and began to enroll Arab members unconditionally. After that Herut and the other Jewish parties also began to accept Arab members (Cohen 1985, 79).

Electoral support for Jewish parties was influenced by many variables, associated with these parties' positions toward the Arabs, the degree of control exercised by the heads of clans and communities, as well as the existence of satellite lists (see below), which attracted most of the votes of this stream. Throughout the years in which the satellite lists were active (1949–1977), most voters of the Israeli-Arab camp cast their ballots for the satellite lists; only about an eighth of their valid ballots were given to Zionist parties. But when the Zionist parties dropped their support for satellite lists and began to accept Arab members, they began to attract direct Arab support. In the elections for the tenth Knesset in 1981, Arab support for Jewish parties jumped to about 40 percent and no satellite list made it into the Knesset. In the elections to the eleventh Knesset (1984), no satellite lists competed and the Jewish parties increased their direct support to about 50 percent of the Arab electorate. In the elections to the twelfth Knesset, the Democratic Arab Party (see below) appeared on the scene and cut into support for the Jewish parties, whose share of the Arab vote fell to about 40 percent.

In the elections to the thirteenth Knesset in 1992 support for the Zionist parties rebounded to 52 percent, because of problems that beset the Arab parties. Most recently, in the elections to the fourteenth Knesset (1996) and to the fifteenth Knesset (1999), Arab support for Jewish-Zionist parties declined to only 37 percent and 30 percent accordinly, because of the change in the electoral system with the direct election of the prime minister, but also because of the Arab parties' improved performance (Ghanem 1998b, Ghanem and Ozacky-Lazar 1999).

Support for Jewish parties remains widespread. Many Arab political activists have strengthened their self-confidence and performance over the years while changing their positions on key issues. Together with members of the satellite lists and of the Democratic Arab Party they manifest positions quite different than those of the other streams.

The Satellite Lists. The Zionist parties, and especially Mapai, unwilling to accept Arab members, encouraged leaders of clans, communities, or regions to set up satellite lists that could attract Arab electoral support. This approach provided the Jewish parties with an instrument for controlling the Arabs and a means for mobilizing their votes and support in the Knesset.

The socioeconomic situation of the Arabs in Israel, who found themselves without a national leadership after 1948, favored the emergence of traditional leaders who were interested in sitting in the Knesset. Because they could not be elected through the Jewish-Zionist parties, they formed alliances with them and served the objectives of the mother party, including through the formation of quasi-Arab lists that were in fact tools of the mother party. The lists had high-sounding names—the Democratic List of the Palestinian minority, Agriculture and Development, Cooperation and Fraternity, Progress and Development, and so on. Most of the lists were established by Mapai under Ben-Gurion. Although Mapam and the General Zionists also set up such lists, only those affiliated with Mapai ever managed to cross the electoral threshold and win seats in the Knesset. Their electoral strength remained very great throughout the period of the military government. They frequently won more than 50 percent of the Arab votes and took as many as six Knesset seats (in 1959). After the abolition of the military government, however, they began to lose voters to the Communist Party and the Zionist parties themselves. Prominent leaders such as Hamed Abu Rabi'a from Al-Naqab, Seif ed-Din al-Zouabi of Nazareth, Fares Hamadan from the Triangle, Jabber Mu'adi of Yirka, Labib Abu Ruqun of Isfiya, Mas'ad Qasis of Mi'ilya, and others, sat in the Knesset at one time or another. Most of them served more than one term and all were subservient to the leaders of Mapai, to the point that in 1961 they voted to continue the military government, in accordance with Mapai's position contrary to the interests of their constituency (see Cohen 1985; Ozacky-Lazor 1996; Landau 1971). By adopting positions scarcely different from those of the mother party, the representatives of these lists faithfully represented those of the Israeli-Arab stream.

In the elections to the tenth Knesset (1981), the Labor Party, the heir of Mapai, withdrew its support from the last of the satellite lists and it failed to pass the threshold (Cohen 1985, 74). To a certain extent the Democratic Arab Party, established by an MK who seceded from Labor, Abdulwahab Darawshe, has assumed their mantle.

THE DEMOCRATIC ARAB PARTY (DAP)

In January 1988, shortly after the start of the *intifada*, Labor MK Abdulwahab Darawshe, from the Galilee village of Iksal, addressing a rally in Nazareth called to protest the government's handling of the unrest in the West Bank and Gaza Strip, announced that he was resigning from Labor and its Knesset faction. Darawshe immediately began to look into the options for continuing his political career. In consultation with a number of local council heads, academics, and others, he decided to establish a new party that would be overtly Arab and aspire to represent the Arabs' problems and ambitions.

The founding conference of the Democratic Arab Party was held in June 1988, with the participation of about six hundred prominent figures from the Arab sector, including some twenty local-council heads and one hundred forty deputy council heads and council members, in addition to leading academics and clerics. This conference helped Darawshe and his associates demonstrate that they had broad support in the Arab sector (Landau 1993, 87).

In drawing up its list for the elections to the twelfth Knesset in 1988, the founders of the new party took pains to include candidates who represented various sectors within the Arab community. The second spot on the list went to Ahmad Abu Asba, head of the Jatt local council, in the Triangle, the third spot to Taleb Elsana, a Bedouin lawyer from Al-Naqab, and the fourth spot to Fahd Ali Hussein, a businessman from Majd el-Kurum in the Galilee.

The DAP platform called for equality for the Arabs in Israel and for the establishment of a Palestinian state alongside Israel in order to solve the Palestinian problem. The platform also explained the logic behind the establishment of an Arab party to capture the votes of the Palestinian minority and represent their interests and accused the Jewish parties of exploiting their Arab voters without making a serious attempt to satisfy the aspirations of the Arabs in Israel. To help disseminate its platform and positions, the DAP founded a weekly, *al-Diar,* distributed in Arab communities.

In the 1988 elections the DAP won only one seat in the Knesset—a good beginning nevertheless. Four years later, in elections to the thirteenth Knesset, the DAP increased its share of the Arab vote from 11.3 percent to 15.2 percent and doubled its representation to two seats (Ghanem 1996d). The party also made significant gains in local elections. In 1989, appearing for the first time, it returned two local council heads and several councilman. In 1993 the DAP elected six council heads and 47 council members, an impressive accomplishment by any standard (Ghanem and Ozacky-Lazor 1994, 19–20).

In 1996 the Democratic Arab Party formed an alliance and joint list with the "southern wing" of the Islamic movement (see below). Together they received 25 percent of the valid Arab ballots in 1996, good for four Knesset seats. In advance of the elections to the fifteenth Knesset it added MK Mahameed, from the DFPE, to its list, winning about 31 percent of the valid Arab ballots and five mandates. This was an impressive achievement in all opinions, which can be attributed chiefly to a solid organizational structure and the ethnic-religious tension among the Arabs in Israel.

The success of the DAP has several roots. Unlike of the Progressive List, it focused on the concerns of daily life while continuing to pay lip service to the general Palestinian cause. In the conditions that prevail today in the Arab sector—the result of the long-term discrimination in education, health care, municipal development, and other fields—its accent on such problems gave the DAP a significant foothold. The party employed a combined approach to advance these causes: in its platform and the speeches of its leaders, including MK Darawshe, it ignored Zionism and the Jewish-Zionist character of the state, to avoid offending the establishment and establish its credential as a potential coalition partner. It was careful to convey the message that the Arabs had to be part of the government coalition in order to have influence from the inside and achieve relevant gains. The DAP expressed its willingness to help put together a large and effective Arab bloc and initiated the establishment of a United Arab List. When this attempt at an Arab grand coalition failed, it nevertheless cobbled together a sort of mini-bloc with several independent groups and, with the help of veteran activists who called themselves the National Agreement Committee, headed by the chairman of the follow-up committee for Arabs in Israel Affairs, to cast the blame for the failure to achieve unity on the Progressive List and its head, Muhammad Miari (Ghanem 1996d).

POSITIONS ON KEY QUESTIONS

Here an attempt will be made to examine the main components of this stream's ideology. I shall focus on how its members relate to the issues of equality between Jews and Arabs in Israel, the identity of Arabs in Israel, resolution of the Palestinian problem, and how the struggle should be waged.

EQUALITY BETWEEN JEWS AND ARABS

For the Israeli-Arab stream, the question of equality—emphatically civic equality (individual rather than national or collective)—is the core around which its struggle is organized. Its adherents stress that in a regime that declares itself to be democratic, discrimination is untenable. Hence democracy is the guiding norm in their approach to the subject. Another guiding norm is pragmatism: the Arabs' demands must be pragmatic and "moderate" if they want to be able to realize them.

There has been no change in how this stream views the question of equality since 1948. In principle it perceives the struggle for civic equality and promotion of the Arabs' daily interests as the heart of the matter. It also draws a clear distinction between the issue of equality between Jews and Arabs, and other questions that are relevant to Arab life in Israel. In particular it distinguishes equality and the struggle to attain it from the Arab-Israeli conflict and its resolution, which they did not consider to be a key question. We may conjecture that the distinction is made because of its members' belief that raising the issue of the Israeli-Arab dispute and its resolution would have a negative impact on their struggle for equality within the state. Clear-cut evidence of how this stream sunders the issue of equality from that of a settlement of the dispute between Israel and the Arab countries is provided in a speech by MK Jabbar Mu'adi of the Druze satellite list affiliated with Mapai. This was in the Knesset debate on the composition and program of the new government in 1966, which preceded the swearing in of the new government of Levi Eshkol.[1]

The demand for equality indicates that for the stream, the progress of the Arab sector in Israel is to be measured by the size of the disparity with the Jewish sector, including what the central government provides to the two sectors in terms of budgets, grants, and so on. Its spokesmen hinted that the discrimination against the Arabs is due to their national affiliation.[2]

Its leaders have emphasized the need to move the Arab sector forward in many areas so that it can integrate more completely in the life of the country. Their forceful demand for integration in national life attested to their desire to be full partners in Israeli society.[3]

This demand for equality was galvanized in the early 1970s and came to include a sharp demand for equality and to have Arabs appointed to positions of responsibility in the management of the Arab sector. Greater prominence was accorded to the demand for full integration of Arabs into the life of the country, manifested chiefly in the demand for abolition of the various ministry departments for Arab affairs, put forward by MK Obeid in the Knesset debate on the subject.[4]

Another demand raised more forcefully in that period was to have Arabs appointed to official posts in various government ministries. It was emphasized that only broad integration could indicate an official intention to help the Arabs progress ahead.[5]

This development illuminates a significant change in the views of this stream and its members. They were no longer content to sit on the sidelines and were no longer willing to concede what they considered to be matters vital for advancing the interests of the Arabs in Israel. The strengthened demand for equality was associated with the view that a rapid advance in the status of the Arabs would improve coexistence with the Jewish majority and thereby contribute to the state itself. The stream demanded concrete steps to accelerate the achievement of equality, as stated by MK Mu'adi in his motion for the agenda on the state of the Arab local authorities.[6] This is further evidence of the evolution in the stance of this stream. Its spokesmen were no longer satisfied with what was offered them but insisted on submitting their own plans to promote the interests of the Arab sector. This attests to a desire to take part in setting policy for the Arab sector, set until then by the Jewish officials in charge of the Arab sector.

Despite the change in the attitude toward equality held by the members of this group, until the middle of the 1970s its view was generally characterized by a quiet and compromising tone, accompanied by periodic expressions of gratitude for the "benefits" that the state of Israel granted to its Arab citizens.[7]

In the mid-seventies this started to give way to a more forceful and harsher tone, as a significant change in the attitude toward the question of equality and full integration into Israeli life began to be evident. This change was manifested chiefly in unequivocal accusations that the Israeli government and policymakers were practicing ethnic and national discrimination against the Arabs (previously the line had been that such discrimination was the result of mistakes by junior bureaucrats). The decline in the tolerance for official manifestations of discrimination reflected intensified politicization. At the same time, the principle of legal struggle continued to be paramount. There were no signs of fatigue with the democratic struggle, only a determination to make better use of the means provided by Israeli democracy.[8]

In addition, members of this group began to express public support for the campaign by Arab local council heads against land expropriation and for equal budgets. This change is important in itself, because it was germane to a very large percentage of the Arabs in Israel, especially in light of the fact that during that period entire villages were fighting the expropriation of their lands. It is clear that the question of land and land expropriation is connected not only with the question of equality, but also has clear national dimensions and links with the Arab-Israeli conflict in general.[9]

The change in the attitude toward discrimination was quantitative and not only qualitative. The members of this stream were no longer content with speeches about discrimination in this or that sector but spoke out about discrimination in every sphere of life, official discrimination against Arabs in favor of Jews. It indicted the government and its bureaucracy for conscious application of this discrimination.

In this view, government policy that discriminates against Arabs causes direct damage to Arab-Jewish relations, because perfect coexistence is possible only between equals. The argument is that as long as there is no equality, coexistence is deficient and even in jeopardy.[10] The claim that the discrimination was practiced on an ethnic and national background and conducted at the government level intensified during the 1980s. The spokesmen of this stream made no bones in their charges that the inferior situation of the Arab sector was the result of the discriminatory policy of the Israeli government.[11]

Here I should comment that throughout the period being studied, the spokesmen of this stream made their peace with Zionism and ignored any connection between it and discrimination against Arabs. This differentiates it from all the other streams, which posit a direct link between Zionism and discrimination against Arabs and present Zionism as the key factor in this discrimination, by virtue of its preference for Jews over all others. Nawaf Massalha, the director of the Arab department in the Histadrut executive and later a Labor MK, asked whether the Arabs had to recognize Israel with all the goals proclaimed at its founding, including the absolute right of Jewish immigration and the automatic citizenship conferred on every such immigrant by the Law of Return, replied: "With all the objectives. Every Arab who has managed to recognize reality knows today that no solution is possible that includes a secular state in Israel."[12] In the nature of things, this acquiescence is a result of these persons' activity inside parties that define themselves as Zionist and of their belief that the struggle must be oriented toward attaining civic equality, convinced as they are that Israel will continue to be a state with a Jewish and Zionist character.

When they intensified the demand for equality in the 1980s, the representatives of this stream emphasized that the Arabs' objective was full integration in the life of the country and refused to discuss any other solutions—such as territorial, cultural, or institutional autonomy for the Arabs in Israel—on the assumption that autonomy is incompatible with integration. They also saw separate Arab-ethnic organizations, such as the council of heads of Arab local authorities and the university student organizations, as tools for further integration. In an interview conducted by Prof. Smooha of Haifa University, MK Darawshe said:

> Our rational propensity as citizens is toward full integration in all spheres of life in the country. But to my great distress, the political and partisan establishment in the country has not permitted the genuine integration of Arabs in the life of the country in all settings, and this is why, as a matter of protest, the particularistic organizations were established in the Arab sector.[13]

The representatives of this stream were resolutely opposed to solving the problems of the Arabs in Israel by means of some form of autonomy. In an interview I conducted with Fahd Abboud, a CRM member of the Haifa city council, he said: "A solution based on autonomy for the Arabs in Israel is out of the question and has no place. This solution is continued integration with the preservation of our uniqueness as Arabs."[14] This opposition to autonomy was explained as reflecting the facts that most Jews are opposed to it and that integration, which they hold to be incompatible with autonomy, is a more effective method to advance the Arabs' status and objectives.

The more strident demands for equality were accompanied by a demand that the authorities recognize the Arabs as a "national minority" who belong collectively to the Palestinian people and the Arab nation, and that they be treated as such. They were no longer content with being recognized as a cultural minority or religious group—a definition they had accepted until then.[15] The demand for recognition as a national minority was accompanied by emphasis that this minority has its own culture, language, and national identity that unite it and distinguish it from the Jewish majority in the country.[16]

As for obligations such as military, national, or civilian service, to which Jews attach great importance, the representatives of this stream long tended to ignore the question. But when the Arabs' intensified demands for equality provoked a Jewish reaction that demanded equal obligations, the representatives of this stream found themselves pressed to state their ideas on the topic. Here they did not display unanimity.

Some are violently opposed to Arabs' doing military, national, or civilian service, for two reasons:

1. Military service will bring the Arabs into confrontation with their Palestinian Arab brothers on the other side of the border. This opposition was overtly tactical and might vanish after the establishment of peace in the region.

2. Civilian or national service would be exploited to turn the Arabs into "servants" of Jewish society while providing no guarantee of advancing the status and objectives of the Arabs.[17]

Other representatives of this stream are opposed to military service for the same reasons, but would accept civilian or national service in a setting where they would be helping Arabs for a limited period in hospitals, schools, or villages. They explain that this kind of service would ultimately contribute to advancing the objectives of the Arabs in Israel.[18]

The establishment of the Democratic Arab Party headed by Abdulwahab Darawshe, who quit the Labor Party, led to a certain "radicalization" of the positions of this stream. In essence, its thinking moved toward the center of the political and ideological map of the Palestinian minority. Members of the DAP, who had freed themselves of direct subordination to the Jewish-Zionist parties, slowly began to voice clear indictments of the Israeli government for its discriminatory policy. Their demands for equality gained strength from year to year, and began to cover broader areas. At the founding conference of the DAP, MK Darawshe said: "We have to organize a political force that can participate in decision-making in order to attain full equality for the Arab people in Israel, in order to deal with problems of land, education, budgets, housing, and employment, to find appropriate solutions for the problem of the abandoned and unrecognized villages, and to find a solution for houses marked for demolition."[19]

The DAP's platform emphasized that the Arabs are part of the Palestinian people and that Israel must be a state of all its citizens, both Arabs and Jews.[20] But its spokespersons continued to reject any discussion of autonomy for the Arabs. In a series of interviews that I conducted with a number of leading figures in the party— As'ad Azaiza (head of the Dabburiya local council), Ahmad Abu Asba (head of the Jatt local council), Ahmad Abbas (head of the Nahaf local council), and Abd al-Rauf Mu'assi (head of the Fureidis local council)—they emphasized that the best solution would be full integration into the life of the country together with preservation of the Arabs' unique identity that stems from their national affiliation; in other words, an improvement of the status quo rather than a demand to abolish it. They stressed that autonomy is incompatible with integration into the life of the country.

This position is somewhat blurred by the fact that many party activists have made significant contributions to the establishment of institutions specifically for the Arab sector, such as the committee of Arab local council heads, or put forward demands that the Arabs be allowed to manage their own affairs in whole or part. Party movers and spokespersons tended to ignore the question of equal obligations, including military, national, or civilian service. Their silence stemmed from a fear of expressing an opinion that might provoke mainstream Jewish elements and hinder progress in the campaign for equality—or arouse Arab antagonists of the idea and produce a schism that undercut the struggle. In the series of interviews that I conducted, however, it was clear that there was a broad consensus concerning equal obligations. They absolutely rejected military service, out of an unwillingness to fight or help in a war against Arab countries or their Palestinian brethren, but they supported the idea of mandatory or voluntary service in Arab villages, hospitals, or educational institutions.[21]

Speakers for the DAP raised the threshold sensitivity of the Israeli-Arab stream with regard to the scope of the inequality imposed on the Arab citizens of the state by the Israeli authorities. Their ever-increasing protests included a sharp indictment of the authorities for conducting discriminatory policies and a demand for rectification of the injustice and parity between Jews and Arabs in the allocation of resources, including budgets for local authorities. These demands began moving closer to the positions of the other streams. Nevertheless, the members of the Israeli-Arab stream did not let the existing discrimination make them despair of integration. On the contrary, there was a far-reaching intensification of their demand for equality and for integration into the life of the state, accompanied by a clear decline in their tolerance for manifestations of institutionalized discrimination against the Palestinian minority.

The Israeli-Arab stream's perspective on the question of equality between Jews and Arabs has changed dramatically since the establishment of the state. Most of the changes have taken place on two levels:

1. There was a clear increase in the activism of the demand for equality. Unlike the start of the period, when its members spoke about the *possibility* of equality in several spheres, at the end of the period the *demand* for equality encompassed every area of life. Their initial silence about institutionalized discrimination and praise for Israeli governments' Arab-sector policy gave way in the mid-seventies to accusations that Israeli governments and agencies

were conducting institutionalized discrimination against the Arabs on account of their ethnic-national origin.

2. Unlike the beginning of the period, the members of this stream refrained from speaking about or referring to "political" topics relevant to the Arabs in general and saw their role as conducting a struggle to attain municipal and civic goals. The leaders gradually freed themselves from this limitation and began to see their role as participation in the "political" struggles being waged by the Arabs in general, especially with regard to land and land expropriation, the Arab-Israeli conflict, and the Palestinian problem.

The new attitude was based on the argument that coexistence pertains only between equals. As long as there is discrimination and inequality, it is impossible to speak of true coexistence. As stated, the campaign to attain equality was the central component in the position represented by the leaders of this stream. The basic logic underlying their position was that an improvement in living conditions and the situation of Arab communities would contribute not only to enhanced coexistence and relations with the Jewish majority, but would also strengthen the Arabs' hold on their lands and villages, and prevent them from leaving.[22]

The metamorphosis in this group's views about equality reflects the politicization that is taking place among the Arabs in Israel. It attests to a better understanding of the Israeli political system and the possibilities of maneuvering permitted by its democratic regime. It manifests a desire to integrate into and belong to the state without seeing the struggle for equality as part of the struggle for national liberation, but only as a campaign to enhance their status and position within the country.

THE IDENTITY OF THE ARABS IN ISRAEL

The question of the identity of the Arabs in Israel is one the thorniest issues with which this stream must contend, especially in light of the fact that they include supporters of the Jewish-Zionist parties. For its spokesmen, however, it is a secondary question that they generally prefer to ignore. All the same, the circumstances in which the Arabs found themselves in Israel after 1948 compel them to go public with their views on this issue. Fundamentally they have spoken of two components—Arab and Israeli—and preferred to use the expression "the Palestinian minority" to describe their group or "Israeli Arab" to describe their individual identity. These are appellations drawn from the Israeli-Jewish terminology for the Arab minority and its members, which assumes that it is a new minority distinct from the rest of the

Arab world and the Palestinian people, an Arab who is "made in Israel."

The result of the 1967 war threw open the frontier between the Arabs in Israel and the Palestinians in the West Bank and Gaza Strip. Just as in the period before the war, however, the representatives of this stream continued to use this bipolar identity, an Arab-national element and Israeli-civic element. In other words, they viewed the Arabs as "the Palestinian minority" or "Arab citizens of Israel." The leaders of this stream did not mention the Palestinian affiliation of the Arabs in Israel, neither in Knesset debates nor in the community. None of the literature they circulated in those days mentioned any affinity between the Arabs in Israel and the Palestinian people.

This highlight on the Israeli affiliation was accompanied by a vigorous demand that the Jews see them as Israelis and that the state of Israel be the state of all its "Israeli" citizens, both Arabs and Jews—a situation that would certainly help them feel more comfortable and at home in the state. In interviews conducted in 1971 by Ellen Gifner with prominent Israeli Arab personalities who supported Jewish-Zionist parties, she heard remarks like: "I belong to the State of Israel and not to the Jewish state. . . . The state begins with the hypothesis that the key item is not its Jewishness but its Israeliness" (Gifner 1974, 138). The view of the Arabs as "Israelis" or "Israeli citizens," while ignoring their affiliation with the Palestinian people, was typical of this stream throughout the decade.[23]

While accentuating their Israeli affiliation, the representatives of this group did not ignore the affiliation of the Arabs in Israel with the Arab nation in general and even emphasized this.[24] They insisted that the Arabs in Israel are part of the Arab nation without associating them with the Palestinian people.

This group saw the identity of the Arabs in Israel as one split between national and civic affiliation, with the realization that this fissure causes tensions and contradictions in the Arab psyche. All the same, they made their peace with this opposition and looked for a middle ground that would permit them and all the Arabs in Israel to live between these two identities.[25] They saw their identity as sundered between their being Israelis and their being Arab, and ignored any possible Palestinian identity. The Israeli identity derived from the fact that they lived in Israel, with all this implies, including achievements associated with living in the state of Israel; their Arab identity stemmed from their historical and cultural affiliation with the Arab world.

This split identity had in essence accompanied this stream and most Arabs from the establishment of Israel, because after 1948, the Arabs for the first time found themselves required to evince loyalty to a state that was at war with the Arab world and their Palestinian people. Throughout this period, which lasted until the early 1970s, the perception was that one had to decide between a single loyalty and affiliation, either with Israel or with the Arab world. This produced the split identity, because this stream wanted to be part of and loyal to both sides at one and the same time, without choosing one or the other. It is noteworthy that statements about this split identity began to appear only in the 1960s, after the recovery from the blow to Arab society caused by the 1948 war and the founding of Israel.

A significant change in how this stream related to the Arabs' identity began to be visible in the early 1970s and gained momentum from the mid-seventies on. This change involved an increasing emphasis on the Palestinian identity of the Arabs in Israel, accompanied by a strong emphasis on their also being Israelis.

Initially this was accompanied by a cautious demand that the Arabs in Israel rethink their affiliation with the Palestinian people. Mohammed Watad wrote that "there is a need for a return to the sources and a reconnection with awareness of the suffering of the Palestinians in Arab lands."[26] But this change was not comprehensive and in general applied only to members of Mapam among the Jewish-Zionist parties. The change gained strength in the mid-seventies and broadened significantly in the 1980s, with an emphasis that this evolution in the identity of the Arabs in Israel did not impair their loyalty to the state of Israel. According to this view, the Arabs in Israel are both Palestinians and Israelis loyal to the state. A clear expression of this change, which crystalized in the mid-eighties, was given by MK Darawshe, then representing Labor, in an interview with Prof. Sammy Smooha of the University of Haifa:

> The Arab citizens in the state of Israel are an integral part of
> the Palestinian people and the same time loyal Israeli citizens.
> I do not think that there is any conflict between being a
> proud Palestinian Arab who is loyal to the Palestinian people
> and the Arab nation and being an Israeli citizen who is loyal
> to the state.[27]

As stated, the accent on the Palestinian affiliation of the Arabs in Israel, as apprehended by the members of this group, did not come at the expense of their Israeli identity. Rather, it was accompanied by an emphasis that national affiliation with the Palestinian people and civic affiliation with the state of Israel were indeed compatible. The spokesmen of this stream made it clear that it is their civic affiliation with Israel that differentiates the Arabs in Israel from the rest of the Palestinian people.[28]

This civic affiliation with Israel and national affiliation with the Palestinians is a hallmark of the stream's attitude to the identity of the Palestinian minority in the 1980s. Unlike the late 1960s and the 1970s, when they were conscious of a conflict and fissure in the Arabs' identity, between the Israeli component and the Arab component, in the 1980s they postulated two affiliations—Israeli and Palestinian-Arab—which together constitute a single complex identity in which the two parts march together and work synergistically rather than overpowering the other. This view of the identity as complex rather than bisected stemmed from a growing awareness of their simultaneous affinity with two spheres, the state of Israel and the Palestinian people, and the desire to preserve both of them. Hence it was emphasized that the civic and legal affiliation was totally Israeli, while the emotional and national affiliation was Palestinian-Arab.[29]

The Israeli-Palestinian identity of the Israeli-Arab stream gathered speed after the establishment of the DAP. One of the cornerstones of the DAP's definition of the identity of the Arabs in Israel is the emphasis on their affiliation with a Palestinian people, in addition to their being loyal citizens of the state of Israel, and the denial that there was any contradiction between the two. According to the party's platform for the elections to the twelfth Knesset, held in November 1988: "The Democratic Arab party is the outcome of a protracted struggle by the Arab masses, which has gone on for forty years. Its principles and platform make it the appropriate context for serious participation in attaining genuine equality within the state, which is the state of all its citizens, and in which the Arab citizens are an inseparable part of the Palestinian Arab people and citizens of the state of Israel."[30]

The identity of the Arabs in Israel, as perceived by this stream, has gone through significant changes and developments since 1948, on two main levels:

1. At the start of the period, the leaders of this group saw the identity of the Arabs in Israel as split between two components—Israeli and Arab. Later they began to emphasize the Palestinian identity of the Arabs in Israel as well, but without retreating from the Israeli identity. Hence the identity of the Arabs in Israel since the mid-1970s has included two key components—Israeli and Palestinian—and both have been gaining strength over the years.

2. At the start of this period, this stream was conscious of a split and even a conflict between the Israeli affiliation and the Arab affiliation of the Arabs in Israel. Later they began to conceive of a complex identity that combined Israeli and Palestinian-Arab elements into a single unity, with no internal fissure or contradiction.

THE ARAB-ISRAELI CONFLICT

The Israeli-Arab stream always viewed the conflict between Israel and the neighboring states as secondary to the issue of equality. As the years passed, however, its importance grew, with special emphasis on how it affected the life of Arabs in Israel.

In the pages that follow I will attempt to present the views of this stream with regard to the Arab-Israeli conflict and its impact on the Arabs in Israel. I will consider their views about specific events, including the wars between Israel and its Arab neighbors, international decisions relevant to the conflict, Sadat's peace initiative, the attitude toward the PLO, the extent to which that organization represents the Palestinian people, and its struggle against Israel, and how they view the link between the conflict, the Arabs in Israel, and their relations with the Jewish majority.

This stream's view of the conflict and its solution evolved over the years, from absolute support for Israel and its positions, including rejection of the establishment of a Palestinian state, or support for non-involvement in issues related to the conflict, toward an emphasis on the need for a solution based on the establishment of a Palestinian state and recognition of the PLO as the sole legitimate representative of the Palestinian people. It even went as far as accusing Israel of responsibility for the perpetuation of the conflict (whereas, at the start of this period, blame was cast exclusively on the Arab states). Similarly, at the beginning of the period no attention was paid to how the conflict impacted on the lives of the Arabs in Israel and their relations with the Jewish majority. Later, especially from the mid-seventies, the representatives of this stream began to link the conflict with the Arabs' life and to see its continuation as the focus of the tensions between Jews and Arabs, and thus as the chief obstacle to stable and full coexistence.

As for the conflict itself, in the period that proceeded the June 1967 war, this stream saw itself as part of the Israeli side. During the days before the outbreak of hostilities, it blamed the Arab states for the situation and expressed its willingness to share in the preparations for the war. In a letter of support sent by *mukhtars* and school principals from the villages of Bir es-Sikka, al-Marja, Yamma, and Ibthan to Yaakov Cohen, the director of the department of Arab affairs in Histadrut, they wrote: "In the difficult conditions besetting the state we proclaim our full support for the steps taken by the government and our willingness to place whatever is in our power at the disposal of the state."[31]

Israel's triumph in the war inspired the members of this stream with a sense of security about the future. They even expressed open feelings of "joy" at the victory and supported the notion that it was the Arab countries that had begun the war against Israel and who refused to make peace, and accordingly deserved to lose.[32]

Even though the representatives of this stream saw themselves as part of the Israeli side, the issues of the solution of the conflict and the appropriate attitude toward it stood at the focus of an internal dispute in which there were two main positions. Some asserted that the solution of the conflict was none of their business and did not even bother to express an opinion on the matter, as in the remarks by MK Diab Obeid, of the Mapai satellite list, Cooperation and Fraternity, when asked about his opinion concerning a peaceful resolution of the conflict: "Peace making does not depend on us [the Arabs in Israel] but on higher political decisions . . . in which I do not get involved."[33] Others saw the conflict as relevant to themselves but preferred to relate to it and the possibility of peace in general terms. They sympathized with the plight of the members of the Palestinian people who had fallen under Israeli occupation after the war, but totally ignored any Israeli responsibility for the state of war and accused the Arabs of causing the situation, telling them that they should "get wise" and come to the negotiating table with Israel.[34]

The pro-Israeli position of the members of this stream persisted even later. After the outbreak of the Yom Kippur war, a meeting of Arab public figures who were supporters of the Jewish-Zionist parties, including MK Seif ed-din Zouabi of the Alignment (Maa'rach) and deputy health minister Abd el-Aziz Zouabi of Mapam sent a telegram to then–Prime Minister Golda Meir: "The hundreds present at the Municipal cultural center in Nazareth support all the steps taken by the Government and see them as a means to attain victory. We all stand ready to help the government with all the means at our disposal in order to succeed in the battle that has been forced on the state, in order to achieve the longed-for peace" (Zouabi 1987, 183–185).

Despite this show of support, in the years after the October (1973) war a significant change began to emerge in this stream's view of the conflict. The idea that the Arabs in Israel should refrain from involvement in issues related to the conflict was replaced by an accent on the need to achieve peace, with support for returning territory and accepting Security Council Resolutions 242 and 338. This position, which first emerged among the Communists after the June 1967 war, began to take clear form among the representatives of the Israeli-Arab stream starting in the mid-seventies. The beginning of the change was reflected in support for returning territory and accepting Security Council Resolutions 242 and 338.[35]

In the mid-seventies, paralleling the slow movement in the Arab world, the first voices were heard in the Israeli-Arab stream to recognize and negotiate with the PLO to achieve peace, accompanied by explicit calls for granting the right of self-determination to the Palestinians.[36] This was a profound change for this stream. Unlike the start of the period, when the Palestinian question was totally ignored, and any calls for peace were general calls addressed to the Arab states, the leaders of this group began to emphasize the importance of solving the Palestinian question. They made a clear demand that Israel move toward the Palestinians and express its willingness to make concessions.[37] In the view of the members of this stream, recognizing the PLO and the Palestinian people's right to self-determination was a paramount Israeli interest. Israel needed not fear taking such steps, since it was clear that Israel would continue to be a Jewish-Zionist state with all this implied. It was obvious to this stream that a solution based on the principle of self-determination for Israel and Palestinians was a final stage, after which there would be no further demands for secession or the establishment of a democratic secular state by the Arabs in Israel.[38]

The new perspective from which the Israeli-Arab stream views the conflict and its resolution are a result of the international political awakening with regard to the Palestinian question and the success of the PLO, especially after Arafat's address to the United Nations General Assembly in 1974. These caused far-reaching changes in the overall position of the Arabs in Israel on the conflict, the Palestinian problem, and the PLO, a position that increasingly supported the need to recognize the PLO as the representative of the Palestinian people and demanded the establishment of a Palestinian state alongside Israel. Members of this stream reacted to these changes as a result of the pressure exerted on them by the Palestinian minority in general and by the other streams in particular.

A new development followed Sadat's initiative and visit to Jerusalem. This stream was the central force among the Arabs in Israel who supported Sadat's initiative and saw it as a step in the direction of peace. They intensified their idea about resolution of the Palestinian problem and their demand for an overall resolution of the Israeli-Arab conflict. In the words of Jamaal Ka'an, a member of the Mapam secretariat, at one of its debates on the condition of the Arabs in Israel: "I would like to begin with a statement of congratulations at the peace with the largest country among our neighbors, Egypt, and I profoundly hope that process will continue and reach the other neighbors and also the Palestinians."[39] They began to say openly that the Palestinians' right of self-determination meant in practice the establishment of a Palestinian state alongside Israel. They also began to speak clearly about the fact that the conflict was one of the causes of the tensions in the relations between Jews and Arabs in Israel. Its resolution would alleviate the condition of the latter and allow them to feel more comfortable and integrated better into the state.[40]

This stream saw the Lebanon war, which Israel launched in 1982 with the aim of destroying the PLO presence in Lebanon, as a mistake, especially in light of the fact that the calamities it wreaked fell mainly on the Palestinians in Lebanon. This war led to a new emphasis that a solution of the Palestinian problem would have to be based on the establishment of a Palestinian state and recognition of the PLO as the representative of the Palestinian people living outside the Green Line. The war crystalized the change that the members of this stream had been undergoing since the middle of the 1970s. Clear evidence of this change can be found in a letter sent by Seif ed-din Zouabi, who in the past had praised Israel's military achievements and given his full support to measures taken against its Palestinian and Arab enemies, to Prime Minister Menachem Begin after the outbreak of the war: "There is no alternative to talking with the Palestinians. . . . I have never been a supporter of Yasser Arafat and am among those who are enamored of him, and I did not recognize his existence. After Yasser Arafat demonstrated that he is the only person who can speak in the name of the Palestinians, why did you not take advantage of this opportunity?" (Zouabi 1987, 258).[41]

The disposition for a solution based on two states—Israel and a Palestinian state—persists among this stream until the present day. It is clear that, as with the other groups, the demand for the establishment of a Palestinian state alongside Israel has become clear and unequivocal.[42]

Like the other streams, the Israeli-Arab stream considers the PLO to be the representative of the Palestinian people in the West Bank, Gaza Strip, and the Diaspora, but resolutely rejects the possibility that the PLO or other elements based outside the Green Line could represent the Arabs of Israel. Its leaders see Israeli actors, including themselves, the Arab members of Knesset, and the government of Israel as the representatives of the Arabs in Israel.[43] Even after Darawshe quit the Labor Party to set up the Democratic Arab Party, he continued to hold the same positions.[44]

The positions of the members of this stream with regard to how a solution of the conflict in general and of the Palestinian problem in particular would influence coexistence and the life of the Arabs in Israel began to crystalize in the late 1970s. The idea is that a solution of the Palestinian problem would remove one of the most serious obstacles that cause alienation and estrangement between Arabs and Jews in Israel. The establishment of a Palestinian state alongside Israel would lead to a sense of relief among the Arabs in Israel, which would help them integrate into the life of the country and enhance Jewish-Arab coexistence.[45] Members of the DAP and those close to it shared this view. In a series of interviews I conducted with DAP activists, there was a clear consensus that a solution to the conflict would alleviate the situation of the Arabs in Israel and contribute to their integration into the country, and improved coexistence between Jews and Arabs in Israel.[46]

This perspective, which has been coalescing since the end of the 1970s, views the conflict as the chief obstacle to normal coexistence between Arabs and Jews. Accordingly, a resolution of the conflict would be a great boon for the Arabs and permit them to integrate more fully into the life of the country.

THE APPROPRIATE MEANS OF STRUGGLE

As I pointed out in previous pages, the leaders of the Israeli-Arab stream wanted to alter the status of the Arabs in Israel. They advocated a resolution of the conflict by means of the establishment of a Palestinian state alongside Israel. This required that they define, for themselves and for others, the appropriate means for conducting their struggle.

Both at the start of this period and later, the leaders of this stream saw their role as advancing the daily interests of the Arabs in Israel. They totally ignored the Zionist character of the state. Their demands, as compared to those of the other streams, were not radical and did not go beyond promoting the Arabs' interests in various spheres.

This stream's conception of the appropriate means for conducting the struggle has changed only slightly since 1948. In the pages that follow I shall investigate its position on this question, and especially with regard to Jewish-Arab cooperation, their status as a junior element in the Zionist enterprise, participation in government coalitions, the advantages of doing so, and various forms of parliamentary and extraparliamentary struggle.

Throughout most of the period, this stream has supported organization as a junior faction within the larger parties, which by the nature of things are composed chiefly of Zionist Jews. There is particular importance to this, because this perspective, according to which activity within the large Jewish-Zionist frameworks will enhance the capacity to nudge the Jewish majority in the direction of greater acceptance of the Arabs' objective, is an important index for distinguishing this stream from the other streams.

When Prof. Sammy Smooha of the University of Haifa asked MK Darawshe about the importance of activity in a large Jewish-Zionist party, such as Labor, the latter replied: "Our problem is not persuading those who are already convinced, but influencing the majority that controls this country. . . . In my opinion the broad framework of a large party is a setting that permits broader influence than a small party does."[47]

The organization of some members of this stream in satellite lists (until 1981) was a tactic aimed at winning Arab votes. After election day, the members of the satellite lists were in practice considered to be members of the Jewish parties that had sponsored the lists and were counted with them in everything associated with ideology and political behavior. The establishment of the Democratic Arab Party was a milestone. For the first time an Arab party was established without the involvement of Jewish parties and perhaps even despite their opposition, with the emphasis that the party was an instrument to improve the lot of the Arabs in Israel. According to an editorial in *al-Diyar*, the party newspaper, "The time has come to highlight Arab power, the power that can have influence for a positive change."[48] Among the reasons Darawshe gave for quitting Labor were his disappointment with the atmosphere in the large party and a strong desire to organize a separate Arab force that could have a direct influence on decision-making in the country. In an interview conducted after he quit Labor he said: "I quit because I felt that I had failed by not managing to exert influence."[49]

As this stream sees things, a common Jewish-Arab struggle is the only way to advance the interests of the Arabs in Israel. Its members felt compelled to work with Jewish circles that were close to them ideologically. Their activity in parties that define themselves as Jewish-Zionist attests to the importance they attach to cooperation with Jews. Their demand for Jewish cooperation has grown stronger over the years. In the early 1970s, only Arabs affiliated with Mapam emphasized this point. Later, however, members of other Jewish-Zionist parties began to advocate the idea.[50] They also deemed it necessary to work unstintingly to mobilize Jews to help them conduct their struggle. A national conference of Arab-sector Mapam activists passed a number of resolutions, of which the most conspicuous was "to continue action to mobilize Jewish public opinion in favor of the just demands of the Arab citizens of Israel."[51]

The ideological commitment to Jewish-Arab collaboration grew stronger over the years. Members of this stream saw it as the only guarantee of success in the struggle of the Arabs in Israel. Consider an article by Qasim Zeid of Mapam, headlined "The Source of Power: A Joint Effort," in which he wrote:

> The struggle must be Jewish-Arab and by no means a separatist struggle or one conducted by Arabs only. . . . The struggle for peace, too, must be a common one. Without Jewish-Arab cooperation, Jewish radicals will accuse Jewish circles of playing into the hands of marginal Arab elements, while the Arabs will be accused of being radicals and secessionists who are

playing into the hands of the PLO. The two sides must work together on an equal basis. Only through joint and equal forces can we win the battle.[52]

The actual position on the best form of organization varies from group to group within this stream. Those who belong to Jewish-Zionist parties totally reject organization on an Arab national basis. The spokespersons of this stream consider such organization to be against the best interests of the Arabs in Israel.[53]

By contrast, those who preferred to organize in the DAP emphasized that they supported cooperation with Jews and deemed it essential. In an interview after the establishment of the DAP, Darawshe said: "By establishing an independent Arab party we are not saying that we want a divorce from the Jewish public. We want to consolidate our forces, but with a clear disposition to maintain the link with the peace camp and Jewish democratic forces."[54]

The Israeli-Arab stream believes that its efforts will be crowned with success only if it works within a Zionist structure. Its members believe that the fact that most Israeli Jews are Zionists requires an appropriate attitude and cooperation with this majority in order to accomplish anything.[55]

The leaders of the Israeli-Arab stream view the parliamentary arena as the chief venue for making gains. They also believe that the Arabs in Israel must be partners in the government, at any price.[56] This idea that the Arabs must be represented in the government coalition is a permanent feature of the stream. MK Darawshe told: "The Arab sector, which constitutes 17 percent of the inhabitants of the state, should be represented in the government."[57] The debate that took place in the second half of the 1980s about the establishment of a national unity government, with the participation of both Labor and the Likud, and the existence of such a government in 1984–1990, posed a serious dilemma for this stream. In Arab eyes, membership in a coalition with the Likud is contrary to their interests and the interests of the Palestinian problem. Hence during those years the position on joining the coalition advanced by the spokespersons for this stream was hesitant or against, with stipulations that focused on the benefits that joining the coalition could bring to the Arabs. When asked, "in your opinion is it important to be part of the government coalition?" MK Fares replied: "Yes, but not in every coalition."[58] The same general line has guided the Democratic Arab Party since its founding.[59]

This stream views the parliamentary struggle as the chief means for the Arabs to wage their campaign, on the assumption that it can bring them to the coalition table and decision-making forums. In the early years of the state the Israeli-Arab stream did not favor legal extraparliamentary methods; very slowly, however, it began to consider this. Like the other streams, it rejected illegal extraparliamentary activity and emphasized that the campaign must be conducted within the law. In the words of MK Fares, "the means that I reject—I do not even call them struggle—every act that contravenes the law. I call that anarchy."[60] Leaders of this stream slowly began to show interest in and even to support demonstrations and strikes, but they continued to utterly reject the use of violence and emphasized that the struggle must be conducted by legal means only.[61]

Here too the DAP remains within the consensus. Its members advocate parliamentary effort and view participation in elections for the Knesset, the Histadrut, and local authorities as essential for influencing the status of the Arabs in Israel and making progress toward a resolution of the Arab-Israeli conflict.[62] They also support extraparliamentary efforts, including demonstrations, general strikes, and rallies. They believe that these are important means for mobilizing the Arabs and creating a force that can deter the establishment from implementing discriminatory policies and make a contribution to the resolution of the conflict. They stress, however, that these methods are a legitimate right that the Arabs may and must exploit.

The DAP rejects illegal mechanisms, such as violence, disturbances, and terrorism, as well as boycotting elections. They argue that illegal methods play into the hands of the authorities and harm the Arabs and their struggle, hence they should be avoided. According to MK Darawshe, "I am opposed to violent activity in Israel, because this is the shared homeland of the Jewish majority and the Arabs and we must preserve this homeland."[63]

Support for parliamentary and extraparliamentary efforts and staying within the law is one of the important indicators of the politicization of the Arabs in Israel. In addition, the increased emphasis on the need for extraparliamentary means—that is, activation of the demand for achieving their goals while employing all the means permitted by the law—is one of the most important components of the politicization process and attests to its depth. The use of many and various forms of activity, while observing the law, is considered to be vital for advancing the interests of citizens in the democratic regime that prevails in Israel.

PROFILE OF THE ISRAELI-ARAB STREAM

The general ideology of the Israeli-Arab stream, as presented in this chapter, draws in part on the four themes presented here. I can sketch its profile on the basis of several indices that distinguish it from the other streams:

1. It favors *organization within the Zionist establishment,* or at least aspires to be part of a government coalition headed by parties that represent this establishment. Leaders of this stream maintain that the Arabs' struggle must be conducted inside the Zionist establishment. Accordingly they opt to join parties that define themselves as Jewish-Zionist or establish Arab lists that are close to the Jewish-Zionist parties ideologically. They strongly prefer that these parties be part of the executive branch, on the grounds that this offers a better opportunity to influence decision-making and resource allocation. Unlike the other streams, they want to work in concert with the Jewish-Zionist establishment in order to promote the interests of the Arabs and those of Israeli society in general. In their estimation, only activity as a junior partner with the Zionist establishment can lead to concrete results. Unlike the other streams that accept or even require the establishment of Arab groups on a separate national basis, or joint non-Zionist Jewish-Arab organization, this stream generally insists that it must be part of Jewish-Zionist organization, because of the solid Jewish-Zionist majority in the state.

2. It places *equality* at the top of its agenda. This stream considers the struggle for civic equality to be its main raison d'être, and progress on this front as its most important goal, even though other issues, especially resolution of the Arab-Israeli conflict and its influence on coexistence, have begun to occupy a central place in their doctrine.

3. It aspires to only *limited changes* (pragmatism). The Israeli-Arab stream recognizes the fundamental fact that Israel is a Jewish country with a Jewish majority. It accepts this existing order and does not demand a change in character of the state. Instead, it focuses on improving the Arabs' status in civic issues such as equal allocation of resources, jobs, and the like. This approach draws on its essential pragmatism, which, along with acceptance of Israeliness and Jewish-Zionist supremacy, constitutes the broad ideological armature of its doctrine.

4. It adopts a *conciliatory tone.* The tone and language generally used by the spokesman of this stream to describe the situation prevailing in the country and region, including demands for change, tend to be accommodating of Jewish sensibilities. They continue

to be much more conciliatory than those of the other streams, although over the years the demand for changes and realization of the vital objectives and interests of the Arabs in Israel has become more forceful.

These four criteria are interrelated. Taken together, they constitute the main tenets of the doctrine of the Israeli-Arab stream. Its commitment to activity within the Jewish-Zionist parties and focus on civic equality as a central value lead it to display a pragmatic approach and call—in a conciliatory tone that expresses a readiness for compromise—for only limited changes in the status of the Arabs in Israel, while avoiding demands for a modification of the Jewish-Zionist character of the state.

The changes in the Israeli Arab stream since 1948 can be summarized as follows:

1. There has been an intensification of its demand for equality and integration in the state. This reflects its desire to belong to the Israeli system and the Israelization on the margins of Israeli Jewish society. This process has been accompanied by a sharpening of the tone of its calls for improving the Arabs' condition and lowered tolerance of manifestations of discrimination against the Arabs by the authorities.

2. A two-part compound identity—Arab-Palestinian national and Israeli civil—has emerged, in which the two components reinforce each other.

3. There has been a strengthening of the demand for the establishment of Palestinian state alongside Israel as the only way to solve the fundamental problem of the Palestinian people. This solution, it is emphasized, will also improve the situation of the Arabs in Israel and enhance its coexistence with the Jewish majority. On this question, too, there has been a clear escalation in the demand that Israel reach an accord with the Palestinians.

4. Support for legal means of struggle in the parliamentary and extraparliamentary arenas has remained constant. The use of violence or illegal means in order to advance the interests of the Arabs in Israel is rejected absolutely.

4

The Communist Stream

The Communist Party, which began as a marginal organization during the period of the Mandate, derived its raison d'être and fundamental positions on social, cultural, economic, and political issues from the broad ideology of Communism. It attained the zenith of international public support between the two world wars, in the wake of the triumph of the Bolshevik Revolution in Russia.

The few Arabs who believed in Marxist ideology at the start of the century were significantly reinforced by immigration to Palestine, in the late nineteenth and early twentieth centuries, of thousands of Jews who advocated Communism and its mission. They had a fervent faith in the ideology and aspired to realize it in the new land they were working to build.

In this chapter I shall consider two different aspects of the Communist stream in Israel: first, the organizational aspect, associated with the Communist Party, its public support and electoral strength; second, its basic positions on the key questions that preoccupy public discourse in the region and Israel in general, and its Arab citizens in particular. These positions were nurtured by the unique situation that prevails in the region, Israel, and its Arab minority. But they were influenced to various degrees by the broader Communist ideology, which in many cases served as a tool to justify or market the positions advocated by the stream.

ORGANIZATION AND PUBLIC SUPPORT

The Communists began to organize in Palestine long before the establishment of the state of Israel. The Socialist Workers' Party, the first organized manifestation of Communism in the country, was founded in 1919. Later, in 1923, it renamed itself the Palestine Communist Party (PCP), joined the Comintern, and began to accept Arab members in addition to its Jewish founders—although the party retained a Jewish majority (Rekhess 1993, 25–26).

Intervention by the Soviet Communist Party to "Arabize" the Palestine Communist Party and the dissolution of the Comintern in the early 1940s led to a split in the ranks of the PCP. Most of its Arab members seceded to form their own Communist national organization, the League for National Liberation. The Jewish group, led by Shmuel Mikounis, Meir Wilner, and Esther Wilensky, continued to be active as the PCP (Rekhess 1993, 26–27).

The two Communist factions, Jewish and the Arab, did not reunite until after the establishment of Israel. At a joint conference in October 1948 they proclaimed the founding of the Israel Communist Party (ICP), known by its Hebrew acronym *Maki*, which immediately set to work to reorganize and act in various ways to promote its platform and objectives, and garner support among both Jewish and Arab citizens of the state.

In the early years, most ICP members and voters were Jewish, and this preponderance actually increased at first because of the good relations between the Soviet Union and Israel in the late 1940s. When the Soviet attitude toward Israel became more hostile in the mid-fifties, and especially after the rapprochement between Egypt and the Communist bloc, led by the Soviet Union and the first arms deal between Egypt and Czechoslovakia, Jewish support for the ICP waned, accompanied by a parallel gradual increase in Arab support, which slowly Arabized the party.

The Communist Party was able to attract Arabs because it functioned as a legitimate political party represented in the Knesset while strongly defending the rights of the Arabs, opposing Israeli positions and policies in both foreign and domestic affairs, and demanding that Israel allow the refugees to return, stop expropriating land, make peace with the Arab states, and implement the other half of the 1947 UN partition resolution calling for the establishment of a Palestinian Arab state alongside Israel (Rekhess 1993, 28–30; Jeryis 1973, 304–309, Qahwaji 1972, 427–430).

In the early years of the state, there was only limited Arab support and voting for the ICP. The party had to contend with the difficult conditions of disintegration and fear that dominated the Arabs after the 1948 war and the influence of the military government, which exercised tight control over Arab communities. There was a ban on the distribution of its newspapers in Arab areas, and its activists found it hard to peddle its ideas and attract new members. The only manifestation that indicated the extent of support for the party was its electoral results. In the first five Knesset elections, from 1949 through 1961, the party was unable to win broad Arab support, which never exceeded more than 20 percent of the Arab vote (see Appendix).

The ICP went through a grave crisis in the mid-sixties when it split in two. One faction, led by Mikounis, continued to call itself the Israel Communist Party (Maki). It comprised most of the Jewish members of the party and a handful of Arabs. The other faction, led by Wilner and Tewfiq Toubi, called itself the New Communist List (known by its Hebrew acronym *Rakah*). Its membership was predominantly Arab. The split had many causes, including personal struggles for power and control of party institutions and assets, as well as ideological disagreements that pitted the Jewish-Zionist tendencies of the circle headed by Moshe Sneh against the Arab national tendencies of the group led by Vilner and Toubi. In his study of the episode, Landau (1971) noted:

> The elements of the dispute also included personal rivalries . . . but these merely highlighted the ideological breach and the differences in tactics. The Jewish-led faction recognizes the rights of the Arabs in Israel and sympathizes with the struggle of some of the Arab states for socialism; it sees the change in the leadership of Israel—following Ben-Gurion's resignation from the government—as an appropriate time for the Communists to recognize Israel's right to exist, a step that would increase their popularity in Jewish circles. By contrast, the Arab-led faction attacks Israel's Arab policy with no qualifications, ascribes greater significance to the struggle of the Arab peoples for socialism and their liberation movement, and prefers to seek popularity in Arab circles. (Landau 1971, 105)

In the elections for the sixth Knesset (1965), held after the split, Rakah came out ahead. It won three seats in the Knesset, with about 75 percent of its votes from Arabs; Maki won only one seat, with negligible (less than 0.5 percent) Arab support (Rekhess 1993, 34). Maki failed to clear the threshold in the elections for the seventh Knesset (1969) and disappeared from the political map, leaving Rakah as the only representative of the Communists in Israel in the parliamentary and public arenas.

The disappearance of the "Jewish" faction of the Communist movement in Israel and changes in the structure and nature of Israeli politics, the status of the Arabs in Israel, and the status of the Palestinian national movement in general, as well as changes in the tactics adopted by the Communist Party itself, gained prominence in the early 1970s. They enhanced the strong position of the Communist Party among the Arabs in Israel.

After the disbanding of Maki, Rakah began garnering an increasing share of Arab support, both with regard to membership and electoral results. In the elections to the eighth, ninth, and tenth Knessets (1973, 1977, and 1981), it took a plurality of the Arab vote. The high point came in 1977, when it actually won an absolute majority of the valid Arab votes (see Appendix).

In his comprehensive book about the Israel Communist Party, Rekhess summarizes the chief factors behind the rise of Rakah:

> The explanation for the rapid consolidation of the Communist Party among the Palestinian minority is to be anchored on four levels: a political and ideological platform that suited the changing situation, the sociopolitical processes of change that ripened in the period in question, the strategy that the Communists developed in response to changing needs, and an excellent and effective party organization. (Rekhess 1993, 219)

In fact, it can be argued that the period from the early 1970s through the mid-1980s was the golden age of the Communist Party among the Arabs in Israel. The chief ingredients of its attraction for the Arabs can be summarized as follows.

1. Starting in the early 1970s, the Communists' initiatives reflected a profound change in its perception of its location and role vis-à-vis the Arabs and other forces active in the field. The party launched activity based on the concept that Rakah was the central force among the Arabs that should lead their struggle. The search for ways to attract other supporters led to the establishment of extraparliamentary committees such as the land defense committee and membership in other committees, whose leadership it aspired to win—for instance, the national committee of local authorities—and presenting the successful candidacy of the chairman of the committee, Hana Mois, who was the head of the Rama local council, as a member of Knesset on the list of the Democratic Front for Peace and Equality (the DFPE, also known by its Hebrew acronym *Hadash*) (Rekhess 1993, 146). This latter organization was in fact the pinnacle of Rakah's efforts to broaden its influence.

The DFPE was established at the initiative of Rakah to serve as an umbrella organization that included, in addition to Rakah, the Black Panthers, led by Charlie Biton, representatives of the committees of Arab university graduates, especially that in Nazareth, representatives of some Arab local authorities, representatives of students, and representatives of other public committees and organizations. Even though the front was essentially controlled by the Communists, they did not insist on the inclusion of "realization of Communism in the country" in the guidelines of the DFPE and settled for a number of points that constituted a minimum platform for all the forces united in the DFPE, namely, "achieving a comprehensive and stable Israeli-Palestinian and Israeli-Arab peace, defending workers' rights, achieving equality for Arabs in Israel, advancing the status of women, abolishing communal discrimination, and protecting the interests of the poor neighborhoods and development towns."[1]

2. In the complex situation in whose shadow the Arabs of Israel live, the DFPE and Rakah at its head offered a platform and positions on domestic and foreign issues that, for that period, were adapted to the needs and demands of the Arabs in Israel and attracted Arabs to support the DFPE and Rakah. This argument is an instructive reflection of the situation of the Arabs in Israel and the emergence of a consensus among them. Indeed, the Communist Party was the workshop that produced the views of other forces in the Arab sector, including the DAP, the Progressive List, the Arab supporters of the Jewish-Zionist parties, some of the Islamic Movement, and to a certain extent even the Sons of the Village, all of whom have moved toward the idea of two peoples and two states, a concept of equality that focuses on closing gaps between Jews and Arabs, and struggle that remains within the confines of Israeli law. There is no doubt, for example, that if the Communist Party still held the view that sovereignty over the parts of Israel that were to have been included in the Palestinian state, under the 1947 UN partition plan, should be reopened for discussion and their inhabitants given the right of self-determination, as it did until 1958, the spectrum of positions among the Arabs in Israel would be different and it is even possible that the evolution of the Palestinian question would have been different.[2]

3. The DFPE and Rakah disposed of a network of Arabic-language newspapers which they used to disseminate ideology and positions, and publicize regular activities. Over the years, many persons were exposed to an aggressive press that was critical chiefly of the authorities and included various shades of political, social, economic, and literary material, something that influenced readers to move closer to the DFPE and Rakah.

4. The DFPE and Rakah presented the Arabs with a secular platform that was suited to the general level of development of the Arabs in Israel. It effectively interacted with the changes that were taking place in Arab society as a result of exposure to Western

media and culture, imported chiefly by the Jewish majority. The platform attracted the growing segment of the Arab population that was interested in these changes and favored their introduction to their community as well.

5. Probably the most important factor in the strengthening and consolidation of Rakah and the DFPE was the excellent and effective party organization, which worked meticulously to build an infrastructure and hierarchy rising from individual members to the central committee and general secretary, a pyramid that worked well and effectively (Rekhess 1993, 224). Rakah membership grew from five hundred after the split in 1965 to sixteen hundred Arab members in 1988. They lived in almost every Arab town or village (5). In addition, in almost every community dozens of activists who were not officially party members were prepared to work in all forums to promote its platform. They were characterized generally by initiative, efficient organization, and a willingness to volunteer to enhance Arab society.

There has been a decline in the status and position of the DFPE and Rakah among the Arabs in Israel since the mid-1980s: a continual falling away of members, a thinning of the leadership ranks, and a struggle on a national, religious, and regional basis within the party. Although it is still too early to eulogize it as the main political force in the Arab sector, it has certainly become weaker. The decline in its strength and status has been reflected at the polls. Ever since 1984 there has been a significant retreat in Arab electoral support for the party, a decline that continued until the elections for the fourteenth Knesset in the summer of 1996 (see Appendix). In those elections the Communist Party, in cooperation with a group from the national stream (the National Democratic Alliance [NDA]—see the next chapter), received a significant fraction of the Arab vote. This change did not necessarily indicate that the party is returning to its glory days. The circumstances depend not on the party but on outside factors, such as the change in the electoral system and its agreement with the NDA.

In the fifteenth Knesset election, support for the DFPE dropped to about 22 percent of the Arab votes, good for three Knesset seats. This result constituted a severe defeat in the eyes of the party leadership and supporters, who had evidently expected to win at least four mandates. Right after the elections a thorough internal debate was initiated in an attempt to understand the factors that had caused the decline in support for the party. In my estimation, the vigorous competition among the various parties and the replacement of the traditional leadership by lesser known faces were among the key factors for its decline in strength.

It seems plausible that if there are no surprising developments, Arab support for the party will continue to drop.

A series of factors, both inside and outside the party, contributed to the decline in the party's status and position. These can be summarized as follows:

INTERNAL FACTORS

On this level one can diagnose the emergence of a crisis within the party itself, which made the largest contribution to the decline in the status of the DFPE and Rakah. There are a number of explanations for this.

1. The creation of the consensus mentioned above as one of the causes of the increased strength of Rakah and the DFPE was also paradoxically one of the more significant factors in the decline of Rakah. Once its views became common property, the party lost its uniqueness. In practice, the platform of the DFPE is hardly different, leaving aside a few Marxist accents, from those of the Progressive List, the DAP, and the CRM, and even the views of many members of the Labor party. The anti-Zionist platform spoken of by Rekhess (1993) has been blurred over the years. There have been few articles published in *al-Ittihad* explicitly denouncing Zionism since the departure of Emile Habibi, its long-time editor. The DFPE and Rakah failed to update their platform and principles. Party members even evince pride that they "advocate principles that do not change every day and night." Despite the severe criticism, both internal and external, of this conservatism, the powers-that-be within the party have still not digested that in the changing situation of the Arabs in Israel, principles that were suited to the 1970s and even to the 1980s, may not be appropriate to the 1990s and should be reexamined.

2. In the same context, the consensus on the issue of equality, in which what was originally Rakah's unique position has been adopted by other groups active among the Arabs, requires movement, expressed in a thorough and meaningful discussion of the substance of equality, which the Communists still avoid while holding to their negative view of equality as no more than closing gaps. For example, the Communist Party has long advocated recognition of the Arabs as a national minority, but it is doubtful whether any scholar or party member can provide a satisfactory explanation of the practical meaning of this concept. Nor is it clear what kind of state Rakah wants Israel to be or its positive interpretation of the collective status of the Arab minority in Israel. A party that claims to represent the Arabs in Israel and still

holds a certain primacy must provide adequate answers to these questions. The least the party can do, but has not done so far, is to offer a positive definition of equality. That is, in a situation of equality, what would be the status of the Arabs and to whom would the state of Israel belong? Would it continue to be a Jewish state, the state of a Jewish people? Or does the Communist Party propose an alternative?

These two factors, both related to the creation of a consensus—on the one hand, the spread of the idea to the other streams and groups, and on the other hand, the failure to advance new formulas about equality, aside from general statements—have left the Communist Party in a worse position than it occupied in the 1970s and early 1980s. Continued stagnation on these questions will contribute to a further decline in the status of the ICP and the DFPE.

3. The party's publications, which played a decisive role in the consolidation of Rakah and the DFPE, have also played a negative role since the mid-eighties, by pushing Arab intellectuals away from Rakah in search of alternate channels for political and cultural expression. For many years these periodicals provided a home for key Rakah personalities who were its mouthpiece to the world. Until recently it used an aggressive marketing technique that could be called a form of intellectual terror against actual or potential rivals and against all demands for organizational or ideological pluralism. Not forgotten is the firestorm directed against the Progressive List, whose members, like others in the Arab sector, were denounced as satellites and pawns of the authorities. In many senses this group was a closed clique that rejected anyone new or "alien" and deterred new adherents. The language that they used, also, turned many uninvolved observers into enemies of the party and its activity in the Arab sector.

In addition, over the years leading members of the party have competed for control of these periodicals, leading to the establishment of rival camps and groups. The moment that represented one camp that came out on top, disappointed supporters of the rival camps, and they withdrew. At least two recent examples can be noted, the departure first of Emile Habibi and later of Salim Jubran, who edited *al-Ittihad* for many years. These rivalries and resignations, in addition to the militant struggle against competitors outside the party, certainly made their contribution to the decline of the ICP and the DFPE.

4. The manner in which Rakah and the DFPE coped with the modernization processes among the Arabs in Israel, which at one stage contributed to their rise, later caused their decline. As a result of policies directed against them, the Arabs in Israel experienced rapid but selective modernization that did not operate in all areas of life. Rakah supported comprehensive modernization and encountered conservative opposition that became more hostile over the years, such as support for social and religious traditionalism, strictness with regard to female conduct, and loyalty to the clan and extended family. In a number of areas, the severe reaction among Arab society caused to Rakah to compromise its stance. The most conspicuous example was the significant alteration in its attitude toward the phenomenon of clans before and after the establishment of the DFPE. The DFPE was set up and functions as a coalition that incorporates the Communist Party, representatives of university graduates, and public bodies, but also representatives of clans who represent, for example, dozens of local authority chairmen and members, elected on a clan and local basis, who appear in public as members of the DFPE and supporters of the ICP.

The change in the attitude toward clans was a result of the desire for representation or control of a larger number of local authorities, for hegemony and control, for using governmental power to distribute benefits and mobilize support for the DFPE in Knesset and Histadrut elections. Today even some senior members of Rakah view this as a significant tactical error. Too many individuals have been elected on DFPE lists whose main concern is for their clan and village or town, with no practical commitment to the issues that Rakah seeks to advance on the country-wide level—people who desert the moment they smell a lure dangled from the other side of the fence. The reliance on clans contributed to the rapid decline in the status of Rakah and the DFPE. Clans that supported the DFPE as a group also seceded as a group. Thus Rakah's experience with selective modernization processes in some senses have worked to its detriment rather than its advantage.

5. Organizational efficiency, which at one point was a factor that attracted support, later worked against the DFPE and Rakah. It seems plausible that the tight structure and "democratic centralism" that guided Rakah activity are no longer as acceptable as in the past. In an age when everything is wide open and people reject compulsory frameworks in favor of the liberal democratic

spirit, the obligations imposed by membership in the Communist Party become a burden the people are glad to cast aside.[3] In addition, interference by party headquarters in branch affairs, which once made the party stronger, has become a stumbling block. For example, the intervention by the national leadership in the municipal elections in Shefa'amre, in favor of the reelection of Ibrahim Nimr Hussein as mayor, on account of countrywide interests, rebounded against Rakah. The party branch in Shefa'amre went through a severe crisis that threatened its existence. Ultimately the interference caused a significant drop in support for the DFPE and Rakah in Shefa'amre.

Taken together, these factors generated an internal crisis that the DFPE and ICP are having difficulty coping with and arriving at an appropriate response.

EXTERNAL FACTORS

The decline in the status of the DFPE and Rakah was catalyzed by external factors as well:

1. Starting in the early 1980s, various political organizations that posed a serious challenge to the DFPE appeared on the scene. The Progressive List, the Islamic movement, and the DAP challenged the DFPE's control of the Arab concentrations. They enjoyed great success in shaking its grip and taking its place in broad segments of the Arab population. In addition, the change in the attitude toward the Arabs of the Zionist parties, especially those that compose the Meretz bloc (the Citizens' Rights Movement, Mapam, and Shinui) and Labor, especially with respect to recognizing the existence of discrimination and showing a willingness to close gaps and solve the Palestinian problem, recognize the PLO, and withdraw from the occupied West Bank and Gaza Strip. These factors strengthened the DFPE and ICP's rivals and undercut its control in the field.

2. A major factor that undermined the ICP and the DFPE in the late the 1980s was the dissolution of the Communist bloc, which had provided significant financial assistance to the ICP by funding scholarships for Arab students in Communist countries and making direct grants to the party and had also provided an ideological and moral backbone for the Israeli party. Its disappearance left a vacuum in these areas, caused perplexity among the party faithful, who had consistently and blindly defended this bloc and its actions, and weakened it in its moral, ideological,

and daily financial struggle against other forces on the left and on the right.

Perestroika, introduced by the last leader of the Soviet Union, Mikhail Gorbachev, posed many challenges for the Communist Party in Israel. The ICP found it difficult to deal with the far-reaching changes in the Communist parties of other countries and lagged behind almost all of them in its willingness to reform. The wave of criticism and purges complicated its life, and reduced and weakened its position (Rekhess 1993, 201–218).

In sum, it seems plausible that the discussion about the Communist Party and scholars' interest in it appeared and gained strength in the 1970s and 1980s because of the key role played by the Palestinian Communists in the West Bank, the Gaza Strip, and Diaspora as part of the struggle of the Palestinian people for liberation and establishment of a state—especially their role in prodding the Palestinian leadership to take pragmatic positions with regard to a solution and the decisive role of the Communists in molding the national and civic consciousness of the Arabs in Israel.

The Communist Party is the most important party for the Arab citizens of Israel. In the 1970s and 1980s it played the key role in developing their consciousness and positions. It was the central political force active among the Arabs in Israel in general which demanded a solution of the Palestinian problem in the guise of a Palestinian state alongside Israel, but also demanded equality for the Arabs in Israel. Over time, these two demands became the linchpins of a broader Arab consensus and were adopted by all streams among the Palestinian minority.

The rise and fall of the ICP, especially among the Arab citizens of Israel, is one of the most fascinating topics in the history of the latter and has been studied by many scholars. In my opinion, the internal and external factors enumerated above worked together to generate a profound crisis within the ICP and DFPE. Its members have still not managed to cope with these factors, and they continue to contribute to its declining prestige and public support.

POSITIONS ON KEY QUESTIONS

Although the Communist stream existed before the birth of Israel in 1948, it has gone through a process of gaining recognition and legitimacy since then, beginning with its holding a seat in the first Knesset for Tewfiq Toubi, which granted legitimacy to the Arab members of the ICP. In 1977, the Democratic Front for Peace and Equality (DFPE) was established to serve as an electoral framework for this stream. Its forces have conducted a consistent struggle against official Israeli policy, especially with regard to equality between Arabs and Jews, and the resolution of the Arab-Israeli conflict.

Its fundamental stands rest on the assumption that coexistence within the state must involve equals; hence it is crucial to fight to attain equality so as to enhance the level of coexistence. The best form of organization to attain the goals of the Arabs in Israel is an egalitarian Jewish-Arab party. This stream resolutely rejects organization on an Arab national basis, which they fear would be viewed as secessionist, thereby harming the Arabs' cause.

The Communists highlight equality and peace as the two key objectives in which all the Arabs' efforts must be invested, while cooperating with Jews who also seek them. For them, the index of equality is the degree of integration enjoyed by Arabs, in addition to the allocation of equal resources to Jewish and Arab communities and recognition of the Arabs as a national minority. These objectives, it is held, will be attained more quickly after peace is achieved and a Palestinian state is established alongside Israel. They reject any talk of secession by the Arab population centers in the Galilee and Triangle.

The Communist stream considers Zionism to be the main obstacle to equality for the Arabs. It argues that the chances of attaining equality are nil as long as Zionism remains the official ideology of the state. Accordingly, Zionism must be dethroned as the official ideology and the Zionist character of the state abolished. In this the Communists differ from the Israeli-Arab stream, which makes its peace with Zionism and prefers to ignore the extent to which it is responsible for discrimination against Arabs.

The Arab-Israeli conflict is viewed as an obstacle to advancing the country and the region. Accordingly great efforts must be invested in resolving the Palestinian problem. The preferred solution is the establishment of the Palestinian state alongside Israel. The Communist stream also supports all modes of parliamentary and extraparliamentary struggle in order to accelerate the Arabs' achievement of their objectives. But it emphasizes that the struggle must remain within the law and that illegal activities would play into the hands of the authorities and damage the Arabs' cause.

The Communist stream over the years identifies two main components of the Arabs' identity—Palestinian Arab national and Israeli civic. They see these two as complementary and reject the contention that they are contradictory or incompatible. Naturally they hold that general Communist ideology guides their positions on concrete issues in Israel.

EQUALITY BETWEEN JEWS AND ARABS IN ISRAEL

Equality between Arabs and the Jewish majority is one of the cornerstones of the Communists' ideology. Since 1948 this stream has waged a consistent struggle for such equality. From the outset the struggle has been unequivocal and uncompromising. This influenced the evolution of the Communists' perception of this issue. Unlike the rapid changes in their perception on other issues relevant to coexistence, and unlike the views on equality of the other streams, here there have been no significant changes.

For this stream, the starting point is that integration of the Arabs in all areas of life is an index of equality, and the degree of equality is an index of coexistence, which should be between equals. They demanded a radical change in all spheres of life.

In the pages that follow I shall examine the Communists' views in the following areas: inequality between Jews and Arabs; the degree of equality that should be attained; the changes required in the status of the Arabs in Israel, including their recognition as a national minority with recognized rights and not merely as religious and cultural minorities; the causes of discrimination; and the link between Zionism and discrimination against the Arabs. I shall also attempt to trace changes in these areas over the years.

The leading edge of the Communists' struggle for equality was the fight against expropriation of the land that remained in Arab hands. In their eyes, expropriation symbolized the zenith of the authority's discriminatory attitude toward Arabs. They demanded that the Arabs be allowed to keep the lands still in their hands as well as the return of land expropriated from Arab owners who still lived in Israel. The Communists considered land expropriation to be part of the Israeli policy that derived from Zionist ideology, which in their view aims at depriving the Arabs of their lands. MK expressed this idea during the second reading in the Knesset of the Lands Law (1969), which the Communists vigorously opposed.[4]

For the Communists, the policy of expropriating Arab land is antithetical to the attainment of equality between Jews and Arabs. They voiced a clear demand for the return of land expropriated from Arabs and an end to all such expropriation. The platform they presented in the elections for the seventh Knesset, in October 1969, stated that "Rakah will work to abolish land expropriation and to stop the dispossession of farmers from their lands, for the return of land to local Arab refugees who were dispossessed of their land and villages" (Rakah platform, elections for the seventh Knesset 1969).

The demand for equality embraced many areas. The struggle for placing Arab local authorities on a par with Jewish communities, including official recognition of unrecognized villages, occupied a major place in the Communists' notion of equality.[5] The same congress passed a resolution about "the need to establish councils in all Arab villages and to expand the area of jurisdiction of Arab villages, to abolish the discrimination in services to Arab citizens and the allocation of government assistance for establishing industrial and professional enterprises in Arab villages."[6]

The Communists carried their demand for equality between Arabs and Jews to debates in the Histadrut, where they insisted that equalizing the conditions of Jews and Arabs was a necessary and prior condition for any discussion of equality, especially between Arab and Jewish workers. They emphasized the importance of the class struggle of Jewish and Arab workers against capitalists and employers who exploit the workers, whatever their national affiliation.[7]

The Communists' struggle against discrimination included vigorous opposition to laws they considered to be discriminatory. They opposed the citizenship law and land laws that discriminate between Jews and others, which they saw as meant to harm the Arabs and limit their rights, and to serve as a tool for continued discrimination against and dispossession of the Arabs.[8]

In the mid-1970s the Communists amplified their demand for equality, as a result of their improved understanding of the Israeli system and the possibilities of maneuvering within it. This included a louder call for a struggle for equality and broadened resistance to the expropriation of lands from Arabs. The Communists evinced vigorous opposition to the program for the Judaization of the Galilee, aiming toward increasing the number of Jews living in the Galilee. This program was published in a report in the name of Koenig, the person responsible for the northern district in the ministry of the interior of Israel. Salim Jubran, a well-known poet and later the editor of the Communist Party paper *al-Ittihad*, said: "The most recent form of the policy to 'cleanse' the country of Arabs is the policy of Judaizing the Galilee. They speak about developing and settling the Galilee, but it is all lies and deception. The government's main objective is to steal the lands of the Arab residents of the Galilee."[9] It is clear from Jubran's remarks that the Communists viewed the Judaization of the Galilee as another link in the ongoing chain whereby the Israeli regime aimed to deprive the Arabs of all their lands.

One of the clear signs of the intensification of the struggle by the Communists and of their view that equality is an essential condition for harmonious coexistence is the extension to other areas—that is, reminding the authorities and Jewish population in general that discrimination encompasses many areas of life and is not merely a "tactical mistake" by mid- and low-level bureaucrats. The notion that discrimination is a policy conducted by the Israeli regime is one of the hallmarks of the Communist perspective, unlike the Israel-Arab stream, which initially saw the discrimination as the unintentional outcome of mistakes and improper action by officials at various levels.

The Communists' view made it easier for them to define the objectives of their struggle to modify official policy, which, in their eyes, is the reason for the Arab's inferior situation vis-à-vis the Jews. In addition to the fight against land expropriation, the struggle included a stubborn and broadening fight against discrimination against Arab local authorities, discrimination in education, and the discrimination produced by various laws.

The first Land Day, in 1976, spurred the Communists to voice their demands for equality with greater energy. (Their vigorous stand against land expropriation in the Galilee had contributed to the expectant tension that led up to that day.) Land Day became, not only a manifestation of Arab opposition to the continued expropriation of their land, but also of protest against discrimination in general. A clear expression of the Communist position on land expropriation was given by MK Zayyad of Rakah, in many speeches and newspaper interviews he gave around then.[10]

The Communists' always strong opposition to land expropriation intensified after the first Land Day. They considered expropriation to be an intentional policy aimed at depriving the Arabs of their few last *dunams* of land. They were also reinforced in their view that expropriation directly harmed Jewish-Arab relations and the fabric of coexistence.

The national land defense committee was established at Rakah's initiative in 1975, and its activists included party members. At its meeting on 7 March 1978, the committee resolved on "the need for a uniform position in the struggle against the official policy whose objective is to deprive the Arabs of their lands. Such a position is the only way to make our voice heard by the world and to stop the policy whose objective is the expropriation of the Arabs' land through pressures and despicable laws."[11]

In the mid-1980s the struggle focused, in addition to the Judaization of the Galilee, on Area 9, a large tract in the Galilee near the village of Sakhnin, whose owners were forbidden to enter it because of its use for military training exercises. Resolutions of the twentieth Communist Party congress condemned "the new government assault on the Arab masses aimed at stealing what remains of their lands, and this in the context of the national discrimination, one of whose manifestations is the program for the Judaization of the Galilee. The political step in this new assault is the announcement of the closure of Area 9 [and] the construction of a fence around thousands of *dunams*. . . . This assault follows the annexation of 180,000 *dunams* to the Misgav regional council in the Galilee, land that belonged to 20 Arab villages."[12]

The Communists continued to see land expropriation and the authorities' discriminatory attitude toward the Arabs as the root of the problem. In an article headlined "The Lands Question and Recent Developments," Marzouk Halabi, a Communist activist from the village of Daliyyat al-Karmil, wrote: "The land problem is the heart of the Middle East problem. If the Arab masses have land they have an existence, and they have a national existence they have rights; and this is what the governments of Israel do not want to recognize."[13] The return of lands to the Arabs in the late 1980s, especially the restoration of Area 9, attracted only limited interest on the part of the Communists, although the restoration was described as the fruit of "the struggle of the Arab masses" whom they led.

The momentum in the struggle against discrimination and on behalf of equality derived, in addition to the land issue, from the daily problems of the Arab citizens, especially equalization of the conditions of the Arab local authorities with their Jewish counterparts, including budgets, education, outline plans, and the establishment of councils in areas of Arab population concentration not officially recognized as villages or towns. With regard to education, too, there was a clear indictment of official policy as aimed at preserving Jewish domination.[14]

The Communists state that the fact that dozens of Arab settlements lack official recognition and local councils to deal with their problems "cannot be explained by the size of the community, because there are many Jewish communities whose population does not exceed hundreds who have received such recognition. This policy is merely a continuation of the discrimination and contempt for the rights of the Arab citizens." The Communists' charges about the need for government recognition of unrecognized Arab settlements were very clear. They unequivocally demanded official recognition of unrecognized Arab settlements, including the granting of municipal status where appropriate.[15] The allegations in this sphere also included the failure to draft outline plans for recognized Arab villages, which was considered to be part of the policy discriminating against the Arabs and aimed at preventing the advancement of the Arab communities. The secretary of the national land defense committee, Saliba Hamis, told an interviewer: "The discrimination includes the issue of outline plans for Arab villages. The Israeli government still has not approved outline plans for Arab villages and had not provided them with either development areas or residential areas."[16]

The intensification of the general claims about inequality and the need to change official anti-Arab policy in order to attain equality is one of the clear signs of the recent period. In late 1980 Rakah called for a "conference of the Arab masses" in Nazareth. The then–prime minister, Menachem Begin, in his capacity as minister of defense, banned the conference. The conference, one of whose objectives was to protest discrimination against the Arabs in Israel, marked a significant aggravation of the rhetoric used to demand equality.[17] Loaded terms like "racism" and "apartheid" were used to describe the situation of inequality between Jews and Arabs.

The Communist stream was one of the central actors that pressed for an "Equality Day" strike on 24 June 1987, with the objective of raising the profile of lawful protest against discrimination. MK Zayyad, interviewed about the plan for a strike by the Arab sector on that day, said: "Striking is a legal right. It is the right of every people to use it against racist policy and national discrimination in order to achieve full equality."[18]

The Communists demanded not only civic equality but also "national" equality—a vague concept whose crux was recognition as a national minority, meaning recognition of the Arabs in Israel as part of the Palestinian people and a group with the right to organize and conduct its struggle as a national entity, and not only as an ethnic group with recognized minority rights. According to the platform adopted by the Communist Party for the elections to the eighth Knesset (1973), "Rakah is working to eliminate all national discrimination in Israel and to guarantee full equality of civic and national rights for the Arab population."[19]

The Communists continued to voice their demand for recognition of the Arabs as a national minority. The eighteenth Party congress resolved that "the Arab masses in the state of Israel are a national minority and part of the Palestinian Arab people. They are fighting for equality of national and civil rights in the state of Israel."[20] Despite this demand, the Communists rejected any talk of institutional, cultural, or territorial autonomy. The also rejected the conversion of Israel into a binational state, taking it as a given that Israel is a Jewish state with an Arab minority. As Salim Jubran told an interviewer in 1989: "We see Israel as a Jewish state by virtue of its having a Jewish majority. At the same time we see it as the state of the Palestinian-Arab national minority that lives in it. Autonomy for the Arabs is out of the question."[21] Antoine Shalhat, the deputy editor of *al-Ittihad*, responding to a question about the optimum solution for the question of the Arabs in Israel, said: "We demand full integration of the Arab population in Israel. We reject any talk of or tendency to autonomy, now or in the future."[22]

The Communists also rejected the argument that the establishment of all-Arab institutions and committees, such as a university and the land defense committee, the committee of Arab local-authority heads, and the follow-up committee, could serve as the basis autonomy in the future. They maintained that these institutions were set up to help solve specific problems in the Arab sector and should not be seen as a basis for future institutional, territorial, or cultural autonomy.[23]

The Communist stand against any form of autonomy is particularly problematic in light of the fact that it was persons identified with this stream who initiated the establishment of Arab-only bodies and insisted on the Arabs' right to occupy key posts dealing with issues relevant to them. It can be explained, however, by the fear that it would be understood by the authorities and Jewish majority as an attempt to undermine Israeli control of Arab population centers in the Galilee and Triangle. In practice, the Communists did encourage trends toward autonomy for the Arabs in Israel.

The Communists' position on Zionism is clear. Allocating greater resources to the Arabs would not be enough; they demand the abolition of Zionism as the official ideology of the state. Unlike the Israeli-Arab stream, they view Zionism as a racist movement and the main impediment to equality. Accordingly its abolition is a necessary condition for attaining it. Their rejection of Zionism makes their demand for equality more radical and constitutes one of the chief reasons why they are not considered for membership in Knesset coalitions.

For the Communists, there is an intimate link between Zionism and discrimination against the Arabs. It is impossible to achieve equality without the abolition of Zionism as the official ideology of Israel.[24] A particularly sharp expression of this position can be found in the report submitted by the central committee of Rakah to the nineteenth Party congress: "The development of the Galilee should be implemented like that of other areas of the country. But the acts of land theft and discrimination represented by the policy of Judaization of the Galilee are among the sordid expressions of the racist Zionist policy that threatens the Arabs."[25] In other words, land expropriation and discrimination in the allocation of budgets and services to Arabs are corollaries of Zionist ideology, which favors Jews over non-Jews. Accordingly its abolition as the official ideology that guides Israeli decision-makers is a sine qua non for equality between Jews and Arabs.

As for equal obligations for Arabs—that is, military or national service—which is an important issue, at least from the perspective of the Jewish majority, on the road to equality, the Communists generally tend to ignore the question, although they cannot avoid stating their opinion when asked directly. They are opposed to military or national service for Arabs, on the grounds that the authorities exploit the demand that Arabs do military or national service as an excuse to evade allocating them equal resources.

This opposition, however, is tactical rather than a matter of principle. It rests on the argument that military or national service would contribute to Israel's war effort against the Palestinians in particular and the Arabs in general. Because they view Israel as an aggressor state, they are not willing to contribute to this effort and find themselves in direct confrontation with their Palestinian kindred. Conditions in the region are not normal; but the establishment of peace would make it possible for them to serve in the army. In the words of the deputy editor of *al-Ittihad*, Nadier Majali: "I am willing to meet all the obligations imposed on me, but there are problems that stem from historical facts. When this state has an army that fights against my people or some of my nation and expresses goals of occupation, it is my right and even my duty not to serve in it."[26]

The Communists also reject civilian or national service for the Arabs in Israel. They argue that the Arabs participate in building the country by working in the Israeli economy, in factories, construction, and the like, and accordingly there is no need for national or civilian service to prove that they contribute to the state. In the Communists' view, the argument that their failure to do military or national service is grounds for denying the Arabs equality is invalid; they counter that equality is a right of all citizens and that it is the duty of the state to enforce it without conditions. In the interview cited above, Nadier Majali said: "I am opposed to any conditions for full equality between Jews and Arabs in the state."[27]

The Communists have been calling for equality ever since 1948. The June 1967 war and its results, however, led to an intensification of the Communists' pressure for absolute equality between Jews and Arabs. The first Land Day, on 30 March 1976, accelerated and amplified this demand. The increasing activism on this front is a sign of the growing politicization of the Arabs in Israel.

The Identity of the Arabs in Israel

The identity of the Arabs in Israel is one of the thorniest questions they must face. The Communists, who are considered to be an illegitimate opposition in Israel and have been attacked at various times by both sides in the Arab-Israeli conflict, located a middle course that takes account of two fundamental points: the Arabs in Israel are part of the Palestinian Arab people, but they are also citizens of the state of Israel. Here I shall attempt to trace the evolution of these two strands.

Unlike the Israeli-Arab stream, which until the mid-1970s considered the Arabs in Israel to be "Arabs" or "the Palestinian minority," the Communists began to see the Arabs in Israel as both Israeli citizens and part of the Palestinian people even before 1967, although the perception was not clearly stated at the time (Rekhess 1988, 147). The June 1967 war stimulated the Communists to hone their concept of the identity of the Arabs in Israel. Indeed, on the one hand there is an emphasis that the Arabs are citizens of Israel and that Israeliness is part of their identity.[28] On the other hand, the idea has gained strength among the Communists that the Arabs of Israel are part of the Palestinian people—that is, that their national identity is Palestinian.[29]

Unlike the Israeli-Arab stream, for which the identity of the Arabs in Israel is split between their Arab national affiliation and their Israeli citizenship, the Communists consider these two components to be complementary. Together they create the identity of the Arabs in Israel, so that they are Palestinian Arabs with regard to their national identity and Israelis with regard to their civic identity. In article on the subject, published in *al-Ittihad*, Emile Touma, a member of the Communist Party central committee, wrote: "The clear national affiliation [of the Arab minority] does not change the fact that its destiny is linked to the destiny of the state of Israel. . . . The Arab citizens do not see a contradiction between their identification with the goals of the Palestinian people with regard to the right of self determination and the return the refugees to their homeland, on the one hand, and their Israeli citizenship, on the other."[30]

Thus the idea that the Arabs in Israel are Israeli citizens and the same time part of the Palestinian Arab people—a complete rather than a split identity—is a cornerstone of the Communist viewpoint. It is fully in keeping with their attitude toward the future of the Arabs in Israel even after a resolution of the Palestinian problem—namely, that the Arabs will remain citizens of Israel with an Israeli identity superadded to their Palestinian identity.

The Communists insist that they are aware of the changes taking place in the identity of the Arabs in Israel, particularly the strengthening of its Palestinian component. They deny that these changes are contrary to the interests of the state of Israel or that they prevent the Arabs from being loyal to the state. Instead, they consider them to be a positive development serving the interest of peace between the two peoples, the Israeli-Jewish and the Palestinian. In their view, the dual identity of the Arabs in Israel can help solve the conflict. A solution of the conflict is an Israeli interest, because Israeliness is part of their identity, and a Palestinian interest, because that too is part of their identity. This buttresses the argument that enhancement of the Palestinian component is not necessarily antithetical to the interests of the state, but is a natural evolution that can promote peace between the two peoples and thereby also benefit the state of Israel.[31]

The 1982 Lebanon war, in which Israel attacked the PLO in Lebanon, directly affected the Arabs in Israel because of the national, village, and even family ties that straddled the Israeli-Lebanese border. The war resulted in greater prominence for the Palestinian element of the Arabs' identity, but without derogating from the Israeli element. Samir Majali, a Rakah activist in Nazareth, wrote about the bond between the Arabs in Israel in the Palestinians in Lebanon: "The Arabs in Israel are an integral part of Palestinian people, and the massacre in the camps affects them directly because many of them have brothers, uncles, and cousins in these camps."[32] After the war, Emile Touma told an interviewer who asked about the identity of the Arabs in Israel and their ties with other Palestinians that the Arabs in Israel are "first of all an integral part of the Palestinian Arab people at the level of national identity, and Israeli citizens second."[33] The reinforcement of both elements continued to accompany the Communists even later, with no contradiction perceived between the two elements.

To avoid being accused of sedition or of challenging the very existence of the state of Israel, as a result of the emphasis on the Palestinian component of the Arabs' identity, the Communists were compelled to specify who, in their eyes, represents the Arabs of Israel. They sharply rejected the possibility that the PLO could represent the Arabs in Israel, by virtue of their being Palestinians. They contended rather that the PLO represents the Palestinians who live outside the borders of Israel but not those living inside Israel. Responding to the question, "does the PLO represent the Arab citizens of Israel?" Emile Touma replied: "No, it represents those who have not managed to realize their right to self-determination. The Arabs in Israel are represented by their elected representatives in the Knesset, the heads of local government, and organizations that work to realize their right to civil equality in Israel."[34] In this view, the Israeli component of the the Palestinian minority' identity is not merely a tactical matter but the outcome of the situation in which the Arabs find themselves, which they see as destined to endure in the future. The PLO does not represent them, nor does the Palestinian component interfere with their loyalty to the state.

In sum, tracing the Communists' perception of the identity of the Arabs over the years reveals a systematic strengthening of both components of that identity, the Israeli and the Palestinian, and rejection of the charge that there is a contradiction between the two.

THE ARAB-ISRAELI CONFLICT AND ITS RESOLUTION

The Communists see the ongoing conflict as the main obstacle to the advancement of Israel, the Palestinian people, and the quality of Jewish-Arab coexistence within the state. It causes tension and abnormal relations because it is a focus of disagreement, source of distrust, and an excuse for inequality between Jews and Arabs. In addition, the occupation of the West Bank and Gaza Strip directly harms its Palestinian residents, with whom the Arabs of Israel identify fully because of their kinship. In the Communists' view, then, a resolution of the conflict is a common interest of the Palestinian people, including the Arabs in Israel, and of the Jews in Israel. A just solution, based on recognition by each people of the other's right to self-determination, would lead to normalization of the relations between Jews and Palestinian Arabs and normal coexistence.

Because the conflict is such an important issue, ever since 1948 the Communists have had to enunciate a clear position on the various options for solving it. The June 1967 war pushed them to greater involvement and a more focused view of the conflict and its solution. Their ideas developed in the direction of mutual recognition of the rights of both peoples, Jewish and Palestinian, to self-determination, with an emphasis that this could be achieved only through negotiations.

The Communists evinced vigorous opposition to the June 1967 war. They blamed Israel for its outbreak and accused its government of having adopted an adventurist policy that exacerbated tensions in the Middle East and inside Israel, especially relations between Jews and Arabs. Remarks in a similar vein could be found in a wide spectrum of Rakah publications as well as in the speeches of its leaders and Knesset members.

The Communists supported their protest against the occupation of the West Bank and Gaza Strip with concrete proposals for solving the problem of the occupation and putting an end to the results of the war. They proposed a withdrawal from the occupied West Bank and Gaza Strip, to be followed by a peace accord that would guarantee that all states in the region, including Israel, could live in peace.[35] A new element that became part of the Communists' view of a solution of the conflict was UN Security Council Resolution 242, which called on the countries involved in the conflict to reach a peace accord based on Israeli retreat from the land occupied during the war.[36]

Their conception of the appropriate solution to the conflict included an explicit demand for recognition of Israel's right to exist. Nevertheless, at the start of the post–Six Day War period the Communists did not raise a demand for the establishment of a Palestinian state alongside Israel. Their rather vague formulations included Israeli recognition of the national rights of the Palestinian Arab people and the rights of the Arab refugees to choose between return to their homeland and compensation, in accordance with United Nations resolutions, but there was no explicit call for a Palestinian state as an expression of the national rights of the Palestinian people.[37] But the October 1973 war, the increased international prestige of the PLO, including Arafat's address to the General Assembly, and the Soviet Union's recognition of the PLO as the representative of the Palestinian people produced a significant shift in the Communists' view. Thereafter they explicitly called for the establishment of a Palestinian state alongside Israel and recognition of the PLO as the representative of the Palestinian people. The Communists' demand for the establishment of a Palestinian state went through many drafts before it attained its final form. It started with a call for granting self-determination to the Palestinian people, without explicit definition of the meaning of this phrase.[38] In the interim, a new element had been added to the Communists' approach to a solution of the conflict—Security Council Resolution 338, which called for implementation of Resolution 242.[39]

The earliest Communist statement I have located that refers to the Palestinians' right to establish a state, an indirect but clear call, was made during the Knesset debate of the government's statement on the report of the commission that investigated events during the *fedayeen* attack on Ma'alot. During that debate, MK Zayyad said:

> The only way to achieve peace in our region is a full withdrawal from the occupied West Bank and Gaza Strip and recognition of the legitimate rights of all peoples of the region, including the Israeli people and the Palestinian Arab people. . . . There is room in our region for the state of Israel and the Jordanian state and for a Palestinian Arab state, if the Palestinian people want to establish one. A just solution of the Palestinian problem is a precondition for the establishment of a just and lasting peace in our region.[40]

The change in the Communists' views after the October 1973 war included a modification of their attitude toward the PLO. Before the war, the Communists had not considered the PLO to be a legitimate representative of the Palestinian people and even ignored the question. After the war, however, the contention that the PLO was the "sole legitimate representative of the Palestinian people" began to be heard among them. It is reasonable to assume that it was the change in the Soviet Union's position vis-à-vis the PLO and its recognition of that organization as the representative the Palestinian people that led Rakah to alter its stand.[41] An explicit call for recognition of the PLO as the representative of the Palestinian people and for the establishment of a Palestinian state alongside Israel appeared in the resolutions of the eighteenth Party congress: "During this period it has been clearly demonstrated that the PLO is the sole legitimate representative of the Palestinian Arab people. . . . Our position calls for Israeli recognition of the PLO as the sole legitimate representative of the Palestinian Arab people and calls for its participation in Geneva conference alongside Israel."[42]

The Communists denounced the peace between Egypt and Israel, which began to take shape after Sadat's visit to Jerusalem. It described as an imperialist plot to isolate Egypt from the Arab world and conclude a separate peace that would not include their solution to the conflict—namely, the establishment of a Palestinian state.[43]

The Communists summarily rejected the idea of a secular democratic state on the entire territory of Mandatory Palestine, even during the period when this was the official stand of the PLO. This rejection was strategic and not merely tactical. They also rejected the "phased plan" and saw the principle of two states for two peoples as the basis for an ultimate resolution of the conflict.[44] Later the Communists maintained that the belief held by some Arabs in Israel in the "phased plan" as leading to the establishment of a secular democratic state had no justification, because the PLO, "the owner of the Palestinian question," had relinquished that line. Accordingly, those Arabs in Israel who believed in such a solution also had to give it up and be more realistic.[45]

In the Communist perspective, a settlement of the conflict would have a decisive impact on Jewish-Arab coexistence. The two-state solution would improve relations by eliminating the main focus of contention between Jews and Arabs in Israel and thereby strengthening trust between the two sides.[46] The Communists emphasize that the Arabs will not leave Israel and move to the Palestinian state when it is established. They strongly advocate the Arabs' remaining in Israel and conducting their daily political, social, and economic life there in Israel.[47]

The important changes in the Communists' view of a solution of the conflict, moving toward emphasis on the need for a two-peoples two-states solution, were accompanied by an increasing vigorous rejection of *fedayeen* assaults on Israeli civilians. The Communists objected vociferously to the sharp upturn in attacks on Israeli civilian targets that followed the June 1967 war, describing them as "terrorist acts" and "crimes" that must be stopped and condemned. They also saw these operations as holding back the peace process and exacerbating tensions between Jews and Arabs in Israel.[48] Members of the DFPE continued to denounce such actions vigorously and to explain the harm they wreaked on efforts to achieve peace in the Middle East and solve the Palestinian problem.[49]

In contrast to the Communists' forceful rejection of such assaults on Israeli civilian targets, they fully supported the right of the Palestinian people under occupation in the West Bank and Gaza Strip themselves to wage a violent and even armed struggle.[50] Later there were stronger statements about the right of armed struggle in the West Bank and Gaza Strip.[51]

The Communists' position with regard to the Arab refugees expelled from Israel during the 1948 war was clear. In their eyes, this was a key problem that must be settled as part of a comprehensive solution of the conflict. Their proposed solution was based on "the right of the refugees to choose between returning and receiving compensation," relying on United Nations resolutions in this vein.[52] The Communists did not believe that implementing this solution would harm Israel, because they estimated that only a minority of the refugees would choose to return, while most would settle for compensation.

The Jewish majority and its mainstream political parties consider the Communists' core positions—blaming Israel for the continuation of the conflict, proposing a solution based on the principle of "two states for two peoples," and support of the Palestinian refugees' right of return—to be extremist. This is why the Communists have never been viewed as potential coalition partners at the national level in Israel.

METHODS OF STRUGGLE

As was shown above, the Communists advocate radical changes in the status of the Arabs in Israel. Within Israel they demand full equality and recognition as a national minority. Externally they call for a resolution of the conflict based on the principle of "two states for two peoples" and on the refugees' right to return or receive compensation. The demand for such radical changes required them to define methods for pursuing their struggle that could benefit the Arabs in Israel. Their preferred methods went through several avatars over the years.

The Communists considered a joint Arab-Jewish struggle based on an organization with fully Arab-Jewish equality as a fundamental and even the only approach that could bring success to the struggle of the Arabs in Israel. They vigorously opposed organization on a national basis, whether Arab or Jewish. From their perspective, cooperation with the Jewish majority promotes understanding and accelerates the realization of the desired changes. The central argument is that the two peoples have the same interests and should cooperate in order to attain their shared goals.

In a question-and-answer appendix to Rakah's platform for the elections to the ninth Knesset, we find: "Q: Why did Rakah propose the establishment of a Jewish-Arab Front for Peace and Democracy? A: Rakah put forward this program in the knowledge that its sections are accepted by many circles and people in Israel who can together establish a peace camp in our land. A united peace camp can be an influential political actor in Israel and promote the chances of peace."[53] The Communists insist that separate organization on a national basis is reactionary and detracts from the struggle of both Arabs and Jews.[54]

The Communists' advocacy of Jewish-Arab cooperation became stronger over the years. It was adapted to the conditions that prevail in Israel, where the Jews constitute the overwhelming majority and ultimately make all decisions about the Arabs as well. For Rakah, Jewish-Arab cooperation per se is even more important than concrete results in the field. Because their Communist ideology holds that the class struggle is the most important arena in society, and that differences of nationality, race, or religion are secondary, it calls for tearing down the boundaries between peoples.[55] A joint Jewish-Arab struggle serves and will continue to serve the interests of both the Jewish majority and Arab minority in Israel. Accordingly the struggle is not a zero-sum game, good for one side and bad for the other.[56]

Even though the Communists described Zionism as racist and castigated it as a colonial movement that worked hand in glove with colonialism against liberation movements throughout the world, and especially in the Middle East,[57] they did not reject cooperation and even a coalition with religious, capitalist, or Zionist groups or individuals in order to achieve concrete results in some areas and also in order to break out of the quarantine imposed on them as a marginal group in Israeli politics.[58]

The Communists continue to hold this position today. In an article published in *al-Ittihad*, Amir Makhoul wrote of the need for negotiations between the government of Israel and the PLO, and the refusal of Peace Now to cooperate with non-Zionists and anti-Zionists on the issue of peace: "It is necessary to reinforce what we have in common. . . . The starting point is that the interest of peace outweighs other interests and ideological differences."[59]

The Communists have tended to ignore the possibility of their sitting in a government coalition, but a close reading of their literature indicates that their basic orientation supports a willingness to do so.[60] Despite their willingness to join a coalition in the Knesset, the Histadrut Central Committee, and the municipal councils in the mixed cities, on condition that these accept or at least approximate the Communists' positions, they have never set this as a primary goal. For lack of choice they have accepted the reality of being a permanent opposition. A clear expression of the willingness in principle to be part of a coalition alongside acquiescence with the status of permanent opposition in practice was given by Salim Jubran:

> In theory we do not rule out participation in a government coalition, but in practice, insofar as this involves the two major parties, to date participation in a government coalition has not been conceivable. We are prepared to support Labor if it needs our support to win the confidence of the Knesset to establish a new government, but we are not prepared to serve as ministers in its government because this would require that we agree with its program. It is illogical for Meir Wilner and Tewfiq Zayyad to be ministers in a Peres government.[61]

In order to achieve concrete gains and realize their objectives and those of the Arabs in Israel, the Communists support lawful parliamentary and extraparliamentary struggle and reject any resort to violence. In their view, the struggle should be waged in the parliamentary arena because the Arabs in Israel are an integral part of the state. They recognize its right to exist and want to be equal participants in it. Arabs should vote and stand for office in elections to the Knesset, the Histadrut, and the local authorities. Suffrage, in this view, is an important means in the struggle for equality and for exerting influence on behalf of a just solution of the Palestinian problem. They believe in the effectiveness of information campaigns, education, and propaganda for winning support and modifying positions. Civil rights are realized through voting and action.

The Communists rejected calls to boycott elections, especially those issued by the Sons of the Village. They consider such an abstention to be surrender and retreat before the authorities. In their opinion, nonparticipation in elections is failing to make active use of a legal right. This is negative, because it prevents the victims of discrimination from protesting against its agents. Not voting is negative participation in elections. As one party activist put it: "In plain language: someone who abstains from voting is denying his national affiliation, retreating and weakening himself before the oppressive authorities."[62]

This stream also supports extraparliamentary struggle, because the parliamentary arena alone cannot achieve equality and peace. In the Communists' view extraparliamentary struggle includes demonstrations, political strikes, protest rallies, and distribution of posters. These are important means to mobilize the masses. They create power centers, deter the establishment from implementing discriminatory policies, produce concrete gains, and contribute to Arab unity. It is not true, according to this stream, that extraparliamentary struggle has a negative impact on Arab-Jewish coexistence in Israel.[63]

For the Communists, the extraparliamentary struggle must employ legal means only. In their opinion, taking advantage of the possibilities provided by Israeli law provides sufficient margin to conduct the Arabs' struggle for changes in their status and the establishment of a Palestinian state. According to Salim Jubran: "We are ideological foes of Zionism in the context of the options afforded us for ideological confrontation."[64]

The Communists' support for joint Jewish-Arab struggle and their willingness to participate with Zionists as a group and as individuals, as well as their support for parliamentary and extraparliamentary struggle within the limits permitted by the law, and rejection of violence, are a striking indicator of their ability to maneuver within the Israeli system and to realize the potential for Arab political participation as a way to improve their situation and status in the country.

The overall conception about valid modes of struggle is quite clear. The Communists perceive a need for united ranks among the Arabs. They view Arab unity as strength and division as weakness. They favor a joint Jewish-Arab struggle, because the Arabs are a minority and cooperation with the Jewish majority is essential to promote understanding, achieve equality, and resolve the Palestinian problem. They argue that the Arabs and Jews have shared interests, and only government policy prevents the Jews from seeing this. They also deem it necessary to collaborate with any Jewish group, regardless of differences of religion, ideology, or belief in Zionism. They are willing to cooperate with Zionists in order to achieve concrete goals and objectives needed by the Arabs in Israel. They accept that they are a permanent opposition for lack of choice, despite their theoretical willingness to participate in a coalition that would support or approximate their positions.

PROFILE OF THE COMMUNIST STREAM

The Communists' overall perspective on the questions that preoccupy the region in general and the Arabs in Israel in particular was nurtured in part by their positions on the four issues discussed in this chapter. A close reading of their literature discloses a direct link between these four topics and coexistence, as well as a growing commitment to make progress in realizing these issues and to Jewish-Arab and Israel-Palestinian coexistence.

The Communists are distinguished from the other streams in a number of ways:

1. *Organization on a Jewish-Arab Anti-Zionist Basis:* The Communists are organized on the basis of a Jewish-Arab equality. They deem this method to be the very best for the success of the Arabs' struggle in Israel. They also express anti-Zionist positions, manifested chiefly in their definition of Zionism as a colonialist and racist movement.

2. *Equality and Peace as Key Objectives:* The Communists see the achievement of equality between Jews and Arabs and peace between Israel and the Palestinians as their primary vocation. This view is accompanied by an emphasis that the issues discussed above constitute a single unit and are closely interwoven, so that progress in one area will lead to improvement and progress in the other areas as well. They reject the argument that progress in one area is liable to detract from the chances for progress in other areas. Progress toward a solution of the conflict, for example, will also lead to greater equality and a broader Jewish acceptance of the legitimate right of the Arabs in Israel to define themselves as Palestinians as well as citizens of Israel. In their eyes, such a solution will reinforce the Arabs' faith in legal parliamentary and extraparliamentary modes of struggle as the appropriate means to advance their quest for equality.

3. *Radical Changes:* Unlike the Israeli-Arab stream, which demands limited changes and generally ignores Zionism and the Jewish-Zionist character of the state, the Communists call for a radical metamorphosis. They explicitly demand the abolition of the Jewish-Zionist character of the state and make no bones that discrimination against the Arabs is inherent in Zionist ideology, which favors Jews over non-Jews. This demand is considered to be extremely radical by the Jewish majority as well as by the Israeli-Arab stream. Unlike the Israeli-Arab stream, whose members are willing to compromise on various matters in order to advance the interests of the Arabs in Israel, the Communists believe that insisting on the realization of all Arab rights, including the right of the Palestinian people to establish a state with its capital in East Jerusalem, is the path most conducive to putting an end to the suffering and war in the region, and to achieving coexistence based on full equality between Jews and Arabs in Israel.

4. *Biting Tone:* The Communists phrase their demands in much sharper tones and vocabulary than the Israeli-Arab stream does. Their terminology describes discrimination against the Arabs as racial discrimination and includes terms like "apartheid" to

describe that discrimination and "repressive occupation" to describe the Israeli presence in the West Bank and Gaza Strip. This rhetoric is considered to be excessive by the Jewish majority as well as by the Israeli-Arab stream, who argue that the use of such loaded terms estranges the Jewish majority from the Arab minority.

These criteria, and especially the demand for major changes and the language in which the demands are voiced, present the Communists in a radical light. But their commitment to joint Jewish-Arab organization and cooperation with Jews, and in recent years even with Zionists, produces a certain restraint in their positions. The Communists' commitment to coexistence, derived from and reflected in their ideology, is much greater and broader than that of the national and Islamic stream, despite their demand for changes in its format.

Over the years, the Communists' stance has been modified in a number of ways:

1. A broadening of the areas in which Jewish-Arab equality is demanded and an increased intensity of the call for equality and recognition of the Arabs as a national minority;

2. A stronger emphasis that the two elements in the Arabs' identity, the Palestinian Arab national component and Israeli civic component, complement each other rather than creating an internal contradiction in the Arabs' identity;

3. Movement from favoring peace in general and abstract terms to a demand for the establishment of a Palestinian state alongside Israel, with increasing emphasis that this solution will enhance coexistence between Jews and Arabs in Israel;

4. Greater emphasis on the need to employ parliamentary and extraparliamentary methods, within the confines permitted by Israeli law, in order to realize the objectives of the Arabs in Israel.

5

The National Stream

Until the establishment of Israel, and especially during the three decades of British rule (1918–1948), the Arab or Palestinian national stream developed in the general context of Palestinian society, which was fighting both against the Jews, who aspired to establish their own state, and against the British, who controlled the country. In principle, the organization and orientation of the national stream had two forms. The first was pan-Arab in nature and had at least an organizational and ideological link with pan-Syrian or pan-Arab organizations and movements. The second stream had a particularly Palestinian orientation that emphasized Palestinian identity and the need to encourage the Palestinian national movement in preference to a pan-Arab or pan-Syrian affiliation.

The national camp among the Palestinians was hit hard by the 1948 war; most of its leadership left the country or was killed. The Arab minority in Israel was left without a national leadership or clear national orientation. The first postwar attempts to reform or establish serious national organizations failed. An organized appearance by this stream was delayed for at least a decade after the establishment of Israel. Even these initial attempts were not particularly successful, as I will show below.

ORGANIZATION AND PUBLIC SUPPORT

The conditions that hindered the appearance of the national stream, including the outcome of the 1948 war, the dispersion of the Palestinians, the sundering of links between the Arabs in Israel and the Arab world, and the rest of the Palestinian people, and Israeli policy toward controlling its Arab citizens—manifested in the 1950s and 1960s by the military government and later in other ways (Ghanem 1998a). These are the same conditions that obstructed the founding of a united organization representing the national stream until the recent appearance of the National Democratic Alliance (NDA), which I will discuss later.

First I will survey the main organizational manifestations of this stream from the 1950s through the early 1990s.

The Arab/Popular Front

In Israel, the establishment of Arab political organizations with a national bent was delayed by factors associated with a result of the 1948 war, the imposition of a military government on Arab communities, and the close surveillance of the Arabs in Israel. In consequence, all attempts to establish an Arab party during the first decade of Israeli independence failed (see Qahwaji 1972, 423–425; Landau 1970, 90–94). The first serious initiative was the founding of the Arab Front. On 6 June 1958, meetings were held in Nazareth and Acre to proclaim the establishment of the Arab Front. Two separate meetings were required because the military government prevented people from Nazareth from traveling to Acre. The participants decided to publish a joint manifesto and elect representatives to function as the secretariat of the Arab Front (Jeryis 1973, 316).

The main components of the new body belonged to two streams in the Arab population of those years—the Communists and the Nasserite nationals. Later this dichotomy was the main factor in the disintegration of the front, when the representatives of the national stream quit the group and established al-Ard movement, against the background of the rift between the president of Egypt, Jamal Abdul Nasser, and president of Iraq, Abdul Karim Kassem, who was close to the Communists. The classification of the Arab Front with the national stream stems chiefly from the fact that this was the first serious attempt to establish an Arabs-only association. Members of the national stream controlled the organization and determined its positions. As its chairman the front elected a neutral, Yani Yani, head of the Kufr Yassif local council. He maneuvered in the ground between the two components of the front until his death in 1961.

We can learn about the objectives of the front from its guidelines, which were published (Qahwaji 1972, 439–446), and from interviews with Yani Yani. In an interview published in *al-Ittihad*, the organ of the Communist Party, he outlined the front's objectives: "The Front will demand implementation of the Arabs' rights, such as abolition of the military government, the return of the refugees to their homes, the abolition of the policy that discriminates between citizens and attaining equality. In addition, the Front will demand the return of the Arab refugees who were expelled from Israel in 1948" (quoted in Murkous n.d., 170).

The most important struggle waged by the front in its short period of activity was directed against the expropriation of Arab land. The

Israeli authorities acted in various ways to convert lands controlled by Arabs into state lands. They relied chiefly on a set of laws that provided a firm basis for expropriation (see Ghanem 1990, 52–53). Opposition to this policy was the main focus of activity by the front, which demanded the return of lands expropriated and the repeal of various laws passed to further this goal. This was an essential element in the front's guidelines, publications, and manifestos, which generally also included information about how much land had been expropriated.[1]

The front also worked to abolish discrimination and to achieve equality for the Arabs. This sphere took up two of the six principles enunciated in its guidelines: a demand to abolish discrimination and establish equality in all areas; a demand for equality of status and treatment between the Arabic and Hebrew languages in Israel. Yani Yani told an interviewer that the front's objectives were achieving Arab rights, abolishing the military government, returning the refugees to their homes, restoring expropriated lands, and attaining equality.[2] Its various publications made the point that the military government and discrimination impeded the Arabs' integration into the state (Murkous n.d., 3–28).

The front devoted much of its effort to the issue of education and the Arabic language. It highlighted the discrimination against Arab education and pointed an accusing finger at the authorities and military government as the cause for this. This issue included all aspects of Arab education, including the number and condition of school buildings, the shortage of equipment and teaching materials, overcrowded classrooms, hygiene, quality of teachers, and vocational and technical education. The front insisted that the situation in all these areas was bad and required fundamental attention.[3]

The front employed various means in pursuit of its objectives; taken together, these were meant to constitute an appropriate response to their demands and situation in the field. The front initiated regional and countrywide conferences, mainly in cities like Acre and Nazareth, at which its members discussed their demands and ways to achieve them. The most important countrywide conferences, of which there were four, met with a hostile response from the military government, which took various measures to disrupt them, such as forbidding delegates to travel to the site of the conference.

The front published various publications that were distributed in Arab settlements in order to explain its objectives and inform the public of the steps it was taking. Its members made sure to be interviewed and to appear at public meetings. The front went so far as to send a memorandum to the president of the state, in which it deplored the situation of the Arab population under the military government, enumerated its objectives and demands, and even requested a meeting in order to explain the situation to him. At the same time they met with public officials at various levels, including members of the Knesset, to explain the objectives and activity of the front (Ghanem 1990).

The front also took far-reaching measures (relative to the period) to press the system to respond to and satisfy the front's objectives. Its members organized conferences and meetings without official approval and even proclaimed a general strike of the Arabs on 28 February 1961. The principal source on the strike is a book by the secretary of the front, Emile Touma, who later became a central figure and ideologue of the Israel Communist Party. He writes that the organizers were pleased with the Arabs' response to the call for a strike, indicating, in his opinion, that the Arabs were prepared to come out against the military government and its policies (Touma 1982).

The military government endeavored to deter people from supporting the front and tried to prevent activists from participating in its regular activities. It was even forced to change its original name, the Arab Front, following the intervention of the area commissioner, who alleged, on the basis of a Mandate-era regulation, that the name was "racist." The new designation was the Popular Front. Prime Minister David Ben-Gurion gave vent to the authorities' antagonism toward the Arab/Popular Front on a number of occasions (Jeryis 1973, 316–317).

The Arab/Popular Front disbanded, as mentioned above, against the background of the strife between its two components, the Communists and the Nasserite nationals, reflecting the struggle within the Arab world between President Nasser of Egypt and President Kassem of Iraq. The Communists returned to activity in the Communist Party, while the Nasserites joined with others to set up the al-Ard movement.

AL-ARD MOVEMENT

When the Arab/Popular Front broke up, the national group, led by Mansour Qardosh and Habib Qahwaji, announced it intention to continue to function as an Arab group. They proclaimed the establishment of Asrat al-Ard (the Family of the Land)—which came to be known the al-Ard movement—a name selected to symbolize the strong bond between the Arabs and their land (Jeryis 1973, 318; Qahwaji 1972, 446).

Al-Ard sponsored conferences and meetings in various places. It preached Arab unity and organization on an Arab national basis, drawing heavily on Nasserite ideology, which reached its zenith in the 1960s and had many supporters throughout the Arab world. To disseminate its positions the movement published single-issue newspapers that came out in several editions and under different names, chiefly because the authorities refused to grant it a permanent permit to publish a regular newspaper. To guarantee budgetary sources the movement set up a commercial arm, the al-Ard Company, Ltd., whose shares were sold to members and supporters of the movement. Among its other activities, the movement drafted a memorandum describing the problems confronting the Arabs in Israel as a result of official policy, and sent to the secretary general of the United Nations, foreign newspapers, diplomats, and representatives of foreign countries in Israel (Jeryis 1973, 319–322; Qahwaji 1972, 455).

Later the members decided to register as a political party whose basic principles highlighted the bond between the Arabs in Israel and the Arab world in general, and the Palestinian people in particular. It emphasized the need for a solution of the Palestinian problem in a way that could satisfy the "aspirations of the Palestinian people and Arab nation." It stressed the need for adequate attention to the problems of the Arabs in Israel.

Both the authorities and the Communists reacted with hostility to al-Ard's activities. The Communists turned a jaundiced eye on the new group and saw it as threatening its own primacy in the Arab population (Jeryis 1973, 318–319; Qahwaji 1972, 447–472). The authorities, who alleged that the newly organized group was Nasserite and had the goal of inciting the Arabs against the state, issued orders restricting its activists. The Communists worked openly against the new movement because they thought that its call for Arabs to boycott Knesset elections was directed chiefly against electoral support for the Communist Party (Jeryis 1973, 319–320).

In the wake of al-Ard's request to register as a political party, the authorities acted vigorously to "deal with" the movement once and for all. The Haifa strip commissioner issued an order banning the organization on the grounds that it "harmed the existence of the state of Israel" (Qahwaji 1972, 59). The members appealed to the high court of justice, which upheld the commissioner's decision and ruled that al-Ard was an organization "hostile to the state and its existence." Immediately thereafter some of its leaders were arrested. The defense minister announced that in accordance with his authority under the Emergency Defense Regulations he was declaring al-Ard and its commercial arm illegal organizations, an action that led to steps against members and supporters of al-Ard. Later, in 1965, when members of al-Ard set up the Socialist list to contest the elections for the sixth Knesset, this order was exploited to ban the list. This led to the final breakup of al-Ard (Jeryis 1973, 324–328; Qahwaji 1972, 473).

According to Habib Qahwaji, one of the founders of al-Ard, the experience "demonstrated the connection between the Arabs in Israel and the Arab national movement and the fact that they were part of the

Arab world. . . . It illuminated the difficult situation of the Arabs under Israeli rule . . . and proved that was impossible to organized freely on an Arab national basis in Israel. . . . It paved the way for the start of a new period in the struggle of the Arab masses in Israel" (Qahwaji 1972, 474–475).

THE SONS OF THE VILLAGE *(IBNAA AL-BALAD)*

During the years preceding the 1967 war, two Palestinian Arab national organizations were set up in Israel, the Arab/Popular Front and al-Ard. The outcome of the war caused a momentary paralysis in the activity of the Palestinian national streams. The Israeli victory over the Arab armies came as a great surprise to members of the stream, who were in a state of shock after the defeat, and paralyzed the efforts to establish a Palestinian-Arab national organization among the Arab minority in Israel. On the other hand, the results of the war led to renewed contact between the Arabs in Israel and the main concentration of the Palestinian people in the West Bank and Gaza Strip, who fell under Israeli control. The renewed contract stirred a Palestinian national awakening among the Arabs in Israel. This, along with exposure to various streams in the Palestinian national movement, provided fertile ground for the establishment of a Marxist Palestinian national group in the early 1970s, the Sons of the Village *(Ibnaa al-Balad)*.

The Sons of the Village movement was established in 1972 by nationals from the village of Umm al-Fahm in the Triangle, under the leadership of a young attorney, Muhammad Kewan. The decision to set up a new local organization was spurred by the Communists' support for the incumbent council and its head, who was identified with the Labor party.

The Sons of the Village boycotted Knesset elections, calling for Arabs not to vote in them. In the 1973 local authority elections, however, the list won a single seat on the fifteen-member village council, which it deemed a significant achievement and a launching pad for countrywide activity. The movement establish branches in other communities under other names—the al-Nahda movement in Tayyibe, the al-Fajr movement in Ar'ara. In the 1978 local authority elections the movement doubled its representation in Umm al-Fahm to two councilors and also won single seats in Tayyibe, Kabul, Mi'ilya, and Baqa al-Gharbiyya. In the 1983 local elections it won nine seats on various local councils (Landau 1993, 78). In 1989, however, the movement suffered a severe defeat, winning only three seats throughout the country and failing to make the council of Umm al-Fahm, which by then had municipal status. In 1993 the movement regained some of its strength, winning a total of eight seats, including two in Umm al-Fahm and two in Makr-Judeida (Ghanem and Ozacky-Lazar 1994, 18).

The Sons of the Village took the initiative to augment their activity among Arab university students in Israel. The campuses, protected by their own rules, and the young students willing to take risks, provided fertile ground for their activity. The campus branches of the Sons of the Village called themselves the National Progressive Movement (NPM). They focused on disseminating the movement's doctrines and increasing the students' commitment to national activity, in the hope that they would continue to be active after they returned to their homes. At the same time the groups worked to solve student problems such as housing, studies, and cultural and social activities. They competed for control of the Arab students' committees, which were not recognized by the university administrations but provided an address for Arab students. Most of these committees were dominated by Rakah; the lists put forward by the NPM constituted its chief rival for control of the student committees.

In 1976, the NPM was at its zenith, winning a majority in the elections for the Arab students' committee at the Hebrew University (Rekhess 1993, 113). In the late 1970s and early 1980s the NPM faltered and the DFPE recovered. After the appearance of the Progressive List (see below), its supporters on campus joined with the members of the NPM to set up a joint National Action Front, which posed a more effective threat to the DFPE. In the late 1980s and early 1990s the front made significant gains in the Arab students' committees.

The activities of the Sons of the Village were backed by a network of weekly and periodical newspapers that sought to disseminate its opinions and ideology. The most important of these were *al-Raya,* a weekly that was closed by a military order from the Israeli authorities, and then *al-Midan,* a weekly, and many one-time publications. In recent years the movement has stopped publishing a newspaper and resorted to posters or articles placed in mass circulation Arabic language weeklies.

The Sons of the Village waged their struggle on two levels. The first, oriented toward the outside of the Arab society in Israel, was against the Israeli authorities and on behalf of "the establishment of a democratic secular Palestinian state on the territory of Palestine." Initially the issue was equality with the Jewish majority in Israel; later, however, and especially after the outbreak of the *intifada*, the Sons of the Village tried to reformulate their objectives. The movement's political program, drafted in February 1988 and approved at its conference held in Nazareth that July, speaks of "the right to determine our destiny in the context of a Palestinian state," without defining the boundaries of the state, and of activity "on behalf of equal rights with no distinction of nationality, religion, sex, or color" (quoted by Landau 1993, 80–81). On other occasions representatives of the movement spoke of a willingness to implement Security Council Resolution 242 and voiced an explicit demand for the establishment of a Palestinian state in the West Bank and Gaza Strip alongside Israel. This implies a significant change in the attitude of the Sons of the Village toward the very existence of Israel and their preferred solution for the Palestinian problem.

On the second level, facing inward, the Sons of the Village worked to introduce changes into Arab society itself. They actively opposed clan domination of Arab local governments and the ascendance of the traditional leadership, and those who collaborated with the Israeli authorities and the Jewish political parties. They emphasized the importance of local government for improving the condition of the Arabs in Israel. They called for additional changes in Arab society, for example, in the status of women.

In 1982, against the background of disagreements about participation in Knesset elections and the attitude toward the PLO and its various constituent groups, the movement split. One faction, headed by the founder, Muhammad Kawan, adopted the name *Jabahat al-Ansar*. They favored Arafat's leadership, supported Fatah, and advocated participation in Knesset elections. The larger faction retained the old name, supported the Popular Front for the Liberation of Palestine, and continued to call for a boycott of Knesset elections.

The 1990s saw the start of a general decline in the activity of the Sons of the Village. The many changes in the region, which also affected the Arabs in Israel, diminished the organization's room for maneuver and spurred them to consult with other actors about their future path. In advance of the elections to the fourteenth Knesset, in May 1996, the Sons of the Village, in cooperation with other national groups, established a new party, the National Democratic Alliance, with which I will deal below.

THE PROGRESSIVE MOVEMENT

The genealogy of the Progressive Movement can be traced to Nazareth, where, against the background of disagreements with the local branch and faction headed by the then-mayor, a handful of activists decided to succeed from the DFPE and set up a new movement, the National Faction, known later as the "Progressive Movement–Nazareth." The new group competed against the DFPE in the 1983 municipal elections in Nazareth. Its candidate for mayor, advocate Kamal al-Dahr, won about 25 percent of the vote, and it captured four of the seventeen council seats (Landau 1993, 84–85). This was an impressive accomplishment for the Progressive Movement and spurred it to organize on a countrywide basis.

Before the elections for the eleventh Knesset, in 1984, the Progressive Movement began organizing throughout the country in order to contest the elections. The initiative was joined by public figures, university graduates, local authority heads, students, and existing groups in other Arab communities, such as the al-Ansar association in Umm al-Fahm. The founding conference in Nazareth proclaimed the establishment of the Progressive Movement, which, as the elections approached, reached an agreement with the Jewish "Alternative group," led by Dr. Matti Peled and the journalist Uri Avneri, to set up the Progressive List for Peace (PLP). Its mixed candidate list was headed by attorney Muhammad Miari and Matti Peled.

In its platform, the Progressive List emphasized support for full equality for the Arabs in Israel, with an emphasis on their Palestinian national identity. It also demanded Israeli recognition of the PLO as the sole representative of the Palestinian people and the establishment of a Palestinian state alongside Israel. Its various publications and spokesmen emphasized the Palestinian national affiliation of the Arabs in Israel as well as the need to arouse the Palestinian component of their identity.

The Progressive List encountered criticism and a counter campaign waged by Arab opponents, and was also attacked by the authorities. DFPE activists who felt that the Progressive List threatened its standing in the Arab sector launched a massive counterattack on the upstart, accusing it of being a satellite of the authorities and serving their schemes. The authorities, for their part, alleged that it was a radical national group promoting the interests of the PLO and representing elements hostile to the state and the Jews. The Progressives, through their spokespersons and periodicals, *al-Tadamun* and *al-Watan,* disseminated counter-propaganda explaining their positions and platform.

The Palestinian national platform, the personality of its leader, Muhammad Miari, and the hostility manifested from all quarters proved to be great advantages for the Progressive List and brought it a signal triumph in the elections for the eleventh Knesset—two seats, one held by an Arab, the other by a Jew.

As the elections for the twelfth Knesset approached in 1988, the central elections committee disqualified the Progressive List on the grounds that it did not support the state's being the state of the Jewish people and wanted to turn it into "the state of its citizens," in contravention of section in Amendment 9 to the Basic Law: the Knesset, enacted in 1985, according to which "a candidates' list shall not participate in elections to the Knesset if its objects or actions, expressly or by implication, include . . . negation of the existence of the state of Israel as the state of the Jewish people" (Kretzmer 1992, 177). The party appealed to the high court of justice, which ruled in a majority decision that the PLP could contest the elections because its demand for full equality did not necessarily contradict the characterization of the Israel as "the state of the Jewish people." The two justices in the minority argued that the PLP's platform and positions did negate Israel as the state of the Jewish people and accordingly it should be disqualified.

In the elections that year, the PLP won only one seat, held by Muhammad Miari. During the term of the twelfth Knesset the Jewish-Arab partnership came to an end. In 1992 the PLP ran a Knesset list that was overwhelmingly Arab, including the first three candidates.

In the 1989 local elections the Progressive Movement lost its representation on the Nazareth city council and did very poorly elsewhere. It was left with only three councilors of the 692 in all Arab communities (Ghanem and Ozacky-Lazay 1993, 20). In the elections for the thirteenth Knesset, support for the Progressive List plummeted to only 9.2 percent of the Arab vote, down from 14.3 percent in 1988 and 17.6 percent when it first ran in 1984. It did not receive enough votes to pass the threshold and lost its only Knesset seat. This result, which confirmed preelection expectations, was the result of a number of factors. First, the Progressive Movement always suffered from defective organization. It did not concentrate on recruiting members, establishing branches, or putting out a party organ on a regular basis. As a result, its connection with its voters was weak and even sympathetic activists switched to other groups and parties. The movement had a severe leadership problem, too; its chairman, Muhammad Miari, was frequently accused of behaving like a dictator and of acting without consulting with the movement's institutions and other leaders. The main branch in Nazareth split because some members, who disagreed with Miari's path, felt they had been neutralized. Second, ever since its founding the Progressive List had trumpeted the Palestinian national identity of the Arabs in Israel. In fact, this emphasis was felt to be the party's main mission (see Rouhana 1986, 137–143).

Since 1967, due to a number of factors, especially the renewed contact with the Palestinians in the occupied West Bank and Gaza Strip and the enhanced status of the PLO internationally, the Arabs of Israel had begun to adopt a Palestinian definition of their identity. This gained momentum throughout the 1980s; after the establishment of the Progressive Movement, which highlighted the "Palestinian roots of the Arabs in Israel," the message was absorbed by most of the Arab population and a significant shift took place in how the other parties, especially the DFPE, defined the Arabs' identity. In this way the Progressive Movement's ideological success led to its own political demise. The movement's failure to change and offer new ideas led to stagnation, disinterest on the part of potential voters, and a significant decline in its strength.

Unlike the other parties and movements, the Progressives devoted major effort to dealing with the overall Palestinian problem, even at the expense of attention to the daily interests that preoccupy the Arabs in Israel. Even when it did raise issues relevant to the Arabs and their status in the country, such as the demand for autonomy or self-management, they did so in a bare bones fashion with insufficient detail. This was another factor that ultimately cost it its voters.

THE NATIONAL DEMOCRATIC ALLIANCE

The National Democratic Alliance (NDA) is the last organized expression of the Palestinian Arab national stream. It is composed of a number of small left-wing political groups that had previously operated in Arab towns and villages, including the Sons of the Village, the Equality Alliance founded by Azmi Bishara of Nazareth (a lecturer at Bir Zeit University in the West Bank and a researcher at the Van Leer Jerusalem Institute), the remnants of the Progressive List, and various other local groups such as the Socialist Party from the village of Maghar, the al-Ansar movement from Umm al-Fahm, the al-Nahda movement of Tayyibe, the Bni al-Tira movement, and various Arab public figures. The alliance received approval to register as a political party.

Its members present the NDA as the representative of the Arab and Palestinian national stream in Israel. It demands that Israel redefine itself as the state of all its citizens rather than as the state of the Jewish people. It also demands that the authorities grant special status to the Arab minority, expressed in institutional autonomy and the possibility of managing its own affairs. The NDA also expressed overt and veiled criticism of the peace accords between Israel and the Palestinians. They are decidedly dissatisfied with the Palestinian regime of Arafat and his supporters. This platform is unique; the ideas it presents, although popular among the Arabs, had never been advanced in the form of a political agenda backed by a significant bloc demanding its implementation.

In advance of the elections for the fourteenth Knesset the NDA ran for the Knesset on a joint list with the DFPE. Its representative, Bishara, received the fourth place on the joint list. During the term of the fourteenth Knesset profound differences emerged between Bishara and the other members of the faction, which spilled over into the two parties and thence into the media. The attempts at reconciliation before the elections failed. The NDA ran alone for the fifteenth Knesset, reinforced by Ahmad Tibi's movement and won about 17 percent of the valid Arab votes, a fine achievement that gave it two Knesset members (Bishara and Tibi) and a strong position to continue the consolidation of the national camp among the Arabs and the party itself. It seems, nevertheless, that the NDA did not realize its full potential because of its conspicuous organizational weaknesses and lack of a collective leadership.

POSITIONS ON KEY QUESTIONS

Although the Palestinian-Arab national stream has existed since the birth of the state, there were long periods during which its adherents maintained a low profile and worked quietly, as against others when they worked openly to occupy their appropriate place. Their most prominent attempt since 1967 was the establishment of al-Ard, which wanted to run for the Knesset but was disqualified by the central elections committee and the high court of justice. After that, its members scattered; some were arrested or exiled from their places of residence.

The general outlook of this stream is based on the assumption that the Arabs in Israel are Palestinians in every respect and that there national identity is no different from that of other Palestinians. Accordingly their future is to be reunited with their Palestinian kindred, either in a single political framework or at least in their aspirations and desires. Following this line, its advocates long saw the establishment of a democratic secular Palestinian state on the entire territory of Mandatory Palestine, where Jews and Arabs would live in equality, as the preferred solution for the Palestinian problem. These two key points of their philosophy, the Palestinian identity and establishment of the Palestinian state, are intimately bound up with Palestinian and Arab nationalism as the broader ideology that guides them on issues of coexistence.

The struggle for equality, which acquired legitimacy and occupied a larger focus in the perspective of the national stream, was long viewed as part of the struggle for national liberation. Progress on that front would contribute to the development and advancement of the Arab sector and provide it with tools for participating in the national struggle of the Palestinian people for the liberation of Palestine and establishment of a secular democratic state. In pursuit of their objectives, the members of this stream generally opted for organization on a Palestinian Arab basis. They did acknowledge a need for a joint Arab-Jewish struggle and even cooperation with Zionists on the practical level, but with the caveat that any such framework must be anti-Israeli and aspire to uproot the Israeli system and build the foundations for a democratic secular society in its place.

For many years, Jewish-Arab coexistence in its present format was considered unacceptable by this stream. It aspired for a different type of coexistence in the framework of the secular democratic state to be set up on the territory of all of Mandatory Palestine, with absolute equality between Palestinians and others.

In the wake of the June 1967 war and the defeat of the Arab armies, the representatives of this stream vanished from the field for a number of years. They began to reappear as individuals in the early 1970s. The Sons of the Village movement was established in 1972, and came to be considered the most consolidated force in the national stream. But its ideology, and that of the stream in general, really began to crystalize only in the late 1970s and early 1980s, especially after the Sons of the Village captured positions of authority in local authorities, such as Umm al-Fahm, Kabul, and Mi'ilya, and among Arab students on the campuses.

In addition to the Sons of the Village movement and those close to it, we may count as members of this stream those who were active in al-Ard in the 1960s and continued their activity in the 1970s and 1980s without being organized in a single political group. The Progressive Movement appeared in the 1980s as an alternative to the Sons of the Village in representing the stream. Finally, recent years have witnessed a rapprochement between the Sons of the Village and the Progressives, especially after the Oslo accords and their implementation in the field. Ever since then, or even since the start of the *intifada*, the Sons of the Village have been undergoing a gradual change, moving closer to the political mainstream of the Arabs in Israel. The Progressives went through a process of rethinking expressed in its demands to convert Israel into the state of its citizens and to grant institutional autonomy to its Arab citizens.

In the pages below an attempt will be made to examine the ideology of this stream. I shall consider its views on the four key issues presented before, and how these views have evolved over the years. I shall show that it has in fact moved closer to the Communists' perspective but that, unlike the latter, it derives its ideas from Palestinian and Arab nationalism.

EQUALITY BETWEEN JEWS AND ARABS

The question of equality between the Arabs in Israel and Jews long occupied a marginal place in the views of this stream. It considered the problem to be secondary to the other important issues. It is clear, however, that its perspective went through many modifications over the years. Its focus for many years on activity on the local level does not indicate that the struggle for equality and municipal improvements was the only thing that preoccupied its members. Rather, it stemmed chiefly from the fact that this was the only channel in which it could be active, in keeping with its ideology, which ruled out activity on a countrywide basis, including participation in Knesset and Histadrut elections.

Unlike the other streams, which saw the call for equality as a strategic demand reflecting their desire to integrate into the life of the country, for this stream it was tactical; that is, the struggle for equality was only an avenue for helping the Arabs in general, and the nationals in particular, reach the ultimate strategic solution to the Palestinian problem, as will be discussed below.

In the nationals' view, the chances for achieving equality between Jews and Arabs are very slim. "Zionism" and the "nature of Zionism" are the keywords used by representatives of this stream to buttress their argument. They perceive an essential opposition between Zionism and equality. As long, then, as Zionism remains the official ideology of the state, the ideology of the Jewish majority, equality is out of the question. Mansour Qardosh, one of the leaders of al-Ard in the mid-1960s and later a key figure in this stream, told an interviewer:

> Zionism is identified with expansionism. The attitude toward the Arabs cannot be one of parity, because this is the general nature of Zionism and of most people in Israel, and with this there is no way to attain equality between Arabs and Jews. (EEP 1976, 74)

This conviction did not prevent Qardosh from declaring: "I am in favor of returning lands, in favor of full equality between Jews and Arabs" (EEP 1976, 94). In other words, for this stream discrimination is part of the essence of Zionism, a means it employs to achieve its objectives, one of which, they believe, is to provoke the Arabs to emigrate. Salah Baransi, another leader of al-Ard, told an interviewer: "Zionism is an ideology based on racism and discrimination. It used the method of racial discrimination to achieve its objectives and goals" (Sharabi 1981).

Unlike the other streams, which compared the situation of the Arabs in Israel to that of the Jews, this stream, seeking to demonstrate the intensity of discrimination, made systematic comparisons between the situation of the Arabs in Israel and that of their Palestinian kindred elsewhere. In a pamphlet published by the National Progressive Movement at the Technion, we read:

> The Zionist authorities are applying a policy of national ignorance against us. . . . If we take, for example, the percent-

age of those with an education among our people, it is among the highest in the world. For every 100,000 Palestinians there are 3,500 university students; whereas among us, there are 350 students for every 100,000 persons. We are aware of this racist policy and are also aware of the grave responsibility that falls on our political and social institutions to stand against this policy and defeat it.[4]

This movement draws an analogy between what Israel does to the Arabs in Israel, that is within the Green Line, and in the West Bank and Gaza Strip, which are considered to be occupied West Bank and Gaza Strip under military rule. In both cases they see Israeli policy as intended to leave the Arabs in an inferior position and encourage them to leave the country. This attitude is derived from how the stream views the identity of the Arabs in Israel, as will be discussed below.[5]

There was a significant metamorphosis in this stream's view of the issue of equality in the early 1980s, and especially after the Lebanon war. Organizationally this was manifested in the appearance, alongside the Sons of the Village, of the Progressive Movement for Peace, founded by activists who seceded from the DFPE in Nazareth, and which a year later turned into a countrywide movement with branches in most Arab communities and ran for the Knesset. Its spokespersons helped pull the stream toward the center of the Israeli Arab political map with regard to equality and other issues, as will be seen below. In practice they founded a new substream within the Palestinian national stream, whose positions for many years remained distinct from those of the Sons of the Village. But the latter, too, slowly came around to the notion that equality could be achieved in Israel. The struggle for equality won broader legitimacy in the movement, with the accent that achieving equality would represent a tactical step from which it would be possible to proceed to national liberation and a strategic solution of the Palestinian problem.

According to a poster distributed by the Arab students' committee at Ben Gurion University, when it was controlled by the Sons of the Village:

> the very fact that we are in the Zionist entity forces us to carry with us "variable dialectic knowledge" that will be manifested in opposition to all the plots while using many methods that can be adapted to all the novelties of the daily situation, while taking into account that our very existence and continued possession of our land are means for a struggle that meets with other shades of our daily struggle and lead to equality in all spheres of life and as such become part of our strategic struggle.[6]

This change provides no relief for the Arabs, in the eyes of the nationals. They deemed equality to be antithetical to the essence of Zionism and accordingly held that the bulk of their efforts should be devoted to removing the obstacles in their path, with Zionist ideology at their head. They also recognized that the struggle for equality is protracted and that many years would pass until it could be won.[7]

Opposition to Zionism and the policies derived from it was also voiced later by members of the Progressive Movement. When I interviewed Ahmad Jarbouni, the head of the Arraba local council and a member of the central committee of the Progressive Movement, he denounced Zionism as a "racist movement" that favors Jews over Arabs, forcefully demanded "the nullification of the Zionist character of the state," as well as "full parity for the Arabs in determining the nature and goals of the state." He also maintained that "the continuation of Zionism as the official ideology of Israel is contrary to the physical presence of the Arabs in Israel."[8]

The view of the struggle for equality as part of that for national liberation grew stronger, as this stream emphasized discrimination and the need for equality while insisting that its true goal was not equality but a solution of the Palestinian problem in accordance with their prescription.[9] They raised demands for a clear strategic path for the future of the Arabs in Israel, while continuing to assert that the struggle for equality between Arabs and Jews must be part of the struggle of the Palestinian people to establish a secular democratic state.[10]

For this stream, discrimination against the Arabs is part of official Israeli policy. They assert that the policy is derived from Zionist ideology, one of whose objectives is to get the Arabs to leave the country. They underscore that this discrimination encompasses all areas of life, and with malice aforethought.[11]

At the top of the agenda of the Palestinian national stream is its fight against land expropriation. As they see it, Zionism views taking control of land as the first step in asserting its hegemony; accordingly the Arabs must firmly resist all attempts to take over their land. Muhammad Kawan, the founder of the Sons of the Village, told an interviewer: "We have been and remain an element discriminated against since the beginning of the Zionist enterprise. Zionist came to 'redeem the land,' and for us this means dispossession and the theft of our lands."[12] This view led the representatives of this stream to emphasize a united struggle against land expropriation and the need to keep the land in Arab hands.[13]

As for civic obligations, such as military, national, or civilian service, the literature of this stream tended to neglect this question. This silence stems from a fundamental unwillingness to accept the status quo and an aspiration to alter it fundamentally, so that any talk of military, national, or civilian service—even opposition to them—would not serve their objective. It is clear, however, from my interviews with activists of the stream (key figures in the Sons of the Village: Raja Aghbaria, Waqim Waqim, Ghassan Aghbaria, and Muhammad Kewan), that their absolute rejection of any military or national service as a condition for equality or equal rights for the Arabs. Waqim Waqim, a member of the national leadership of the Sons of the Village, said: "We absolutely reject any military, national, or civilian service. I cannot contribute to the struggle against my people."[14] Representatives of the Progressive Movement spoke in a similar vein against national or military service for the Arabs in Israel, arguing that the Arabs participate in the building of the state by working in the Israeli economy—in factories, construction, and the like—so there was no need for national or civilian service to prove that they contribute to the state. Riah Abu al-Asal, the national secretary of the Progressive Movement, told an interviewer: "National or civilian service is out of the question for us. We contribute our obligation in the context of our work in various areas of the Israeli economy."[15]

The National Democratic Alliance, founded in 1996 by the Sons of the Village, remnants of the Progressive Movement, and various national circles, continued the fundamental accent on the goal of equality. According to the NDA's guidelines, "the party will struggle to turn the state of Israel into a democratic state and the state of all its citizens and guarantee human and civil rights on the basis of equality for all citizens, without discrimination on a national, religious, or racial basis, including equality before the law."[16] The NDA explicitly stated its hope "for official recognition of the Arab citizens in Israel as a national and cultural minority with the right to conduct their own affairs . . . especially in educational and cultural matters."[17]

The NDA's general perspective on equality between Jews and Arabs in Israel long ignored the influence of equality on Jewish-Arab coexistence in Israel. It is clear, however, that whereas at first they deliberately ignored the question of equality and saw the struggle for equality as empty and useless, because Israel and Zionism would never grant the Arabs equality, since the early 1980s their view has been changing. Members of the stream increasingly emphasize the importance of a struggle for equality and consider that it may be possible to make progress on this issue. In this they are moving closer to the Communists' view, even while remaining differentiated from the latter by their emphasis that the struggle for equality as part of the struggle for national liberation.

The emphasis by some representatives of the stream that equality is a tactical step for the Arabs in Israel and that the Palestinians must achieve the solution of a democratic secular state on the entire territory of Palestine paints them as very radical in the eyes of the Jewish majority and Israeli authorities, even in comparison to the other streams among the Arabs in Israel.

THE IDENTITY OF THE ARABS IN ISRAEL

The Palestinian national stream saw the Arabs of Israel as part of the Palestinian people in every respect—political, social, cultural. Its speakers do not acknowledge the presence of any Israeli component in this identity. This view, which has accompanied them since their first appearance as an ideological and political stream, began to change after the outbreak of the *intifada*, as I shall discuss below.

This stream sees the Arabs who live in Israel as a national group that belongs to the Palestinian people, from which it was separated by force of circumstances and with which it will eventually be reunited as a single entity in their homeland of Palestine. This affiliation is the key element in this stream's view of the identity of the Arabs in Israel.[18] The conviction that the Arabs of Israel are in every respect Palestinians like all other Palestinians caused this stream to be among the pioneers in proclaiming the PLO as the representative of the Palestinian people, including the Arabs in Israel, and that any solution of the Palestinian problem must also include the Arabs in Israel.[19]

This stream rejects the idea that there is any Israeli element in the identity of the Arabs in Israel, by the mere fact of their living in Israel. This is associated with fact that they see Israel as an ephemeral phenomenon that will vacate its place for the establishment of a secular democratic state in all of Mandatory Palestine. Ibrahim Nasser, a key figure in the National Progressive Movement at the Hebrew University during the years when the struggle concentrated on opposition to participating in the campus guard roster, in 1978, told an interviewer: "We are Arabs who live under Israeli rule. We must inculcate the masses with the recognition that they are Palestinians only and get them to see Israeliness as a passing phenomenon."[20]

This stream also invested great effort in its debate with other forces among the Arabs, such as the DFPE and Communist Party, who do recognize the existence of an Israeli component in the identity of the Arabs in Israel. They rejected this view and saw it as mistaken, informed by ulterior motives, and denying the true identity of the Arabs in Israel.[21]

As already noted, the Progressives nudged the positions of this stream toward the center. In addition to the Palestinian national component, they also highlighted the Israeli civic component of the identity of the Palestinian minority. Muhammad Miari, the head of the list, told the

central elections committee for the eleventh Knesset, meeting to approve
the PLP participation in the elections: "We see the PLO, as we wrote in
our platform and as we say all the time, as the representative of the
Palestinian people outside the borders of the state of Israel. We are
Israelis and are part of Israeli politics."[22] As Miari told a meeting between representatives of the Progressive List and the then–defense minister, Moshe Arens: "The PLO does not represent me. It represents the
Palestinian people. I have representatives on the official level, the government of Israel and Knesset. And on the narrow political level I want
my own representative in the Knesset."[23]

They gave clear expression to the Palestinian element, too. After his
election to the Knesset in July 1984, Muhammad Miari told an interviewer: "We see a need for the existence of a political list to mobilize
the Palestinian masses [in Israel] and to give our public struggle a Palestinian form and identity."[24] Sammy Mar'i, in a lecture at the University of Haifa and as one of the leaders of the Progressive Movement for
Peace, explained his motives for joining the movement: "The movement['s] roots, contents, and aspirations are Palestinian, for this reason
I found myself in harmony with its Stream of thought and I wish it
continuation and progress, and the radiation of nationalism and feelings
of identity."[25] The trend to a strengthening of both two elements continued to be a central tenet of the Progressives, who saw no contradiction between the two.[26]

Unlike the Progressives, the Sons of the Village continued to hold
the traditional outlook. For them, the Peace Day strike held by the
Arabs in Israel on 21 December 1987, as a mark of solidarity with
the *intifada* in the West Bank and Gaza Strip, expressed the oneness of
the campaign being waged by the Palestinians, "wherever they are," to
put an end to the occupation and gain independence for a Palestinian
national state. For them, the strike demonstrated "the shared destiny
and reinforced the saying that the [Israeli Arab] masses are an inseparable
part of the Palestinian people. . . . It is impossible to separate the future
of these masses from the future of the Palestinian people as a whole."[27]

This perception of the identity of the Arabs in Israel, held by the
Sons of the Village, was slowly modified under the impact of the *intifada*.
They came to recognize the existence of a fundamental Israeli component in the identity of the Arabs in Israel. In my estimation, the change
was catalyzed by the *intifada* and the PLO's recognition of Israel and
Arafat's statements on the matter. This recognition stated clearly that
the Arabs who live in Israel will remain linked to Israel. Hence the
members of this stream were compelled to recognize the existence of an
Israeli component of their identity. In a series of interviews, members of
the Sons of the Village made it clear that, in principle, they did recognize

the existence of an Israeli component of identity. Raja Aghabaria, one of the group's leaders, told me: "I am a Palestinian Arab who lives in the state of Israel. I am engaged in politics and involved with institutions. When I go to Kupat Holim (the biggest health insurance company in Israel) or the National Insurance Institute or the university I am considered to be an Israeli."[28] The NDA, too, continued to emphasize fundamental elements of the Arabs' identity as it saw it. According to its guidelines, "the Arab citizens of the state of Israel, who are living in their homeland, are part of the Palestinian people and the Arab nation with regard to their national and cultural affiliation."[29]

THE ARAB-ISRAELI CONFLICT

The Palestinian national stream's view of the Arab-Israeli conflict and its overall solution, including the Palestinian problem and the representation of the Palestinian people by the PLO, is directly associated with the identity of the Arabs in Israel. As noted above, the nationals held that the Arabs in Israel had an exclusively Palestinian identity (although this changed after the appearance of the Progressive Movement and the outbreak of the *intifada*). Hence any solution of the conflict must take account of the Arabs in Israel. For many years, then, they favored the solution of a secular democratic state in the entire territory of Mandatory Palestine, where Jews and Arabs would live together. The movement derived this idea from the Palestinian Covenant, drafted in 1964 by the PLO. In the words of Saleh Baransi: "There will not be a solution through the establishment of a Palestinian state in the West Bank and Gaza Strip. The solution is the establishment of a democratic secular state. We Palestinians are represented by the PLO and this is the solution proposed by the PLO. . . . I state categorically that there will be no peaceful solution with Zionism" (Sharabi 1981, 69).

When this stream first crystalized it rejected any possibility of a compromise between Israel and Palestinians. This was epitomized in the slogan: "The struggle is not about borders, but about existence" (*al-sera' fi mantiqatana liesa sara' hudud wanama sera' wujud*).[30] This position began to change in the early 1980s, when the movement began to admit the need for an interim solution based on the establishment of a Palestinian state or "entity" on any land liberated from Israel (see Sharabi 1981, 83–84). The movement continued to hold this position for a number of years, but always with the accent that the establishment of such a state would be only an interim phase, to be followed by the total liberation and establishment of a secular democratic state on the entire territory of Mandatory Palestine. The change also included an emphasis on the need to persuade the Jews, who constitute the majority in Israel, to support the ultimate solution proposed by the Sons of the Village.

It is indeed an interesting development that the Sons of the Village now want to use legitimate democratic means, including persuasion, to get the Jewish majority to adopt their solution.[31]

Throughout the years the Sons of the Village rejected Security Council Resolutions 242 and 338, which refer to the need for an Israeli withdrawal from the West Bank and Gaza Strip occupied in the June 1967 war and call for mutual recognition of all states in the region, including Israel. A manifesto published by the Arab students' committee at the University of Haifa in 1979, when it was controlled by the National Progressive Movement, stated: "We reject United Nations resolutions 242 and 338 as a basis for a solution of the Palestinian problem."[32]

This stream also rejected the Camp David accords between Egypt and Israel, and saw it as a Western plot to bring Egypt under the influence of Western imperialism.[33] They also evinced vigorous opposition to the steps taken by the PLO, led by Arafat, to conclude a peace agreement in the region, adopted the hard line stance of the Rejectionist Front, and demanded that Arafat renege on the moves in this direction. In a one-time publication of the Sons of the Village, in March 1985, we read: "We denounce the steps of the Palestinian right, its retreat from the decisions of the Palestine National Council at its 16th conference, and support for the compromise proposal. We also denounce the symbol of the right, Arafat, and see his visit to Cairo as deviating from the decisions of the National Council."[34]

As I have already noted, the Progressives held a different view on the key questions, including the solution of the conflict. For them, a solution of the conflict should include the establishment of two states, Israel and Palestine, alongside each other, with mutual recognition of the right of the other group to live in its independent state. According to the PLP platform for the eleventh Knesset, "the Palestinian problem is the most serious problem facing Israel and thus heads the list of problems that must be solved." In the same platform the Progressive List presented its concrete proposals for a solution, including:

1. Mutual recognition by the two peoples of the right of the Jewish people in Israel and of the Palestinian Arab people to self-determination. This requires an Israeli withdrawal from the West Bank and Gaza Strip occupied in 1967, including eastern Jerusalem . . . so that the Palestinian people can establish their state.

2. There will be mutual recognition by the two states and a peace agreement reached through negotiations between the government of Israel and the Palestine Liberation Organization outside the borders of Israel.[35]

The Progressives believed that their preferred solution would also help the Arabs in Israel. They emphasized that it would improve the daily life of the Arabs and help them live in normal coexistence with Jews. They emphasized, however, that the Arabs would not leave Israel and moved to the Palestinian state when the latter is established. They took a clear stand in favor of remaining in Israel and maintaining daily political, social, and economic life within the state of Israel.[36]

The view of the Sons of the Village with regard to the identity of Arabs in Israel and a solution of the conflict led them to see the PLO as the representative of all Palestinians, including the Arabs in Israel. Issa Qesar, a student at Tel Aviv University and a member of the National Progressive Movement, told an interviewer: "The PLO is the representative of all Palestinians, so it is also my representative."[37] This view, which differs from the stance of the other streams, who see domestic Israeli organizations as the representatives of the Arabs in Israel, is considered to be extremely radical by the other streams of Arabs in Israel and by the Jewish majority.

On the question of the refugees and their return to the homes abandoned in 1948, the position of the Sons of the Village is clear-cut: they support the refugees' return to Israel within the Green Line. They see this as a right that should be honored at once and not linked to a solution of the conflict. They emphasize that they do insist that the refugees return to their original homes; they can be resettled in other places until a permanent solution is found for their problem.[38] This stream emphasizes that the return of the refugees will not affect the Jews, because they will not necessarily return to their original homes and in any case their return will not affect the presence of the Jews in the country.[39]

The Progressives' position on the refugees was closer to that of the Communists. In essence they supported the same solution. To quote its platform for the eleventh Knesset elections, it supported "a solution to the question of the Palestinian refugees in the context of a solution of the Arab-Israeli conflict, in accordance with the United Nations resolutions that call for the right of return or payment of compensation."[40] Implementation of this demand, they insisted, would not harm Israel, because only a minority of the refugees would want to return and most would settle for compensation.

As for the appropriate means of struggle to solve the Palestinian problem, this stream long rejected peaceful methods and advocated an armed struggle based on cooperation between the PLO, Palestinian opposition organizations, and the Arab countries. The rejection of peaceful methods was justified on the grounds that Zionism would never accept a peaceful solution and was opposed by its very nature to the use

of peaceful methods. Saleh Baransi told an interviewer: "I state categorically that there will be no peaceful solution with Zionism, because
its nature, goals, and objective conditions lead us to the conclusion that
it is impossible to reach a peace agreement with it" (Sharabi 1981, 83–
84). They saw a comprehensive struggle including armed force as the
only way to resolve the conflict in accordance with their preferred solution.[41]

Unlike the Sons of the Village, the Progressives rejected the acts of
the *fedayeen* against Israeli civilian objectives, although such methods
were considered to be legitimate in the occupied West Bank and Gaza
Strip. As Kamal Dahar, one of the leaders of the Progressives in Nazareth,
told an interviewer: "As for the members of our people who lived in the
West Bank or Gaza, their political future has yet to be determined and
they are fighting for it.... I believe that a Palestinian who lives there
has the right to conduct his struggle, even an armed struggle. There
Israel is an occupying force.[42]

Like the Progressives, the NDA, formed in 1996, emphasized the
need "for a just and peaceful solution to the Palestinian problem, based
on the establishment of an independent Palestinian state in the West
Bank and Gaza Strip occupied 1967, with its capital in eastern Jerusalem." It also stressed the need "for the removal of all settlements established in the West Bank and Gaza Strip ... and a solution of the refugee
problem on the basis of the relevant United Nations resolutions."[43]

This stream's overall perspective on the Arab-Israeli conflict and the
Arabs in Israel is that the Arabs who live in Israel are part of the
conflict, so that their problems stem from and are linked with it. Hence
the solution they advocated would make things easier for the Arabs. It
is clear, however, that this stream ignores the influence of the solution
it has advocated in recent years, on the Arabs of Israel. This stream long
rejected the status quo and called for the establishment of a secular
democratic state in the entire territory of Mandatory Palestine, and
called for the return of the refugees who left their homes in 1948, which
by its very essence poses a grave threat to the character of Israel as a
Jewish state. They also rejected the use of peaceful means to resolve the
conflict and favored an armed struggle as the only way to settle it. In
addition they saw the PLO as the representative of all Palestinians,
including the Arabs in Israel. Despite the changes in their views in
recent years, they still hold more radical positions than the other streams
and certainly than the Jewish majority.

METHODS OF STRUGGLE

Alone among all the streams, the Palestinian national stream demands
extremely radical changes in all three areas I have discussed: equality
between Jews and Arabs, identity of the Arabs in Israel, and a solution

to the Arab-Israeli conflict. This stand forces them to define the appropriate means for conducting their struggle. The view presented by its spokesmen has gone through only limited changes over the years. Here I will shall attempt to investigate what methods are considered legitimate, and what illegitimate, and how this has changed.

When this stream first emerged it rejected any joint Arab-Jewish struggle and insisted on a separate Arab campaign. The key argument was that they were working to strengthen the Palestinian identity of the Arabs and cooperation with Jews was incompatible with this goal. They fiercely rejected the establishment of a mixed Arab-Jewish organization and saw organization on a Palestinian Arab national basis as essential for promoting their objectives. In the words of Muhammad Kawan: "Our struggle is to raise the Palestinian national consciousness among the Arab population of Israel. From this follows our conclusion that there is no place for the establishment of an Arab-Israeli organization" (Iskander 1979, 15). This view went through far-reaching modifications in the 1980s. The change began with a readiness for Arab-Jewish cooperation to achieve certain goals important to the Arabs in Israel.[44] Another step was taken when the Sons of the Village formally proclaimed the need for Arab-Jewish cooperation. This alteration in the outlook the Sons of the Village, starting in the mid-1980s, was accompanied by an increasing emphasis on their commitment to Arab-Jewish struggle in order to achieve their preferred solution.[45]

The change in the views held by the Sons of the Village during the second half of the 1980s had been part of the Progressives' agenda since they first appeared on the scene. As stated, it set up an electoral bloc for the elections to the eleventh Knesset in 1984 with the alternative movement headed by Matti Peled and Uri Avneri. This act was given declaratory expression by the spokesmen for the Progressive Movement.[46]

This stream always rejected cooperation with Zionists and insisted that Zionism is a racist movement with which collaboration is impossible. But this stand, like that on Arab-Jewish cooperation in general, has been softened somewhat in recent years. Today members of this stream entertain the idea of cooperation with Zionists and with Zionist organizations, and even see it as essential for making concrete gains in certain domains that are important for the Arabs in Israel. Waqim Waqim, responding to a question about the willingness of the Sons of the Village to cooperate with Zionists, told me: "There is a need and importance, and not only willingness, to cooperate with Zionist forces in order to achieve certain things in the daily life of the Arabs in Israel. . . . But it is clear that we will not cooperate with Zionists in order to reach the final resolution we demand for our struggle."[47]

Until the Progressives emerged, the national stream, in stark contrast to the three other streams surveyed in the previous chapters, who saw parliamentary struggle as the appropriate means for advancing the interests of the Arabs in Israel and realizing their preferred solution of the Palestinian problem, rejected the parliamentary arena and asserted that participation in elections meant recognition of the "Zionist entity." According to it, voting for the Knesset, the highest institution in the state, was tantamount to recognition of the state and recognition of Zionism. It also argued that participation in Knesset elections would not help solve the problems of the Arabs in Israel. On this count they were particular fierce in their assault on ICP, which called on the Arabs in Israel to participate actively in the electoral process. In advance of the elections for the tenth Knesset, the National Progressive Movement, in a poster distributed in Umm al-Fahm on 21 June 1981, called for a boycott of the elections on the grounds that "the Knesset is an institution of repression against the Arab and Jewish communities in the state. This Knesset approved all the racist discriminatory policies and laws against us in employment, education, development, and civil freedoms.[48] This stance, calling for a boycott of elections and denouncing voting as an illegitimate act, actually gathered strength over the years, with the added emphasis that a mass boycott involving a large percentage of the Arabs in Israel could be an effective means of exerting pressure.[49]

The Progressives took a substantially different tack. Obviously they did not boycott the Knesset elections; nor did they reject the possibility of supporting a Labor-led coalition. Its representative in the Knesset in the twelfth Knesset expressed a willingness to support such a government "from the outside," on condition that it work for the convening of an international conference for peace in the Middle East and pass a law banning discrimination (Reiter 1989, 76).

The Sons of the Village linked their call for boycotting Knesset elections with other methods. They called for a broad public struggle that would embrace the entire Arab population—a mass phenomenon that the Israeli authorities would not be able to withstand. They generally said nothing about violence, either pro or con, except for isolated cases when the Sons of the Village were under pressure and stated that they were calling for a political struggle, not physical violence. In a poster circulated before the elections for the tenth Knesset in Umm al-Fahm, they wrote: "We must work seriously to solve our problems through a public struggle, through defending our lands. . . . We must develop and advance our nationalism and our Palestinian affiliation and continue the intensified public struggle."[50]

As already noted, in isolated cases the Sons of the Village related to the use of violence and favored a public political struggle including general and partial strikes, protest manifestos presented to domestic and international organizations, and so on.[51]

Although the Sons of the Village still hold this view today, it has become increasingly clear, unlike the other streams, that their support for a legal and nonviolent public struggle is not strategic but merely tactical. Should conditions change, they would be open to the option of using violent means and an armed struggle to alter the status quo. Raja Aghabaria told me: "We do not use violent means. We fight according to our conditions, and our conditions permit us a public struggle with a clear national patriotic substance."[52]

Most Arabs, the other streams active in the Arab sector, and the Jewish majority, view the Sons of the Village as radicals among radicals. Their willingness to consider violence places them far outside the Israeli consensus. Here too, however, their stance has been modified since they first coalesced into a group, becoming more moderate and closer to that of the other streams. It now takes greater account of the objective conditions that exist in Israel, where the majority that can make decisions about questions that affect that the Arab minority is Jewish and Zionist.

This stream's view of the legitimate methods of struggle, in the parliamentary and public arenas, has undergone modification. Whereas it originally rejected parliamentary activity, today the NDA and remnants of the Sons of the Village and the Progressives favor a broad political struggle, with added emphasis that it must be conducted within the law and in the room for maneuver permitted by Israeli democracy. Ever since the founding of the Progressive List in 1984, this stream has sent representatives to the Knesset to conduct its struggle both inside and outside the Knesset.

PROFILE OF THE NATIONAL STREAM

The overall ideology of the Palestinian national stream on issues related to the life of Jews and Arabs in Israel demanded a radical modification of the status quo, which they almost totally rejected. For many years the stream did not really have much to say about the lives of Jews and Arabs in Israel in the stream situation. They focused on their demand for an essential change in the status quo and the construction of a new society in which the relations between its component groups, Jews and Arabs, would be totally different. When they did relate to other issues relevant to contemporary Jewish-Arab relations, such as equality between Jews and Arabs in Israel, the identity of the Arabs in Israel, the Arab-Israeli conflict and its resolution, and the appropriate methods for realizing their agenda, it was emphasized that dealing with these issues would ultimately lead to the emergence of their model society in all of Mandatory Palestine—the territory occupied today by the West Bank, the Gaza Strip, and Israel.

I can summarize the basic traits of the Palestinian national stream, some of which distinguish it from the other streams, as follows:

1. *Organization on an Anti-Israeli Basis:* This stream is organized chiefly on an anti-Israeli, Arab national basis, which rejects the Israeli system and the very existence of the state. It demands a change in the overall situation in the region, in pursuit of its objective of the establishment of a democratic secular state on the entire territory of Mandatory Palestine. This distinguishes it from the other streams, who consider themselves to be part of the Israeli system and favor its preservation. This radical anti-Israeli stance began to crumble after the appearance of the Progressive Movement and has weakened further even among the Sons of the Village since the mid-1980s.

2. *Palestinian Identity and Palestinian Nationality as Key Goals:* The Palestinian national stream sees the identity of the Arabs in Israel and peace as they imagine it—including the establishment of a democratic secular state—as key values. For them, the Arabs in Israel have the same identity as all other members of the Palestinian people; they consider the dissemination of this view to be their main mission. In their eyes, this issue has major influence on the other questions relevant to coexistence and will determine the future of all residents of the country. Their views on these two questions are derived from the broader ideology of Palestinian nationalism.

3. *Call for Revolutionary Changes:* Unlike the other streams, the Palestinian national stream demands revolutionary changes that are epitomized in their demand for the establishment of a democratic secular state in the entire territory of Mandatory Palestine. In addition to the fact that most Arabs see this demand as unrealistic, it is considered to be subversive by the Jewish majority. There has been some change on this front, too, since the appearance of Progressive Movement. It penetrated the Sons of the Village after the outbreak of the *intifada*.

4. *Tough Tone:* The demands of this stream are voiced in extremely fierce rhetoric, as compared with the Israeli-Arab stream and even the Communist stream. Their tone includes the use of loaded terms to describe the status quo and their demands for change. For example, the very existence of the state of Israel is

described as "an imperialist plot," aided and abetted by Arab reactionaries, while the status quo in the region is referred to as "colonialism."

Throughout this long period, the Palestinian national stream has rejected the existence of the state and has not ruled out the use of violence by the Arabs in Israel. It has preferred to organize on an Arab national basis and evinced no strong commitment to cooperation with the Jews or a desire to be part of the Israeli political system. It is clear, however, that this stream has changed significantly over the years, in part because it has acquired a better understanding of the nature of the Israeli system and the possibilities of working within it. I can point to limited changes that have affected the members of this stream over the years and a movement in the direction of the broader Israeli-Arab consensus. This limited process can be described as follows:

1. The call for equality has become louder. Although this stream views the campaign for equality as part of the larger struggle for national liberation, the importance of the former has increased over the years, as the demand for equality was extended to additional spheres of life.

2. It now recognizes the existence of an Israeli component in the identity of the Arabs, albeit with many reservations and qualifications.

3. It now offers limited support for joint Arab-Jewish struggle and even cooperation with Zionists. This development, too, reflects a better understanding of the Israeli system and the composition of Israeli society and recognition that the majority in Israel, which is Jewish-Zionist, can help promote the objectives and interests of the Arabs if it wishes to do so.

6

The Islamic Stream

"Political Islam" began organizing in Mandatory Palestine before 1948. The Muslim Brotherhood, founded in Egypt in the 1920s did not take an interest in events in Palestine until in the mid-1930s. Especially after the eruption of the Arab revolt against the British, and Jewish immigration in 1936, movement delegations and activists came from Egypt to encourage the Palestinians in their struggle. The first local branch of the Muslim Brotherhood was founded in Jerusalem in 1946. During the 1948 war, three battalions of volunteers from the brotherhood enlisted in the Egyptian army (Shabi and Shaked 1994, 41–46).

The results of the 1948 war, the dispersal of the Palestinians, and the establishment of Israel, which imposed a military government on the Arab communities in Israel, limited the activity of political and partisan Islam. In practice one cannot point to any such organization by Arab citizens of Israel in the 1950s, 1960s, and 1970s.

After 1967, the renewed contact between the Arabs in Israel and the Palestinians in the occupied West Bank and Gaza Strip, the existence of fundamentalist organizations in the West Bank and Gaza Strip, and the presence of religious seminaries there, created new conditions for the development of political Islam among the Arabs in Israel (Meir 1989).

ORGANIZATION AND PUBLIC SUPPORT

A number of young people who completed high school and were attracted to religious sites and Islam preferred to continue their studies in the Islamic colleges and institutes that prepared them for the title *sheikh*. These young men began unorganized activity to preach religion in their home, including sermons in the mosques and meetings in Israel where there were concentrations of Muslims (Meir 1989, 10–11). Their activity paved the way for the Islamic stream to organize in the form of a political and social association.

The history of Islamic religious organization in Israel can be divided into two periods. The first period (1979–1981) featured a semimilitary underground organization composed of a small core of people who believed in armed struggle against the Jews and the state of Israel; they called themselves *Asrat al-Jihad* (the Family of Jihad). This group was rounded up by the Israeli security forces in 1981; the imprisonment of its leaders put an end to this period. The second period, from 1983 through the present, began with the emergence of Sheikh Abdallah Nimr Darwish of Kafr Qasim in the Triangle as leader of a new organization, which called itself the "Young Muslims." The group began to organize in almost every community where there were Muslims and established voluntary associations to promote social activity and gather contributions for these activities. Its members also began to organize on a countrywide basis. In general the mosques served as the meeting place for its members and a place where they could preach the need for a return to the sources and attract new members.

Until recently, the Islamic Movement did not participate officially in Knesset elections, even though it did not formally boycott the elections either. Before election day it would call on its members to act in accordance with their conscience. Before the elections to the fourteenth Knesset (1996), however, the Islamic Movement set up a joint list with the Democratic Arab Party; two of its representatives won seats in the fourteenth (out of four seats for the joint list) and the fifteenth (out of five seats for the joint list) Knesset. Some members of the movement succeeded to protest its participation in the elections and established an alternate movement, led by Ra'ad Salah, mayor of Umm al-Fahm (Ozacky and Ghanem 1996).

The Islamic Movement concentrates its efforts on the municipal level. This effort goes back to 1984, when the movement ran for and won control of the local council of Kafr Bara in the Triangle. In 1989 it run for a number of local authorities and managed to elect the head of five councils—Umm al-Fahm, Kafr Bara, Kafr Qasim, Jaljulya in the Triangle, and Rahat in al-Naqab—plus forty-six council members. A year later it added the head of the Kabul local council to this list. In the 1993 municipal elections the Islamic Movement again won six races for council head, losing Rahat but winning Kafr Qara in the Triangle, as well as a rotation arrangement in Kafr Kanna in the Galilee. It also elected fifty council members, including some in the mixed cities of Acre and Lyde (Ghanem and Ozacky 1994, 17–20).

In addition to running the local government in these communities, the movement focused its effort in the field in spreading its doctrines and providing the services associated with the institutions of civil society. Ever since its founding, the Islamic Movement has been providing essential services to the local population in every community in which it is active (see the list in Aburaiya 1989). These include an educational network to supplement the state system, libraries, computer centers, community centers, preschools, rehabilitation centers for ex-convicts and addicts, medical and dental clinics, and so on. These can be found all over the country (including towns where the Islamic Movement is not part of the governing coalition): Umm al-Fahm, Kafr Qasim, Kafr Bara, Kafr Kanna, Nazareth, Kabul, Nahaf, and others.

The movement employs various means to manage and fund these institutions. It focuses on volunteer activity and mobilizes its members for various objectives, including volunteer days to build facilities. Where these did not exist they relied on the mosques, found in every communities were there are Muslims, to host their projects. They also took control of projects for collecting the *zakat*, which is the tax that every Muslim is required to pay to support for the poor; the movement used these funds to underwrite a large portion of its activities. In localities where the movement could draw on other financial sources, including governmental—especially in places where it controlled the local council—it did so.

Today, with the Islamic Movement firmly rooted and even institutionalized, it faces different challenges, especially the hostility toward it evinced by the authorities and Jewish sector, and by the staunchly secularist streams among the Arabs of Israel. The movement is substantially different from fundamentalist movements in the Arab countries around Israel, aware of its limitations in view of the two adversaries just mentioned. Its prospects of growing and attracting new members are rather slim, given the wave of modernization and secularization among the Arabs in Israel. It is unlikely ever to become dominant countrywide among the Arabs in Israel. Its members will have to find less religious allies in order to stand firmly against its opponents among the Arabs themselves and the Israeli public in general.

POSITIONS ON KEY QUESTIONS

The Islamic stream is represented by the Islamic Movement, which crystalized only in the mid-1980s. This late birth made it easier for the leadership to present firm positions on the main issues relevant to the questions that interest them, such as the situation in Israel, equality, the identity of the Arabs in Israel, resolution of the Arab-Israeli conflict, settlement of the Palestinian problem, and the appropriate methods for realizing the aspirations of the Arab citizens in Israel.

The doctrines of the Islamic stream rest on Islamic sources and rationales. Their struggle for change is guided by the slogan "Islam is the solution." This motto is featured prominently on the movement's publications, and festoons banners and posters at its public gatherings and other Israeli-Arab events, such as a Land Day. Almost every speech and article by the movement's leaders begins with the catch phrase, "in the name of Allah the merciful and compassionate," and they season their words with Qur'anic verses and sayings of the Prophet and his followers. This reflects the primary source of the views they are attempting to disseminate, which is of course the Islamic religion and its ancient sources.

EQUALITY BETWEEN JEWS AND ARABS

For the Islamic stream, the Arabs in Israel are a minority who must fight for equal rights. They recognize the state and the fact that the Arabs are a minority in a country with a Jewish majority. In an interview with Ibrahim Sarsur, the head of the Kafr Qasim local council, he said: "We are not speaking about state within Israel. That's foolish. It has been decreed that we live in a state which is fundamentally a Jewish state. We accept this fact. . . . We accept the fact that we are minority in the state of Israel."[1] This stream also deals with the argument that Islam itself does not permit recognition of the existence of the state of Israel, demands its liquidation, and does not allow Muslims to live in a state under foreign, non-Muslim rule, in which Muslims constitute only a small minority (see Interview with Sheikh Darwish, the leader of the movement, *Jerusalem Post*, 16 October 1987).

This acceptance of the existence of Israel leads to a demand for equality with the other citizens of the state, the Jews. The members of this stream have had to deal with the question of whether they feel oppressed in Israel. In the words of Sheikh Darwish: "There is some degree of repression and humiliation. It is impossible to have coexistence between slaves and masters, between strong and weak. A bridge has to be built between equals."[2] A later manifesto published by the movement noted that "the apathy of the government and its lack of concern must come to an end and the government must allocate larger resources."[3]

Some members of the stream have gone further; they indict Israel for its unwarranted discrimination against the Arabs ever since its founding and the attempts by the security agencies to harass Arab political activists. According to Sheikh Juma'a al-Qasasi, the head of the Rahat local council, "the authorities, ever since the founding of the state in 1948, have worked to Judaize the Bedouin in various ways, expelling them from their lands and expropriating it on the basis of various laws. . . . Members of the Islamic Movement have been subjected to harassment in the form of detention and exile from one place to another and even being discharged from work."[4] Sheikh Kamal Khatib of Kufr Kanna raised the demand even more clearly: "They tell me that I'm a citizen, but I have not received all the rights to which I am entitled. I am discriminated against in the most basic matters, such as educa-tion. . . . We should receive all the rights to which we are entitled."[5]

Some of the charges that members of the Movement direct against the authorities involve the negligent care of Muslim holy sites, to the point of intentionally changing these places to designations that are incompatible with their sanctity. "As a result of the policies of the Israeli authorities, not even the mosques and cemeteries in the areas of 1948 have escaped intact, especially those in the mixed cities such as Beer Alsaba', Jaffa, Lyde, Ramle, Haifa, and Acre, and the mosques in the coastal cities. . . . In addition to the digging up of cemeteries and construction of hotels on them and their use for purposes rejected by logic."[6] The movement considers these sites the property of the Muslim *waqf* taken over by the state in its early years, as belonging to Muslims; it wants "to use all legal means, including a public campaign accompa-nied by demonstrations,"[7] to restore them to Muslim control and have them administered by committees selected by Muslims.[8]

Unlike the other streams, the Islamists, in addition to demanding equality, also emphasized the Arabs' own duty to improve their situa-tion. Consequently they developed the concept of volunteer activity extensively and endeavored to organize the fund-raising mechanisms and volunteer days needed to implement what they deemed to be essen-tial projects. According to Sheikh Darwish:

> If the state is not prepared to give me my due, we will help ourselves. The Islamic Movement has set up not only a soccer league, it has also founded self-help associations in the vil-lages. The public sees the results and donates generously. . . . We supplement the public schools with courses in religion, repair roads in the villages, build mosques, and invest heavily in religious services. . . . From time to time we organize vol-unteer labor camps, which resemble a large wedding that lasts for a week or ten days."[9]

For Sheikh Sarsur, "the Islamic labor camps are one of the mani-festations of the return to Islam in the shadow of the scarcity of gov-ernment allocations."[10]

With regard to the issue of the property of the Islamic *waqf*, too, they have shown initiative and established the Al-Aqsa Association to Deal with the Property of the Islamic Waqf. According to Sheikh Kamal Rian, the head of the Kafr Bara local council, it focuses on "the demand to apply *waqf* assets to the preservation and development of neglected sites."[11]

In summary, equality is a key issue in the philosophy that this stream has endeavored to disseminate. In practice it has displayed a broad and solid position that is very similar to that of the other streams among the Arabs in Israel.

THE IDENTITY OF THE ARABS IN ISRAEL

From the outset, the leaders of the Islamic Movement had to offer definitions of the identity of the Arabs in Israel. These differed from those of the other streams in that they stressed the Islamic religious component, though of course without ignoring the other components of the identity of the most Arabs in Israel identity.

Sheikh Abdallah Nimr Darwish sketched out the line that defines the identity of the members of the movement and of all the Arabs in Israel. For him, the Arabs are a minority in a state with a Jewish majority, and thus have four circles of identity: Muslim, Arab, Palestinian, and Israeli.[12] This order of presenting the circle of identities is usually adhered by Darwish and the other leaders of the movement. The circle given the most emphasis is in the Muslim, and it always appears with other formulas for defining identity. Thus, for example, for Sheikh Hashem Abd al-Rahman, the deputy mayor of Umm al-Fahm, "I am a believing Muslim and a law-abiding citizen of the state of Israel."[13] In a rare appearance in front of a Jewish audience, Umm al-Fahm mayor Ra'ad Salah, who generally does not appear in the Jewish sector, told a symposium in Givat Haviva, "I define myself as a Muslim in my outlook on life, the universe, and the need for a regime and faith that realize the humanity of people. . . . I am also an Arab. At the same time I have third link, the Palestinian link. I also have a fourth dimension— I am a human being who aspires to realize human objectives." He also emphasized, on the same occasion, the fact that he is Israeli citizen who abides by the laws of the state and demanded to receive the rights to which he is entitled.[14]

These same components of identity, with various emphases, were featured in a series of interviews conducted by Nadim Rouhana of Harvard University with seven prominent leaders of the movement as part of a comprehensive study of the identity of the Arabs in Israel, which he made available to me for the present work.[15] In those interviews, the leaders of the Islamic Movement were certain that the Arabs cannot be Israelis like the Jews, because they do not want to be, but chiefly because the state and the Jewish majority do not want them to be. Sheikh Darwish, asked for his opinion of an Arab who defines himself only as an Israeli, retorted that for him such a person "does not understand what identity is."[16] On the same occasion, Sheikh Darwish explained that for the Arabs, Israeliness is an official and legal component of their identity, but not an emotional component linking them strongly with the general population of the Jewish state. This is the result of the Jewish-Zionist character and definition of the essence and objectives of the state, ignoring the existence of its Arab citizens.

THE ARAB-ISRAELI CONFLICT

The Islamic Movement recognizes the existence of the state of Israel as a matter of principle and its right to continue to exist. Although there are nuances in this recognition, which varies from one group to another within the movement, this may be inferred from an analysis of Rouhana's interviews.

The mainstream, represented by Sheikh Darwish, takes a moderate stance. On many occasions Darwish has expressed his recognition of the state of Israel and its right to continue to exist. He even proposed that the Palestinians recognize Israel in exchange for its recognition of their right to set up their own state. He told an interviewer, "I propose the principle of mutual recognition—Israeli recognition of the Palestinian people's right to self-determination, which includes, of course, the right to establish a Palestinian state, and Palestinian recognition of Israel's right to live in peace."[17] In the context of such an agreement, Darwish believes, the Palestinians would make their own decision about the nature of their state and its regime.[18] But like all the leaders interviewed by Rouhana, he demands the Israel state proclaim itself to be the state of its citizens and not of the Jewish people, which means conceding its Jewish-Zionist character and its main vocation: serving the Jewish people throughout the world. But even if it does not do so, according to the Sheikh, it still has the right to exist.

This stream also deals with the argument that Islam itself does not permit recognition of the existence of Israel, demands its liquidation, and forbids Muslims to live in a state under foreign, non-Muslim, rule in which Muslims are only a small minority. Confronting the demand of radical Islam in Lebanon and Iran to eradicate Israel from the Middle East, Sheikh Darwish told an interviewer:

> Why Islam can't exist in a state that is not Muslim? I want to ask them this, and I can state that they have no answer. . . . Yes, I believe that we should establish a Muslim state in the entire Arab Muslim world, . . . But there cannot be an Islamic state in a country that has a Jewish majority.[19]

For the Islamic Movement, the Palestinian problem is a pan-Islamic issue. Its solution is associated with the entire Muslim world. That is, the Muslim states must all participate in finding a solution. This should be self-evident and accepted by the Palestinians, who must work to ensure the involvement of the Muslim states.[20]

As stated, the various streams within the movement recognize Israel at some level, so that their position on a solution to the conflict starts from the idea that Israel will continue to exist as a separate entity in the future. This starting point does not spare the various streams from debating the limits of an accord between Israel and the future Palestinian state, and especially whether that state should include the Galilee and Triangle, or whether these areas should continue to be part of Israel.

An analysis of the answers given to Rouhana and statements published in the media about a solution of the Palestinian problem indicates that there is a consensus among the leadership of the Islamic Movement. Whatever stream they belong to, they support the establishment of a Palestinian state alongside Israel as the means for settling the Israeli-Palestinian conflict.

The mainstream takes a position identical to that of most of the Arabs, which is considered to be one of the two points of consensus among the Arabs (Ghanem and Osacky 1990). It demands the establishment of a Palestinian state alongside Israel, on the West Bank and in the Gaza Strip.[21] Sheikh Darwish has frequently emphasized that both peoples, the Palestinians and the Jews, dream of a large state stretching from the river to the sea. For him, however, these dreams run up against basic and intractable facts, which entail a compromise whose crux is mutual recognition and agreement on the right of each people to live in its own state.[22]

Darwish believes that in order to reach an agreement, Israel must initiate recognition "of the right of the Palestinian people to self-determination and the establishment of an independent Palestinian state." This is important "to persuade the Arab Muslim world that Israel truly wishes to live in peace in the region."[23] In the context of a peace agreement, Sheikh Darwish demands that Jerusalem be the capital of both states, Israel and Palestine, but he does not go into details about how this would work in practice. He does not specify whether Jerusalem should be redivided or whether an agreement could be devised so that the city would serve as the capital of the two states. He told an interviewer, "peace must be based on just principles: the establishment of a Palestinian state with its capital in Jerusalem, which will also continue to be the capital of the state of Israel."[24] The agreement, according to Darwish, would be achieved as a result of an international conference with a participation of representatives of Israel and the PLO.[25]

Darwish rejected the oft-heard contention that the Arabs are threatening "to throw the Jews into the sea." He countered with the inverse fear from the Palestinian side: "We don't want to throw the Jews into the sea, but we want to be confident that they won't throw us into the desert. Come, let us test the Palestinian and give him rights, and then see if even the radical remains radical."[26] In the context of such a settlement, Darwish told Rouhana, the Palestinian refugees who left the country in 1948 would have to be allowed to return to their lands and villages, because this is their fundamental right. Sheikh Kamal Khatib told an interviewer, "we have to receive our due rights, including the right of return of the refugees to the places where they lived before 1948. It is their right to return to their homeland."[27]

Sheikh Darwish believed that negotiations with the Palestinians, led by the PLO, would prove to be the only way to reach an agreement. Accordingly he rejected a solution of the conflict and the Palestinian problem as the outcome of talks between Israel and Arab states without the participation of the Palestinians and the PLO.[28] As for the future Palestinian state, Darwish would allow its residents to decide what type of regime it should have.[29]

Sheikh Ibrahim Sarsur is more rigid then Darwish. He believed, before the signing of the Oslo accords between the Palestinians and Israel, that the Palestinians should not negotiate with Israel unless it publicly announced, in advance, its recognition of the Palestinians' right to establish their own state. "Israel has to recognize the right of the Palestinian Arabs to an independent state. On this matter I am not prepared for compromise. I am not willing for there to be any negotiations before the Israeli leadership recognizes this. I do not believe that the Palestinian leadership should begin negotiations until Israel recognizes this. It is the right of the Palestinian people to continue its legitimate struggle, the *intifada*."[30]

He also espoused a more extreme position than Sheikh Darwish with regard to the borders between Israel and the future Palestinian state. He hinted that his preference was for the lines of the 1947 partition plan. In any case, however, the borders could only be determined in negotiations to begin after Israel recognized the Palestinians' right to establish their own state. But Sheikh Sarsur made it plain that he did not agree with the idea advocated by the hard line faction of the Islamic resistance movement, Hamas on the West Bank and Gaza Strip, that an Islamic state should be established on the entire territory of Mandatory Palestine. "There are several factions within Hamas. One faction wants all of Palestine, from the sea to the river. . . . I am closer in my views to the other faction, the more rational one, which is prepared to resolve the problem in the context of the existing borders."[31] When asked whether this settlement would be based on the 1967 borders, he replied, "Why make any commitment to 1967 borders? What if the two sides agree on the 1947 partition borders?"[32]

The Islamic Movement viewed the *intifada* as a "natural" step in reaction to the protracted occupation of the West Bank and Gaza Strip, manifesting the inhabitants' fierce desire to escape Israeli control. In the words of Sheikh Darwish: "Occupation is something that cannot be borne. Occupation is not enlightened; it is a darkness. The Palestinian people in the West Bank and Gaza feel that they are occupied and the *intifada* is something natural."[33] The leadership of the Islamic Movement always emphasized its sympathy with the *intifada* and support for its main objective, the establishment of a Palestinian state. The movement sees itself as duty-bound to provide financial and moral support to the Palestinian people on the West Bank and in the Gaza Strip by conducting propaganda campaigns and sending food and medical supplies. As Sheikh Kamal Rian, the head of the local council in Kafr Bara in the Triangle, told an interviewer:

> The position of the Islamic Movement on the *intifada* is that we support the right of our people to liberty and independence in its land. This principle has guided the Islamic Movement to support our people in the occupied West Bank and Gaza Strip with the food and medicines they need. What is more, we arrange press coverage of the events of the *intifada* in the weekly *Sawt al-Haq* and the monthly *al-Sarat*.[34]

As for the role to be played by the Arab citizens of Israel in the context of a resolution of the Israeli-Palestinian conflict and their role in the state after such a settlement, there are no disagreements within the movement. It believes that the Arabs must make every effort, using legal means, to find a solution to the conflict. The Arabs in Israel have an important role to play in the struggle for peace because they can constitute, if allowed to, a bridge for peace between Israel and the Arab world.[35] The Arabs can play this role to the utmost if they achieve equality with the Jews in Israel.[36]

METHODS OF STRUGGLE

The Islamic Movement advocates action within the law that does not cross "its limits." This position is derived from its view that the Arabs in Israel are a minority and will remain such even after the establishment of the Palestinian state. Sheikh Sarsur made it plain to an interviewer that, even as part of a two-state solution, "the Arabs of Israel will live as a minority in the state."[37] In another interview he emphasized that this minority will obey the law and not cross any red lines: "It has been decreed that we live in a state that is fundamentally a Jewish state. We accept this fact. We will not allow ourselves, some day or other, to deviate from the law. We have red lines. We are aware of our ability, respect the decisions of the majority, and accept the fact that we are a minority in the state of Israel."[38] This orientation was reinforced by Sheikh Darwish, who emphasized that the law is a shield for the minority against the despotism of the majority: "I know that we are a minority in the state of Israel. Every citizen must obey the law, and in addition minorities have no better defense than the law."[39]

According to Darwish, respect for the law by the Jewish majority, too, is a condition for harmony within the state, even if the majority and minority "hate" each other. There is no danger to coexistence as long as all obey the law. "Things depend on both sides. If each side obeys the law, the two peoples can live together. We Muslims can live with people who hate us on condition that they keep it inside themselves."[40] The leadership of the movement expressed its opposition to any expansion of the *intifada* to Israel proper and Israeli Arab involvement in it. Sheikh Juma'a al-Qasasi, when asked whether the movement would import the *intifada* within the Green Line, said: "I'm convinced that this will not happen, because the Islamic Movement came to power democratically and we will observe the law."[41]

There are disagreements within the movement about the need for Arab-Jewish cooperation to promote a solution in the region. Sheikh Darwish believes that it is necessary and prefers cooperation between a united Arab bloc and the Jewish peace camp, which "recognizes the right of the Palestinian people to self-determination and realization of its national rights in a free state." He does not reject the idea of a joint Jewish-Arab list.[42] Sheikh Sarsur, by contrast, believes "that our movement must work exclusively in internal Arab frameworks."[43] These different approaches are associated with the degree of pragmatism, which includes a willingness for Jewish-Arab cooperation, and the fact that the stream represented by Sheikh Darwish advocates a solution to the Palestinian problem that resembles that favored by the Israeli peace camp.

This stream even expressed a willingness to participate in Knesset elections and did not reject the idea for ideological reasons—an unwillingness to recognize the Knesset as the highest governmental organ in Israel and thus nonrecognition of the state of Israel as a matter of principle. On 10 October 1988, three weeks before the elections for the twelfth Knesset, the Islamic Movement published an announcement to its members stating that it did not favor a boycott and emphasizing that every member of the movement was free to vote for any party, list, or movement contesting the elections.[44] Sheikh Darwish himself repeatedly emphasized his support for participation in Knesset elections and for turning the Islamic Movement into a significant force on the Israeli political map. He believes that Israeli parliamentary democracy is the legitimate forum for activity by the movement and is accordingly willing to recognize the legitimacy of the regime, which is both Zionist and secular.[45] Sheikh Abbas Zakur, a member of the executive committee of the *waqf* in Acre, also expressed support for participation in Knesset elections and estimated the strength of the movement: "If the Islamic Movement decided to run for the Knesset, something that I support personally, it would win no fewer than six mandates."[46]

Sheikh Hashem Abd al-Rahman, deputy mayor of Umm al-Fahm, similarly expressed his estimate that the Islamic Movement could hold the balance of power between the two large camps in Israeli politics, those led by Labor and by the Likud. He hinted that the movement would support Labor, saying that it would support those who favor the formula of "West Bank and Gaza Strip for peace."[47] On the other hand, Mohammed Rian, the head of the Kabul local council, believed that the movement had three options for participating in Knesset elections: "In the form of a separate Islamic Movement or party, as part of a joint Arab list except for the Communists, or by supporting persons from outside the movement and electing them to the Knesset." It was clear from his remarks that he preferred the first option, on condition that it "not require members of the movement elected to the Knesset to give up their faith and religion."[48]

Before the elections to the fourteenth Knesset in May 1996, a slender majority of the executive committee of the Islamic Movement voted to run candidates for the Knesset and to set up a joint list with the Democratic Arab Party of MK Abdulwahab Darawshe. This led to a walkout by the staunch opponents of the idea.

The group that supports electoral participation is opposed by another faction that, despite its recognition in principle of the state of Israel and its right to exist, has more reservations. Circumstances being what they are, these reservations are not expressed freely and find public outlet only on rare occasions. The arguments center on the notion that participation in Knesset elections is contrary to "the spirit of Islam." The most prominent advocates of this line are Sheikh Ra'ad Salah, the mayor of Umm al-Fahm, and Sheikh Kamal Khatib of Kafr Kanna (Malik 1990). Sheikh Samir Aasi, the imam of the mosque in Judeida and a member of the Islamic Movement, expressed vigorous opposition to the idea that the movement might run candidates for the Knesset:

> I do not accept an Islamic party. I believe that enlightened Muslims, those who believe without reservation in the principles and objectives of Islam, will be fiercely opposed to the idea of a Muslim party that runs for the Knesset. Every Muslim who knows what is written in the Koran will reach the same conclusion. I reject the Knesset because in my opinion we cannot achieve the objectives of Islam through it. Quite the

contrary: in the Knesset things will be forced on us and we will have to surrender some of our principles. We do not agree that someone else be responsible for us. We owe an accounting only to God, to Muhammad, and to the believers.[49]

On other occasions he made it perfectly clear that he believes that voting in Knesset elections "is contrary to the law of Islam."[50]

These arguments rest, as might be expected, on Islam as understood by the members of this stream. The decision to participate in the 1996 Knesset elections, the result of internal and external pressures on the movement, led to a split that had previously been avoided because leadership avoided participation in the elections as a separate force or as part of a particular political bloc.

PROFILE OF THE ISLAMIC STREAM

The belated appearance of the Islamic stream, especially the consolidation of its organizational expression, the Islamic Movement, helped it present firm positions from the outset on issues associated with the Arabs in Israel. This stream resembles the others in some respects and differs from them in others:

1. *Organization on an Arab and Islamic-Religious Basis:* The movement favors organization on Arab national basis and prefers organization on Islamic basis. It is split on the question of participation in Knesset actions.

2. *Islamic Identity as the Chief Goal:* The Islamic stream emphasizes Islamic-religious element of the identity the Arabs in Israel and sees its reinforcement as its chief goal. It does not, for that, deny the other components of the identity of the Arabs in Israel, as Arabs, Palestinians, and citizens of Israel.

3. *Rhetoric:* The Islamic stream, which came of age in the mid-1980s, emerged into a new situation in the history the Arabs in Israel. This made it possible for its spokesmen to phrase their demands of the authorities and the Jewish majority in harsh and frequently uncompromising rhetoric. They did not hesitate to demand that the Palestinians themselves take action on behalf of their own future and implemented this demand in practice.

7

Local Politics: The Clan as an Alternative Stream

As a result of the 1948 war and the establishment of Israel, the existing Arab local authorities were destroyed or totally paralyzed by the hostilities and the expulsion of some of the local leadership. When local government was consolidated in Israel after independence, the Arab municipal sector was extremely small. Most Arabs lived in villages that lacked municipal status. The village regime was based on the sociopolitical solidarity of families and on the traditional leadership, whose existence was legitimized by its social standing in the clan *(hamula)* and the community. This was reinforced by their ties with the authorities and the officials of the military government. This situation was advantageous for the authorities and ruling parties of that era, chiefly Mapai. They intervened, through the military governor and their representatives, in the proceedings in Arab localities, whether in the appointment of *mukhtars* or by granting favors to their allies, whether individuals or groups (Lustick 1985).

The decision to grant municipal status rested with the minister of the interior, generally after consultation with the ministry official in charge of the population and with local figures (Weiss 1972, cited by Al-Haj and Rosenfeld 1990a, 29). The declared objective of policymakers was to develop Arab localities and improve the standard of living there. Accordingly they set to work to establish Arab local authorities. Between 1950 and 1954, Arab local councils that had existed under the mandatory government were revived. These included Shefa'amre, which had been granted municipal status as early as 1910, Nazareth (1877, renewed in 1934), and Kufr Yassif (1925). Eight other local authorities were set up (Al-Haj and Rosenfeld 1990, 29).

Examination of the list of localities that were the first to acquire municipal status reveals that the decision to set up a local authority in a particular place was strongly influenced by considerations of size, location, and ethnic composition (Al-Haj and Rosenfeld 1990a, 29). The local governments set up during this period faced many problems. In most of them, the inhabitants were subject to the military government, which restricted their movement. Entire areas were proclaimed to be closed. Entering or leaving them required a permit from representatives of the military governor. During the first decade after independence, the *mukhtars* continued to be active, even in places where local councils had been set up. In many cases, *mukhtars* who did not play an active role in the administration of the council impeded its operations because they saw it as a challenge to their status. On more than one occasion they bypassed the council head (Al-Haj and Rosenfeld 1990a, 29).

Between 1956 and 1960, another fourteen Arab local councils were set up, five of them in the Triangle and nine in the Galilee; between 1960 and 1965, a further thirteen were set up, and thirteen more between 1966 and 1975. Today there are 107 recognized Arab localities, eight of them recognized as cities, fifty localities have local-council status, thirty-eight are part of a regional council, and eleven localities are administered by a *mukhtar* (Al-Haj and Rosenfeld 1990a, 28-33). There are another eighty-one localities that have no municipal status or official recognition, the so-called "unrecognized villages"—fifty-three in the Galilee, Emeq, and Triangle, and twenty-eight in Al-Naqab (see Ghanem 1993, 18–19, 80–92).

In many senses, the period since 1975 has been marked by the consolidation of Arab local government in Israel. From that date it becomes possible to speak of local government that fulfills the main functions incumbent upon it. Local government has gained prominence as the most important channel of sociopolitical development by the Arabs in Israel.

The importance of local government for the Arabs in Israel has been noted in many studies, some of them focusing on that topic in particular, others on the historical development of the Arabs in Israel in general (see Al-Haj and Rosenfeld 1990a; 1990b; Paz 1989; Rekhess 1985; Elazar 1987). The chief reasons for this importance, according to the studies, can be summarized as follows:

1. The Arabs in Israel, as a minority that has come to terms with this status within the state, do not have any real ability to exert an influence equal to the Jews' on the political center in the country and on the delineation of the nature of the general welfare. These matters are in practice the unique province of the Jews, although they occasionally rely on minimal assistance from some of the Arabs, as in the case of the change of government

after the elections to the thirteenth Knesset (Ghanem 1998b). This situation has encouraged the Arabs, or at least some of them, to view local government as the main channel for influencing domains associated with their social, political, and economic development. According to Al-Haj and Rosenfeld (1990a & b), Arab local government is important because of the Arabs' minority status. Local government has become the only political nexus in which the Arabs have direct influence. Paz (1989) argues that local elections have always been important in the Arab sector, as shown by the high participation rate, compared to that for Knesset elections. He maintains that "the Arabs of Israel, who are not participants in the management of foreign, defense, and economic policy, see the local level as the main arena in which they can express their desires in the most effective manner" (Paz 1989, 5). Elazar (1987) maintains that it is a mistake to minimize the importance of the role and influence of local government in Israel; it plays an important function in Israeli society, especially with regard to the ability to control developments directly related to inhabitants. Local government has the same significance for the Arabs. He holds that, for the Arabs, the official institutions of local government have become means to achieve increasing control over their immediate destiny. Even though they do not have to, most Arabs continue to participate voluntarily in the sociocultural system that is protected and maintained by local government in the villages, such that local government becomes a meaningful channel for preserving this involvement (Elazar 1987, 19).

2. In a situation where there is clear and significant discrimination against the hiring of Arabs to fill official positions in the civil service—except for the salaried employees of the ministry of education, because the need for Arab teachers—the number of Arabs employed in other branches of government service is extremely small. As a result, local authorities and local government have become the main employer of Arab university graduates and intellectuals. The establishment and development of the local authorities required the integration of these persons in its various branches; hence, in addition to being a venue where many among the Arab intelligentsia can realize a maximum of self-fulfillment, local government is another source of employment and livelihood for them (Al-Haj and Rosenfeld 1990a, 1990b).

3. After the establishment of the committee of Arab local council heads in 1974 and of the follow-up committee for Arabs in Israel affairs in 1982 (about which more later), local government became

the main track for the heads and members of councils to become part of the national leadership of the Arabs in Israel (see Al-Haj and Rosenfeld 1990a, 130–154). The sharp rise in the status of the follow-up committee during the 1980s led many to aspire to membership on it. This ambition was reinforced by the fact that in a number of cases the local level proved to be a springboard for prominence on the national level; for example, the election of Hashem Mahameed, the former head of the Umm al-Fahm local council, as a Knesset member representing the DFPE, and the placement of Saleh Morshed, the head of the Ibillin council, in the fourth slot on the DFPE list for the thirteenth Knesset.

LOCAL ELECTIONS

This chapter is based on material collected about local elections in the Arab community since 1975. It was in the mid-1970s that Arab local government in Israel stabilized and took on more or less its present form. That was also the year when a significant change in the method of election of local authorities was introduced. Until then, the council was elected by proportional representation, and its members then selected the chairman from among themselves. Since then, there have been separate direct elections for the council members and for the mayor or council head. The information has been gathered from archives and publications of the ministry of the interior and of the central bureau of statistics.

Below I shall refer to aspects associated with how Arabs vote in local elections, the scope of electoral participation, and the results and breakdown of the balloting.

Voter Participation

The data on the level of voter participation reveal a continuing rise in the turnout for local elections, as a percentage of eligible voters. I believe that this points to three developments. First of all, there has been a sharp increase in the attractive force of the clan and its ability to mobilize members in competition with rival clans or coalitions of clans and political parties. Second, there is intensified interest in local government as an arena that can provide an alternative to the central government. Finally, there has been a growing process of localization, as more and more young adults are persuaded that the main arena for their activity is local rather than national, where the Arab influence is infinitesimal.

Voting data (Ghanem 1996a) point to a rather high level of participation in local elections and a consistent rise over the years. The high

Table 7.1. Participation in Local and Knesset Elections

Knesset Elections		Local Elections	
Year	Participation Rate in Percent	Year	Participation Rate in Percent
1977	74.40	1978	87.87
1981	68.00	1983	88.88
1984	72.00	1989	90.29
1988	74.00		
1992	69.70	1983	91.00
1996	76.00	1998	91.00

SOURCE: Ghanem 1996a; Ghanem and Ozacky-Lazar 1999; The figures of the local elections of 1998 are based on personal calculations by the author depending on the official documents of the Israeli National Elections Committee.

participation, as compared to the Arabs' turnout in elections for other agencies, such as the Knesset and Histadrut, points to a significant gap in the participation in local government and Knesset elections. This further reinforces my thesis about the increasing importance of local government for the Arabs (see Table 7.1).

According to the figures presented in the table, the difference in the participation rates for Knesset and local elections is around 17 percent, a rather significant figure. The large turnout for municipal elections stems, in addition to the clans' ability to mobilize voters, from the great importance of local government to Arabs in Israel, as noted before.

COMPETENTS

The struggle for control on the local level is focused in overt and covert competition between two key players: the traditional agents, such as the clan and religious confession, along with their representatives and leadership, on the one hand; and the countrywide political parties and movements, with their representatives and leadership—or groups created by electoral cooperation or coalitions among representatives from these two categories. In addition, a third factor has appeared recently, which presents itself in principle as an alternative to the first two and is based chiefly on the independent organization of young adults who organize and operate on a local basis because of their disappointment with the two traditional groupings. These include *Tamra el-Gad, Mi'ilya el-Gad, Abnaa Arrabe,* and *Abnaa Shafa'amre,* in Tamra, Mi'ilya, Arrabe, and Shafa'amre, respectively—all of them in the Galilee. This factor became prominent only in the local elections of November 1993.

The Clan as a Traditional Player in Local Government. The traditional leadership, whether of the clan or of the confession, had reservations about the establishment of local councils—a new institution whose authority is derived directly from the electorate. The central government was viewed as a threat to the power and position of the traditional leadership, which also feared that the establishment of councils would intensify the authorities' involvement and increase the tax burden (Elazar 1987, 163). The power centers in the Arab community were traditionally controlled by the heads of families, the village notables, and the property owners. Nevertheless, in the absence of any formal political alternative, the introduction of local government strengthened the clan structure and augmented the competition around local government.

As the process of municipalization of the Arab sector intensified, the clan remained the chief framework of loyalty and the basis on which local elections were usually decided (Rekhess 1985, 1). Winning a majority on the council, before the introduction of direct election of the council head and even afterward, gave clan leaders an advantage over their local rivals, alongside a significant ability to influence the administration of day-to-day life in the community. Over time, both during and between election campaigns, the clan competition became a synonym for the local political system in the Arab sector. For a long period there was a distinction between Knesset elections, which were decided by political parties, and local elections, which were controlled by the clans (Rekhess 1985, 2).

Incomplete processes of modernization, in constrained conditions, have modified the functioning of the clans in their social, economic, and political roles. Over time it has lost some of its weight on the social and economic levels, where the nuclear family has become the basic unit. By contrast, on the political level, the role of the clan has actually increased, as we shall see below. In many Arab localities there is a clear overlap between clan affiliation and support for a particular national party in Knesset elections, even though some parties, especially Mapai, as the ruling party until 1977, frequently provided behind-the-scenes support for rival clans in the same locality, in order to garner the maximum number of votes in Knesset elections (Landau 1971, 221).

The National Parties in Local Government. The national political parties and lists have always played a key role in municipal government in Arab localities, even though that role was often played offstage. The parties involved were mainly Mapai and Mapam, which later formed the Alignment (Mapam split from the Alignment in 1984 because of the establishment of the National Unity government with the Likud; in 1992, before the elections for the thirteenth Knesset, it joined with the

Citizens Rights Movement and Shinui to set up Meretz); Maki and later Rakah, established in 1965 following the split in the Communist Party, and the DFPE, established in 1977; the Likud, particularly after it came to power in 1977; the National Religious Party, which for many years controlled the interior and education ministries, which have direct and close contacts with the Arab sector; the Progressive List for Peace, established in 1984; the Democratic Arab Party, established before the elections for the twelfth Knesset in 1988; the Sons of the Village, established in the early 1970s as an extraparliamentary movement and which made a heavy investment in attempts to gain control on the local level; and the Islamic Movement, which coalesced in the early 1980s—it too as an extraparliamentary movement—and also focused on local politics.

Mapai always tried to consolidate its ties and control among the Arabs. In the main it was usually successful in implementing its intention of establishing ties through traditional channels, such as bonds and mutual dependence with *mukhtars* and other traditional notables (Al-Haj and Rosenfeld 1990a, 51). Over time, Mapai was able to consolidate its position among the Arabs through a broad network of activists. Eventually, however, the process of politicization and the rise of other forces forced it to change its tactics. While still fostering their links with traditional elements, Mapai and its successors, the Alignment and the Labor Party, began emphasizing the interests and welfare of the community at large.

Mapai representatives harped on the "danger" of a takeover of local government by the Communists and other radical elements and of the destructive effect that could have. On the other hand, its relations with the field were not always stable, because its representatives could always transfer their allegiance to other parties and often maintained contacts with more than one national party (Al-Haj and Rosenfeld 1990a, 52–53). This situation is in practice an inversion of the situation that prevailed in the 1950s and 1960s, when one party nurtured relations with a number of elements in the same locality, sometimes even with rivals, in order to win wall-to-wall support in national elections.

In recent years, Mapam, the Citizens Rights Movement, Shinui, and Meretz have also played a role in local government. Mapam was the first Zionist party to open its ranks to Arabs as full members and worked to foster a young and educated local leadership. Before the most recent local elections, intensive activity by Meretz was evident. It set up a central municipal team to follow and intervene in the campaigns of Meretz members and competed even in localities considered to be bastions of the DFPE or the Islamic Movement, such as Shafa'amre and Nazareth.

The National Religious Party, which historically controlled the interior ministry, set up a network of activists and supporters and even ran slates for the local council in a number of Arab communities. Even today it retains a seat on the Nazareth city council, elected chiefly by a clan but presented formally as a member of the National Religious Party.

The Likud began to consolidate its position among the Arabs the moment it came to power in 1977. In practice it began to use the same methods previously employed by Mapai, such as accords with traditional elements and support for favorable council heads in return for their promise to support it in national elections. In the elections for the thirteenth Knesset, a number of local council members and heads declared their support for the Likud, evidently because of promises that if returned to power it would see that they received funding (Ghanem 1992b, 30).

The Communist Party has always tried to win seats on Arab local councils. Its elected representatives constituted the scaffolding that supported a major part of its activity in various localities. For many years, though, it had minuscule representation; its weakness was evident in its scanty success in winning seats on local councils (Rekhess 1993, 96–97). The establishment of the DFPE was a step forward, from its perspective, in its quest for representation in local government. Pacts that the Communist Party and DFPE concluded with local elements, such as students' committees, clans, and confessions, bore fruit in elections. Unlike the lists supported by the Jewish parties, the DFPE always sought to give its local platform a countrywide national hue, which also helped to consolidate its position in Arab local authorities (Rekhess 1993, 99).

The Progressive List for Peace was founded on a local basis, when some members and supporters of the DFPE in Nazareth withdrew and established it as an opposition to their previous home. In the local elections, it won seats on the Nazareth council and set its sights on other Arab localities. Until the most recent local elections, it held the chair of two local council, in Arrabe and Ilabun, and seats on other local councils.

The Democratic Arab Party, established in 1988, immediately set to work on the local level. In fact, its founders included a number of heads of local authorities, and some were reelected in 1989. But it is clear that they owed their victories to local factors and usually did not highlight their membership in the DAP. Before the most recent elections, DAP activists conducted intensive consultations to identify places where they had prospects of winning council seats.

The Sons of the Village, founded in the early 1970s, rejected a priori participation in Knesset elections and concentrated its efforts on the local level. Its accomplishments, always minimal even there, have recently contracted even further.

The Islamic Movement was a set up in the early 1980s. It does not see Knesset elections as a challenge and invests most of its efforts in local elections. In 1983 its candidate was elected head of the council in Kafr Bara in the Triangle; subsequently it showed impressive gains elsewhere (Paz 1989, 1–3). Before the 1998 local elections its activists planned to contest the communities in which it had run in 1989 and 1993, as well as other places.

RESULTS OF LOCAL ELECTIONS BETWEEN THE CLAN AND THE PARTY: HOW THE LOCAL LEADERSHIP IS ELECTED

Since the mid-seventies, and especially since the first Land Day in March 1976, there has been the start of a new era in the history of the Arabs with regard to their political organization and the first emergence of party and organizational pluralism, in various ways: there has been increased protest by Arabs against civil and national discrimination. The Arabs have become a more important force on the Israeli political map because of the balance between the Jewish political camps, evident since the first change of regime in 1977. Local government has become more entrenched, thanks to the existence of a broad network of local councils in most Arab localities. Before the 1978 local elections there was a major change in the nature of local elections. Until then, voters cast their ballots for the council; that is, they elected the members of a council, who in turn selected one of themselves as council head. Until then, accordingly, the head of the authority always had to have the confidence of a majority on the council, was considered to be merely the first among equals, and owed the council regular reports. For our purposes, there has been a significant change in the strength of the clan and the formation of coalitions between parties, clans, and even confessions in some localities. Until then, a person won office on the basis of his or her ability to persuade the electors within the clan, if it had enough votes, by creating a coalition with smaller clans, or on a "pure" partisan political basis. Since then, winning election as council head, who in practice holds all the reins of power, has required attracting as many votes as possible. The easiest way to do this is through a direct appeal to clan or confessional sentiment, while creating clan or party-clan coalitions. In practice, the parties that inscribed on their banners a war against clannishness and organization on a traditional basis were undercut by this change; the simplest remedy was significant cooperation with clans and traditional circles. Below I shall analyze the results.

Analysis of Local-Council Elections. Data on the results of all local elections since the introduction of the direct election of council heads in 1975 and consequent separation between the campaigns for council head and council members (in 1978, 1983, 1989, and 1993 [Ghanem 1995], as well as 1998), seem to show stability in the representation of lists affiliated with Zionist parties, a declining tendency for lists associated with "Arab" parties, a significant rise in the weight of the Islamic lists, and a steep and consistent drop in the important clan-affiliated lists of the 1980s, followed by a recovery in 1993. The decline of the clan lists in the 1980s is true if referred exclusively to pure clan-affiliated lists. But the decline is more than a little misleading and conceals the willingness of the national parties and movements to cooperate with clans in various localities in order to garner a maximum share of council seats. Hence the increased strength of lists affiliated with national parties and movements actually represents a gain for a joint—party and clan—force. The rise in the strength of the clans in the 1993 elections reflects the national parties' failure to form alliances with clans and a process of clan segregation, manifested by a desire to run independently, with no assistance or dictates from national parties. In addition, the 1993 elections were marked by the appearance of local lists of younger elements who organized to protest the clan domination and the parties' willingness to join forces with the clans. These lists received one-third of the votes. This attests to the beginning of the emergence of an accelerating internal polarization in Arab society in Israel.

An analysis of the data over time reveals a significant change in voting patterns in the 1993 elections (which was continued in the 1998 elections). Until then, ever since 1978, there had been a gradual but almost linear decline in support for pure clan-affiliated lists, alongside a rise in support for party or joint party-clan lists. In the 1993 elections, however, the trend reversed sharply. In this campaign the clan lists again received the majority of the votes. This change is relevant for various cross sections of Arab localities (Ghanem 1993). The same trend dominated the results of the 1998 November elections; most Arabs voted for lists that called themselves "independent." In practice they are clan-affiliated lists that represented narrow interests of clans, families, and confessions. The common interest of the locality or of the entire Arab minority has not played a significant role when Arab voters decided whom to vote for (see Table 7.2).

The last two campaigns were contested by new lists protesting the clan domination and the willingness of national parties and movements to join forces with the clans in order to win maximum support in local elections. This phenomenon, which had first appeared earlier, became extremely common in the 1993 and 1998 elections and attests to the beginning of a change that will evidently bring more power to the

Table 7.2. Distribution of Votes in 1978, 1983, 1993, and 1998

Year	Valid Ballots	Lists Affiliated with Zionist Parties	Lists Affiliated with Non-Zionist (Arab) Parties	Clan-Affiliated Lists
1978	95,726	6.5	29.9	69.1
1983	117,718	6.3	32	61.4
1989	149,666	6.7	38.3	24.8
1993*	210,500	6.7	20.3	71.6
1998	313,100	5	13	82

*Lists of young activists who organized on a nonclan and nonparty basis received 1.3 percent of votes in these elections.

Source: Ghanem 1996a; Ghanem and Ozacky-Lazar 1999; the figures of the local elections of 1998 are based on personal calculations by the author depending on the official documents of the Israeli National Elections Committee.

younger generation and those who support organization on the basis of collective or individual interests and not on the basis of clan affiliation and sentiment.

Elected Local Council Heads. An examination of the list of local council heads elected during the period being studied demonstrates the depths of the clan underpinnings of municipal elections in Arab localities. Since the introduction of the law for the direct election of local council heads, every candidate has had to attract maximum—at least 40 percent of the vote when more than two candidates run, and more than 50 percent when there are only two candidates. This requires maximum mobilization of political machines where they exist, and in any case mobilization of the social systems dominated by the clan and confession within the Arab sector.

The list of council heads and mayors reveals that most of them were elected largely thanks to the support of a clan or confession, or at least relied heavily on their assistance (representatives of local lists or so-called independent lists), with no more than four or five exceptions (Tewfiq Zayyad in Nazareth and Nimr Morkous in Kafr Yassif from 1975 through 1998, Hana Ibrahim in Ba'ana between 1978 and 1983, and Ra'eed Salah in Umm al-Fahm since 1989)—candidates who won on the basis of their affiliation with a national parties or movement and whose support transcends clan boundaries and rests chiefly on organizational or personal support for them. Almost all the other council heads have been elected with a clear reliance on clan support, even

Table 7.3. Affiliation of Arab Local Council Heads

Year	Number of Officials	DFPE	DAP, NDA PLP	Islamic Movement	Zionist Parties	Local Groups
1978	51	17	–	–	7	27
1983	46	20	–	1	6	19
1989	48	18	6	6	6	12
1993	55	12	6	6	15	16
1998	58	7	2	6	3	40

SOURCE: Ghanem 1996a; Ghanem and Ozacky-Lazar 1999; The figures of the local elections of 1998 are based on personal calculations by the author depending on the official documents of the Israeli National Elections Committee.

though in many cases their formal organizational affiliation was national Zionist or non-Zionist political groupings(see Table 7.3).

Notes from the 1998 Local Elections. The chief conclusions that can be drawn from the November 1998 elections reinforce my key argument concerning Arab politics and the intensification of the process of division and disintegration of Arab society on the collective level. This was furthered by the incomplete and extremely superficial processes of modernization experienced by the Arab community under Israeli rule. In particular, it can be argued that the election results attest to four phenomena that buttress my thesis of increasing distress and crisis, as expressed in the disintegration at the level of local elections.

First, the widespread use of sophisticated means in the run-up to the elections, including the use of the print and electronic media in election propaganda, is foreign to the very essence of local political activity. During and after the campaign, we are in practice dealing with a stubborn competition involving traditional and primordial forces; the progressive and modern forces, by comparison, are quite marginal and are frequently recruited to join the ranks of the former.

Second, there has been a significant increase in the status of individuals who have no social or national link and are willing to present themselves as the embodiment of political activity and, for the sake of success, are willing to mobilize all forces around them and to use every means of manipulation available in order to win. These individuals present themselves as local leaders and contest the elections at the head of a particular camp as candidates for council head or council members. In practice, these candidates are willing to rely on any political force, even those which they described as illegitimate, such as the clan and confession—anything in order to be elected.

Third, the allegations made about a struggle between political and ideological forces for control of a number of Arab local councils has no basis in the field or any significant foundation (except for the cities of Nazareth and Umm al-Fahm, which to some extent deviate from the context in which the Arabs are developing, because they are big cities who enjoyed a long historical and active experience of political life). The struggle in the Arab localities is between individuals who enlist the clan, confession, and even local branches of national parties in service of their personal effort to be elected, and clans that attract the support of individuals and "compel" them to exhibit political herd behavior.

The clan and confession received a significant injection of encouragement in the 1998 elections. There is no doubt that there was a significant decline in the strength of the nationwide parties and local organizations with an ideological cast in favor of primordial, clan, or confessional organizations, which won in a big way, even in comparison with the 1993 elections.

Fourth, elected officials in most Arab localities (except for the most veteran among them) generally lack experience in the administration of systems similar to local government. Their previous careers have been in education, the law, medicine, other liberal professions, or various unsophisticated positions. Their previous status did not provide them with experience in complex systems like local government. This severely limits their ability to cope effectively with the problems of Arab local government, which suffers from grave problems on three levels: interaction between the authorities and the inhabitants, relations with the central government, and internal administration.

In addition to the characteristics enumerated above, election campaigns in the Arab sector have laid bare a number of processes that characterize the general situation in the country: the national parties have almost lost their relevance on the local government level; the ability to infer anything about the health of the national parties from the results of local elections is extremely limited; and campaigns are extremely expensive, which prevents many poor or marginal social forces from having any chance of winning significant representation in the forums of local government.

The main conclusion is that Arab local government and its areas of responsibility are extremely important for the future development of Arab society in Israel. The abandonment of local government to representatives of clans or confessions, totally devoid of experience and ability to administer local government systems, and the deepening schism against a traditional and primordial background—these will severely impair the future of this society and endanger its continued existence as a national group with common needs and aspirations. There is an urgent need for the younger, professional, and responsible forces to organize so that they can work together to save local government from those who are running it today.

An examination of the trends over time reveals a number of phenomena:

1. a persistent and steady decline in support for pure clan-affiliated lists during the 1980s and renewed support for them in the 1993 elections, preserving their dominance;

2. a steep rise to a plateau of support for non-Zionist parties in the 1980s, followed by a drop in support in the 1993 elections;

3. a small increase in support for lists affiliated with the Zionist parties;

4. steady support for the lists of the Sons of the Village;

5. a significant rise in support for Islamic lists in the late 1980s, followed by a significant drop in support for them in 1993.

The foregoing survey can be summarized as follow:

1. The change that seemed to begin in the mid-1970s—a decline in the status of the clan—was illusory. The real change took place not in the clan but in the political parties, which became increasingly pragmatic and more willing than in the past to cooperate with the clans and even to support them in pursuit of victory on the local level and participation in the government of the various localities. The clan became part of the establishment and a significant political actor. At the same time, however, one must not minimize the importance of organization on pure political and ideological basis as part of local or national organizations, phenomena that took hold in a number of localities, especially with the DFPE in Nazareth and Kafr Yassif.

The rise in the power of the clan has not only been quantitative. It had also been qualitative. For the first time, primary elections were held in a number of Arab localities in 1998. These elections, which have a partisan political basis in the United States and Israel, were imported to the Arab sector and conducted within clans in various localities—Tamra, Sakhnin, Tira, and elsewhere. From the perspective of the clan and those victorious in their primaries, the prospects for winning the general elections may be better than when a candidate is chosen without an evaluation of his or her popularity within the clan. From the perspective of the locality, however, the phenomenon can be extremely destructive if that candidate actually wins.

The first commitment of such a candidate is to the members of the clan, for two reasons. First of all, they were elected in the primaries and the general election with a clear dependence on the votes of the members of the clan. Second, because they want to be reelected five years hence and because they must first of all—because the system worked—go through the clan primaries and win the confidence of the members of the clan, they are almost forced to distribute benefits, in the form of jobs and services and even monetary payments, to members of the clan. This leads them to knowingly make irrelevant and even damaging decisions. The clans' recovery began in the 1993 elections and they became the chief source for satisfying the leadership. This became possible chiefly because of the distress besetting the Arabs with regard to political organization and the frameworks that seek to replace the clan on the political level.

2. The manner in which the local leadership is selected and its social sources pose a large question mark as to the ability of this leadership to serve as agents of change in the context of the Arabs in Israel, including on the countrywide level. Their ability to maneuver in the Israeli political system is extremely limited and requires broad knowledge and expert maneuvering capability, but it is doubtful whether this exists among the vast majority of the Arab local leadership. Accordingly, the committee of Arab local authority heads serves as an assemblage of local leaders and not as a national leadership, even though its leaders clearly have national aspirations. This sheds light on the distress that exists among Arabs at both the local and national leadership levels.

3. The Arabs in Israel are developing in the midst of contradictions, some of which can also be found in some of the development of the local leadership. Despite the growing power of the clan, this process was accompanied by a rise in the percentage of young adults who became part of the local leadership and a decline in the percentage of the older generation, as well as a rise in the average educational level of the local leadership. Latent in this contradiction is the willingness of the younger and better educated generation to run as representatives of a clan, and not of a political or social stream.

THE COMMITTEE OF ARAB LOCAL COUNCIL HEADS AND THE FOLLOW-UP COMMITTEE FOR ARABS IN ISRAEL AS CONSENSUS-BASED ORGANIZATIONS

The conclusions of the report on the Arab local authorities, prepared by a committee headed by Dr. Sami Jaraisi, were published in early 1974. Their crux was the determination that there was an immense disparity between the Jewish and Arab sectors in the scale of government assistance and allocations. The national committee of Arab local council heads was established in June 1974. Its declared objective was to work on the local level, chiefly to equalize the size of government allocations to local authorities in the two sectors (Cohen 1985, 89–90). The committee selected that head of the Rama local council (Galilee) Hana Mwies, as its chairman. He served until his death in 1981, when he was succeeded by the head of the Shafa'amre municipal council, Ibrahim Nimr Hussein.

The first Land Day, on March 30, 1976, was a watershed in the history of the committee, which until then had limited its activity to local fields such as health, education, and budgets. From that time the committee began to involve itself in issues related to all Arabs in Israel, including problems associated with Arabs who are not part of any particular municipal government and the general problems on their agenda, including political and ideological questions. After Land Day, the committee send an official memorandum to the then–prime minister, Yitzhak Rabin, in which it insisted on the right of the Arab minority in Israel to official recognition as a national minority and as part of the Palestinian people, rather than merely as religious-cultural minorities of Muslims, Christians, and Druze. The committee also demanded the return of the lands expropriated by the state (Al-Haj 1988b, 109). Since that time the committee has conducted intensive activity related to general political issues, in addition to the daily problems that confront Arab authorities and localities.

A significant change in history of the committee occurred against the backdrop of the Lebanon war in 1982, when the follow-up committee for Arabs in Israel affairs was set up as an umbrella organization of the heads of local councils, Arab Knesset members, members of the Histadrut executive committee, representatives of the Islamic movement and of the Sons of the Village movement, representatives of the Arab students unions on university campuses and of the secondary school pupils' association, a representative of the national Arab parents' committee, and representatives of Arabs living in the mixed cities. As a result of this broad representation, the committee came to be considered to be the "parliament" and most representative organization of the Arabs in Israel, with supreme responsibility for the conduct of their affairs in Israel, including the conduct of the struggle for equality with the Jewish majority. The initiative for the establishment of the committee originated with the chairman of the committee of local council heads, Ibrahim Nimr Hussein, who explained the act by the need "to form up the ranks in order to achieve more" (Cohen 1985, 91).

The prestige of the follow-up committee peaked in the mid-1980s, accompanied by broad and comprehensive public activity whose zenith was the proclamation of two general strikes in 1987. The first, a protest against discrimination and call for equality, was designated "Equality

Day." The second, to protest the occupation in the West Bank and Gaza Strip and show identification with the *intifada*, which broke out at the end of 1987, was called "Peace Day." In both cases, the response to the strike call was comprehensive and included many citizens and the vast majority of public institutions in Arab localities.[1]

The follow-up committee has subcommittees that focus on the status of the Arabs in various domains. Three main subcommittees are active, dealing with education, social conditions, and health. Each committee comprises members who represent follow-up committee and are involved in its specific area of activity; its head is a professional who relies on experts who are not necessarily members of committee. From time to time these committees hold conferences, conduct information campaigns, and exert pressure on the authorities to improve their performance.

The prestige of the follow-up committee and its subcommittees began to decline in the early 1990s, for a number of reasons. First, the committee, which had led the Arabs' struggle for equality and peace, had soon deteriorated from a body that discussed problems and attempted to reach a broad consensus into one in which representatives of the various political organizations sniped at one another without offering original ways for dealing with the extremely difficult problems that confront the Arabs in Israel. Second, the decisions—reached by consensus rather than by majority vote—generally expressed paralysis and a desire to maintain what existed, out of an aspiration to preserve domestic harmony at the expense of raising substantive issues and reaching significant decisions about them. Third, most of the members of the follow-up committee are heads of local authorities, elected chiefly on the basis of their clan affiliation and not because of their personal suitability to their position. This did not add to the prestige and even detracted from the standing of the follow-up committee in the eyes of the general public, which, unlike the council heads, became more modern and achievement-oriented over the years. Fourth, the committee and especially its subcommittees did not work diligently enough to improve their working methods and raise the level of the demands they made of the authorities. When the authorities satisfied their basic demands, which focused on increased budgets, they failed to make new substantive demands related to education, society, and health. The subcommittees found themselves unprepared and restricted by organizational constraints and an inadequate level of expertise.

Part III

The Political Distress of the
Palestinian-Arabs in Israel:
Looking for Ways Out of the Predicament

8

The Political Distress of the Palestinian-Arab Minority as a Reflection of the "Jewish State" Apparatus

Political activity connotes the totality of the behavioral or verbal steps taken by individuals or citizens in order to express their active or passive position with regard to the political, social, cultural, and economic systems. Sometimes there is a close connection between the actor and these systems; at other times there is no direct link and their position or behavior is intended to exert a positive or negative influence on the systems (for details see Barness and Kaase 1979; Kendrick, Fleming, Eisenstein, and Burkhart 1974).

According to the "individual and group needs approach," political activity by a national or ethnic group occurs as a response to its members' desire to express their needs as individuals or as members of the group. The occurrence and scope of their political activity reflects the intensity of the group's demands and needs. A minority group whose members suffer discrimination can use political participation to protest against that discrimination on the individual or group level (or on both levels). The degree and compass of the discrimination and of the demand for its rectification dictate the level and nature of their political activity (Gurr 1993; Horowitz 1985).

STATE AND MAJORITY COMMITMENT TO THE ZIONIST-JEWISH NATURE OF ISRAEL: EXCLUDING THE ARABS

The Arab citizens of Israel employ various modes of political activity to give vent to their needs and demands; but all of them have only a limited capacity to work a serious change in their living conditions, status, and circumstances. This limitation stems chiefly from the iron wall erected by the Jewish-Zionist character of Israel. The Jewish state's commitment to further the interests of the Jews, whatever the cost to its Arab citizens, prevents any significant alteration in the condition of the latter. For the Arabs, this commitment finds clear expression on three levels (Ghanem 1998a):

THE IDEOLOGICAL AND DECLARATIVE LEVEL

The state of Israel was founded to be the state of the Jewish people. It has a Jewish-Zionist character and its objectives, symbols, and policies all rest on the basis that it is the state of the Jewish people, while denying the existence within it of a Palestinian national minority. This situation was exacerbated by the passage in 1985 of Amendment 9 to the Basic Law: the Knesset. It added section 7a, which bars Knesset lists that negate the existence of Israel as the state of the Jewish people. During the debate that preceded passage of the amendment, formulas submitted by MK Tawfik Toubi of the DFPE and MK Mati Peled of the Progressive List, to the effect that the state of Israel is "the state of its citizens," or "the state of the Jewish people and of its Arab citizens" were rejected by large majorities.

Not only does this situation, which results from the need to give the Jews a sense of primacy in their state, engender discrimination against the Arab citizens of Israel on the day-to-day level and nullify the theoretical possibility of their achieving equality with the Jews. In practice it leaves the Arab citizens of Israel, both legally and formally, without an entity that is officially defined as their state. They find themselves in a quandary concerning their status; for example, Are they citizens like the Jews? Is the state also their state? What are the prospects for achieving equality within the state? This uncertainty causes the Arabs and their leaders a sense of distress that goes beyond the level of emotions and belonging.

The Arab citizens of Israel are also deprived when it comes to the dominant values and symbols of the state and its institutions. Compared to the Jews, who treat the symbols, values, and institutions state as their own bailiwick, see them as part of their heritage, and identify with them, Arab Israelis feel nothing for these exclusively Jewish and Zionist symbols. They cannot identify with many of the symbols of the state whose citizenship they hold, because these symbols are rooted exclusively in the religious and ideological heritage of the majority.

THE STRUCTURAL LEVEL

The Arabs are involuntarily excluded from Israeli institutions, which function as the property of the Jews and are supposed to serve Jewish-Israeli or general Jewish objectives rather than Israeli objectives associated with all citizens of the country, including the Palestinians among them. On the structural level, this exclusion has many modes, such as the exclusion of the Arabs from the centers of political decision-making, their nonconscription into the army as a means of exclusion, the non-employment of Arabs in senior positions, the existence of special offices to deal with Arabs, the structure of Arab education, which is discriminatory as compared to other groups, the discrimination against them in the public media, and so on.

POLICY AND ITS IMPLEMENTATION

This includes various forms of discrimination against Arabs and their exclusion from consideration as first class citizens, such as discrimination in the law, in the allocation of budgets, and in the allocation of land. Israeli law enshrines fundamental discrimination in favor of Jewish citizens and to the detriment of Arab citizens. The state pays a significant price, on the official level of its law book, to emphasize its ethnic, Jewish-Zionist nature. This discrimination relates to the fundamental objectives of the state as they are expressed by its leaders and the Jewish majority. Thus, for example, the law of return and the citizenship law are two statutes intended to preserve and augment the Jewish majority in the state; their clear objective is to diminish the number of non-Jews, including Arabs. This is compounded by the special legal status accorded to non-Israeli Jewish institutions, and by Amendment 9 to the Basic Law: the Knesset. In addition, a whole string of legal arrangements discriminate against the Arabs and give preference to the Jews on the symbolic and substantive levels—chiefly laws that accorded a preferential status to Jewish religious and ethnic symbols and values.

With regard to the allocation of budgets, the Arab citizens of Israel suffer continuing discrimination in practically every sphere of life. The various domains of discrimination have been documented in many studies and official reports, as well as in reports published by various private organizations.[1] Despite changes for the better in recent years, as noted in various studies, up-to-date comparisons between the two sectors reveal that the gaps in various areas, which stem chiefly from discrimination, still exist and evidently will continue to do so for many years to come.

There is ongoing discrimination with regard to the division of territory and national and regional development plans. Most Arab-owned land has been expropriated during the years of Israeli independence. The state has applied various means to deprive the Arabs of their property and turn most of the country into "state lands" administered centrally by national and regional planning agencies. The planning committees include permanent representation of the ministry of defense, the ministry of construction and housing, the Jewish agency, and the Jewish national fund. The last two are funded by Jewish communities outside Israel and are supposed to serve their objectives, or those of Jews in Israel, and are committed to excluding Arabs from any consideration as potential beneficiaries of state lands. Even the Israeli agencies represented on these committees demonstrate no concern for the interests of all citizens on an equal footing and give distinct preference to Jews. In practice, Israeli planning policy is designed to serve Jews and exclude Arabs, preserving the benefits of planning for Jews only. This is despite the fact that it was the Arabs who paid the historical and moral price for the realization of various Israeli plans. The planning policy serves as a tool for controlling the Arabs and preventing "their expansion." It is accompanied by the wholesale establishment of new Jewish localities endowed with reserves of land for future expansion and development.

The ethnic character of the state of Israel is strongly reinforced by the overwhelming support that the Jewish majority expresses for it. This all but rules out any significant change in the foreseeable future. From the results of a survey conducted in late 1995, it is clear that the ethnic state and its policies garner extremely broad support from the Jews. Their massive support for it insures the perpetuation of the ethnic system that discriminates in favor of the Jewish majority and against the Arab minority.[2]

According to the survey, a majority of the Jews in Israel support the ethnic state and its policies toward the Arab minority. The Jews view Israel as a Jewish state and even as the state of the Jewish people and want to preserve its Jewish majority. An overwhelming majority (96.4 percent) want to perpetuate this situation and the general outlook that stands behind it and reinforces it on various levels. Some 72.1 percent of the Jews believe that Israel is the homeland of the Jews only; a similar percentage (72 percent) agrees with the legal definition of Israel as the state of the Jewish people, without the inclusion of the Arab citizens in this definition. Only a minority (27.9 percent) accepts the formula that Israel is the shared homeland of the Jews and the Arabs. Some 59.1 percent of the Jews believe that the Jewish-Zionist character of the state should be reinforced; 35.6 percent support leaving it as it is. A large percentage of the Jews (68.1 percent) believe that the law of return, which grants every Jew in the world the right to immigrate to Israel and automatically acquire first class citizenship, while denying this to others, including the Arabs, should be preserved; only 3 percent support its repeal.

With regard to the state and its Jewish and democratic character, most Jews, when asked to chose between the two, opt for Jewish rather than democratic. Some 58.1 percent would prefer to live in a Jewish though nondemocratic state rather than in a non-Jewish democratic country. A majority of the Jews (74.1 percent) believe that the state should manifest great or some preference to Jews over its Arab citizens.

With regard to the Jewish hegemony over national symbols, most Jews are unwilling to make any alteration in them so as to include the Arabs and give them representation on the symbolic level; 85.6 percent are opposed to any change in the symbols of the state, such as the flag or national anthem, so that Arabs too could identify with them. This same percentage (85.6 percent) is opposed to any modification of the national anthem to permit the Arabs to accept it. These symbols are Jewish and derive from the Jewish heritage; the Jews in Israel consider them to be their own and are not willing to share them with the Arabs.

A large percentage of the Jews are not interested in institutional integration of the Arabs and support the continuation of exclusive control by the Jews. A large proportion of the Jews (40.5 percent) is opposed to the inclusion of Arab political parties, or Knesset coalitions on an equal footing with full responsibility for policy; almost as many (38.6 percent) would accept the inclusion of Arab parties in a coalition, but only in certain circumstances. Almost a third of the Jews (32.2 percent) believe that only Jews should hold jobs in government ministries; 27 percent believe that both Jews and Arabs should both be eligible, but with preference extended to Jews. Only 21.8 percent believe that Jews and the Arabs should be considered for public employment on an equal footing; 19 percent support the hiring of Jews and Arabs in the civil service in proportion to their share of the general population.

With regard to political parties, a large percentage of Jews support the outlawing of Arab parties and movements, and forbidding others to contest Knesset elections. Nearly half the Jews (45.6 percent) support the outlawing of the Communist Party; only about a quarter (25.3 percent) oppose it (the rest have reservations), even though the Communist Party is a mixed Jewish-Arab group known for its moderate positions (most of its voters are Arabs). A substantial Jewish majority (72.2 percent) agrees or is inclined to agree that the Islamic Movement in Israel, which represents a significant fraction of the Palestinian minority, should not be allowed to run candidates for the Knesset. In addition, 30.9 percent of the Jews believe that Arabs should not even be allowed to vote in Knesset elections. All in all, a majority of the Jews are not happy with the participation of parties deemed to be Arab and that represent Arab interests in Knesset elections. Evidently broad segments think that the Knesset should include only Jewish political parties that represent Jewish interests exclusively.

Many Jews use the excuse that Arabs do not serve in the army to explain the continued discrimination against them. The survey showed clearly, however, that the Jews do not want Arabs to serve in the conscript army and would leave this as the exclusive privilege or obligation of Jews, who benefit from it, as stated, as part of the ethnic policy. Some 60.7 percent of the Jews oppose compulsory military service for Arabs; 54.3 percent are opposed to compulsory military service for Arabs even after peace is achieved between Israel and the Arab world.

Social segregation of Jews and Arabs as part of the structural separation that keeps Jews and Arabs apart and permits the flow of benefits to Jewish citizens is part of the ethnic policy. This policy has broad support among Jewish Israelis. A large proportion of the Jews are not willing to work under an Arab superior; 43.8 percent are not willing to work under an Arab boss and 25.6 percent would do so, but prefer to work for a Jew. Some 56.3 percent are willing to live only in an all-Jewish neighborhood; another 23.4 percent would live in a mixed neighborhood but prefer a Jewish neighborhood.

In the cultural arena, the Jews want to preserve the primacy of Hebrew culture and the Hebrew language, and are not willing to include Arab culture and the Arabic language as partners in the shaping of Israeli culture. They are not interested in cultural fusion with Arabs; almost a third (30.1 percent) believe that there is no need to treat Arab culture as an important component of the national culture in Israel; 39.7 percent have reservations about treating Arab culture as an important part of the national culture. A significant majority (59.9 percent) are opposed to the broadcast of Arabic music on Hebrew radio stations; 70.7 percent believe that there should not be a legal requirement that the names of all streets and localities appear in Arabic as well as in Hebrew on road signs, even though Arabic has the legal status of an official language of the country. A total of 48.6 percent reject or are inclined to reject the possibility that Jews and Arabs in Israel might create shared values and customs.

Recently a number of Jewish politicians rejected equal participation by the Palestinian minority in certain democratic decisions, such as a referendum on whether Israel should withdraw from the Golan Heights, the West Bank, and Gaza Strip, and even eastern Jerusalem. Such views find legitimacy among the Jews. According to the survey, a majority of the Jews (59.9 percent) agree that decisions about the future of the Golan, West Bank, and Gaza Strip should require a Jewish majority; in other words, on such matters the views of Arab citizens should be dismissed, since they are considered to be willing a priori to return these West Bank and Gaza Strip to Syria and the Palestinians.

The ethnic character of the state is supported by a large proportion of the Jews, who wish to maintain the exclusion of the Arabs from all consideration. A majority of the Jews do not include the Arabs in Israeliness; according to the survey, 51.7 percent of the Jews believe that the term "Israeli" applies only to Jews and not to Arabs. A significant group (36.7 percent) are unhappy with the Arabs' very presence and support the idea that the state should look for and exploit every opportunity to encourage the Palestinian minority to emigrate. A majority (53.1 percent) support intensified monitoring of the Arabs in Israel; 39.4 percent favor the expropriation of Arab land within the Green Line to further Jewish development.

The Jews reject the establishment of an egalitarian democratic state in Israel; 91.1 percent do not want Israel to stop being a Jewish-Zionist state and turn into a consociational democracy in which Jews and Arabs are recognized as equal national groups with representation based on their share in the population and function as equal partners in the running of the country. An even larger majority (95.5 percent) oppose the idea of turning Israel into a liberal democracy that does not recognize the Jews and Arabs as separate groups, allows them to compete freely, and permits them to live wherever they wish and intermarry.

The ethnic character of the state and its manifestations for the Arab citizens of Israel has both a direct and an indirect influence on the political evolution of the Arab minority and on the various forms of political activity (organization, behavior, and voting patterns) among them. The Jews are satisfied with the ethnic state, which they wish to preserve and even strengthen. They support and legitimize the ethnic state's policies towards the Arab citizens, who suffer from it and find themselves in a crisis situation as a result of the policies adopted toward them (Rouhana and Ghanem 1998).

THE PREDICAMENT OF ARAB POLITICS IN THE JEWISH STATE

The emergence of political institutions and organizations depends on citizens' willingness to organize in such frameworks. This of course stems from their evaluation that such an organization can improve their personal well-being or the welfare of their society in general. It also depends on the existence of "good citizenship" based on a willingness to contribute to individual and group well-being and the maintenance of democracy that guarantees the free and equal competition of citizens who are equal before the law, while the state plays the "neutral" role of the guarantor of equality and equal rights. The existence of these conditions leads to the emergence of the network of organizations, political parties, and institutions whose consolidation is the conspicuous hallmark of democracy. Theoretically, the existence of discrimination against some citizens in a state, on an ethnic, geographical, or some other basis—that is, turning the state into an agent that intervenes on behalf of a particular ethnic group or particular geographic region—is an obstacle to the emergence and consolidation of political institutions and organizations, even though in some senses discrimination can spur the deprived group or individuals to organize into a significant force, serve themselves instead of the authorities, and close the gap with the favored group or groups, such that these institutions and organizations provide services that the state ought to be providing to its citizens on an equal basis.

In addition, the development of institutions and organizations requires a stable democratic system, even though political institutions and organizations can evolve in nondemocratic conditions and governmental instability, as was the case in Lebanon during the period of anarchy and in the Palestinian West Bank and Gaza Strip occupied by Israel since 1967. In both cases, the institutions and organizations faced a permanent threat; the individuals who spearheaded the organizations were afraid of intervention by the authorities and tended not to make long-term plans because they could not be confident about the future. In such cases, political organization is hesitant and precarious, and the odds favor the destruction of these institutions and organizations by some external force. Israel, as a Jewish-ethnic state, extends preference to one group (the Jews) over others (principally Arabs), uses policy and legal arrangements to guarantee the superiority of the dominant group, and permits it to control the minority and institutions. In this way the state is an agent that intervenes to benefit the Jews and permits the limited and controlled development of exclusive organizations and institutions for the Arab minority. In many cases, overt or covert government intervention intends to prevent the establishment of some political grouping or to disband an existing one. This included bans promulgated in special orders, such as the ban issued by the then–minister of defense, Menachem Begin, on the convening of an assembly of Arab masses in 1980; the legal steps based on various pretexts employed against the al-Ard movement in the mid-sixties, and against the Progressive Movement in the mid-eighties; or the dismissal of political activists from civil service jobs, such as the dismissal of members of the Communist Party throughout the 1950s, 1960s, and 1970s, and, later, the firing of activists for the Sons of the Village movement.

The organs of local government, too, suffer from similar restrictions on account of the ethnic character of the state of Israel. The authorities still have not extended official recognition to around forty Arab localities, thereby denying them municipal status and services. They also delayed the inauguration of a local authority in many Arab communities. When they were established eventually, it blatantly discriminated against them as compared to their Jewish neighbors, both in budgets and territorial jurisdiction (al-Haj and Rosenfeld 1990a, 1990b).

With regard to Arab political participation on the national level, they suffer problems similar to those associated with political organizations. The Israeli political system is based on an electoral regime that permits a proliferation of parties that compete in countrywide proportional elections. Any party that wins at least 1.5 percent of the vote (the electoral threshold) is awarded seats in the Knesset in proportion; the factions then compete to establish a coalition that can command a Knesset majority and support a government. In principle, the Knesset is the staging ground for membership in the government; on the other hand it oversees the government and its activities. The factions that compose the government are known as the "coalition"; those that criticize the government are "the opposition." When a government is sworn in its members become ministers, headed by the prime minister, who generally represents the largest faction in the coalition. This group becomes the highest authority in the country, setting foreign and domestic policy and overseeing its implementation at all levels. Membership in the government is the goal of the various sectors and groups that organize to win benefits or promote their interests. The Arab representatives in the Knesset, whether members of coalition or opposition parties, have never been included in the government; to this day no Arab has ever served as a minister, and of course not as prime minister.

Historically, the "Arab factions" in the Knesset played the role of permanent opposition. They were considered to represent the "hostile" Arab minority, which could not be trusted or included in a government coalition. A partial exception was made for Arab MKs who belonged to Jewish parties that were in the coalition. Despite the Arabs' significant electoral clout, however, there has never been an Arab cabinet minister. The few Arab deputy ministers have been placed in charge of affairs relevant to "minorities" and not the general population, and depended on the good will of the minister who held the portfolio. This status as permanent opposition had three main causes: first, the fact that the parties are Arab; second, that they are anti-Zionist or at least non-Zionist; third, their fierce opposition to the domestic and foreign policy of Israeli governments.

Despite the gradual improvement in the attitude toward the Arabs, Israel continues to be an ethnic, Jewish-Zionist state, that sees attention to issues relevant to Jews, including bringing them to the country, as its chief vocation. The exclusion of Arab factions and Arabs from full participation in the executive branch keeps them from having an active and equal influence on decisions in matters of vital importance for the Jewish people. Historically the "Arab factions"—the DFPE, the Progressive List, and the DAP—took a militant line and adopted an anti-Zionist stance. In their publications they rejected the definition of Israel as the state of the Jewish people and considered it to be unfair to the Arab citizens of the country. They emphasized that it should be the state of its citizens or, in the best case, "the state of the Jewish people and its Arab citizens" (Ghanem 1990). This position in practice matches that held by the majority of Arabs in Israel, who reject the Jewish-Zionist character of the state (Smooha 1992, 54–58).

In addition to the disagreement about the nature and vocation of the state, the "Arab parties" and their representatives in the Knesset disagreed with and openly opposed government policy on vital issues such as the distribution of resources within the state and the solution of the Arab-Israeli conflict in general and of its Palestinian-Israeli component in particular (Ghanem 1990). This dissent, which in practice corresponds to the division between most Arab citizens and most Jews (Smooha 1992), augments the suspicion about the Arabs held by Jews and decision-makers, and reinforces the notion that they are a "hostile minority" and potential "fifth column." This distrust also deters the Jewish leadership from accepting Arabs as full coalition partners, lest doing so undermine their support among Jewish voters. All these factors have channeled the Arabs to the status of permanent opposition in the Israeli governmental system.

At the time of the coalition crisis in March 1990, even though Shimon Peres, who had been asked to form a new government, needed the votes of the Knesset members from the DFPE, Progressive List, and the DAP in order to win a vote of confidence, he and his representatives did not offer these parties full membership in the coalition but asked only for their support from the outside, with a promise of significant improvements in policy toward the Arabs (Benziman and Mansour 1992, 197). Again after the 1992 elections, when the Labor Party needed Arab votes in the Knesset to support its candidate for prime minister, it preferred to rely on them as part of a "blocking majority" rather than as full partners in the coalition.

After the establishment of the Rabin government in July 1992, the Arab factions supported his government from the outside but were not members of the coalition, occupying a status that was intermediate between being in the opposition and in the coalition. Yet this government, too, like its predecessors, did not fulfill the Arabs' expectations and in practice left them at the margins of the decision-makers' interest. They saw little benefit from the change of regime. There are many explanations for this (see Ghanem 1996d), of which the most important are as follows:

First, was the unwilling relegation of the Arabs to the status of part of a blocking majority, even though at least one faction (the DAP) openly stated its desire to join the coalition. Immediately after the elections, when the change in regime became apparent, MK Darawshe announced his willingness to join the coalition.[3] The next year, the members of the DAP wrote a letter to the prime minister in which they again expressed their interest in joining the coalition.[4] These openings met with a cold refusal on the part of the prime minister and his associates. The DAP eventually withdrew its proposal without any progress having been made.

Second, Arab expectations of the government dissipated quickly. The heads of Arab local authorities, who initiated strikes and demonstrations on behalf of equal budgets, found little responsiveness on the part of the government and its members. Arab local authority heads demonstrated outside the prime minister's office in Jerusalem to protest the absence of equality on two occasions—in September 1992 and in June, July, and early August 1994. The compromises achieved, after a twelve-day strike in the first case and a forty-day strike in the second case, did not really satisfy the local authority heads. Neither time was there any significant progress toward equality nor even an explicit promise of such.

Third, the Arab parliamentarians found themselves in a "no choice" situation. They were forced to support the Rabin government even if it did not satisfy their demands in domestic and foreign policy, because it was nevertheless the best possible government for them and was taking steps to put an end to the Arab-Israeli conflict, including the Palestinian problem.

Since then, there have been disturbing signs of a worsening of this attitude, which might even make the Arab presence in the Knesset quite superfluous on critical issues facing the state. MK Kahalani proposal to give the Golan law special status (so that a two-thirds majority of the Knesset would be required to amend or repeal it) was meant chiefly to neutralize the influence of Arab members of Knesset in matters deemed to be Jewish or security-related. Former MK Yoash Tsiddon (Tsomet) explained the rationale for giving this status to the law in a manner that permitted no other interpretation: "The most reasonable democratic solution, in the absence of another way, is to 'buttress' laws that relate to the security or Jewishness of the state, so that the votes of Arab MKs, whose loyalty represents the interests of their constituents, cannot tip the balance in one direction or the other" (*Ha'aretz*, 2 October 1994).

Netanyahu's victory in 1996 returned the Arab factions to their previous status as marginal opposition with no influence on the course of events. The Arab parliamentarians became irrelevant in the contest between right and left, both inside and outside the Knesset. Only in isolated cases were they able to work extremely minor changes in the policy of the Netanyahu government toward the Arabs and the conflict in general.

When the results of the 1999 elections became known, the winners, Ehud Barak and the Labor party, initiated contacts to form a new government. Throughout the process they almost totally ignored Arab parties, even though they and their supporters had brought Barak his landslide victory (he received only 51 percent of the Jewish vote). Barak, who before the elections had shied away from any contact with representatives of the Arabs, lest this cost him support in the center, continued this practice and did not even bother to make a public expression of sympathy for the Arabs and their representatives in the Knesset or thank them for their massive support.

Barak's behavior led to turmoil among the Arabs and their representatives, who began to give public vent to the idea that they were not "in Barak's pocket" and would vote against him when he presented his government, should he continue to ignore them.[5] This made no impression on Barak, whose short experience with the Arab leadership had taught him that it had no real backing. He estimated that in the end the Arab MKs would support any government he put together, as long as it was committed to continuing the peace process and parity between Jews and Arabs.

The attitude toward the Arabs displayed by Barak and his aides during the coalition negotiations stemmed from two main factors. First of all, the Arabs' sweeping support before the elections for Barak's candidacy withdrawal, were not accompanied by any demands. This made it clear to Barak that he had nothing to fear from the Arab parliamentarians. Relying chiefly on Barak's "good heart" and not on their electoral strength, they did not behave like politicians representing a sizable bloc in the Israeli body politic but more like an "auxiliary force" to the Labor party in its efforts to form a government. The Arab parties set the defeat of Netanyahu as their chief objective—a "negative" goal that was not balanced by any "positive" demands. This detracted from their bargaining power after the elections.

Barak was guided by his Jewish-Zionist vision that sought to base his government on a Jewish majority and not to be seen, as Rabin had been, as someone who depended on Arab votes. This perpetuated the attitude of past Labor governments, which considered the Arabs to be an "outside" factor that must not be relied on and whose representatives could not be included in decisions about fateful matters. Barak saw himself as having been elected to restore the traditional Zionist establishment of the Labor party and the Ashkenazi elites, which had been shunted aside by Netanyahu, to power. He could not permit himself to include Arabs as full partners in this process. He relied on their providing support from the outside or even pretending to be an opposition, on the assumption that Knesset members from the Arab parties would not team up with the right to bring down his government, thereby causing new elections in which Barak and his party could lose power. All this demonstrates the limitations faced by the Arabs in Israel when it comes to making significant achievements through participation in Knesset elections. What, then, is the situation of the Arabs in Israel in municipal and local politics? What sort of benefits do they receive as a result of their participation in local politics?

Here too the rewards are limited. The Jewish-Zionist nature of the state and the limited capacity of the Arabs in Israel to amass adequate returns from their participation in parliamentary politics enhances the importance of municipal politics. But precisely this situation, which leads to greater competition in local politics, including the mobilization of all political and social networks to achieve electoral victory, increases the power of the clan and helps elect individuals who are not necessarily suited to administer local councils, towns, and villages. It creates a pressure cooker on the local level, full of violent contests, unprofessional and inappropriate appointments, and so on.

The situation on the municipal level poses another large question mark as to what the Arabs can achieve through political activity. Even on this level the Arab citizens of Israel face a serious crisis that seems to be hard to escape in the current conditions.

The political views of the various ideological streams among the Arabs in Israel, too, suffer severe limitations. The Arabs in Israel are divided into four ideological camps. Three of them—the Communists, the nationals, and the Islamists—draw their inspiration from broader ideologies that existed within Palestinian society before 1948. Only the Israeli-Arab stream is of more recent vintage, and it is the most hesitant and most willing to accept the inferiority of the Palestinians in the Jewish state. This group displays a significant degree of submission without raising demands for genuine and fundamental equality between Jews and Arabs in a binational Israel, such as the demand raised by the Canadian Franco-Phone National Movement in the last fifty years.

In practice, until recently no stream among the Palestinian minority demanded full equality for the Arabs in Israel in a way that required a frank self-examination by the state, the Jewish majority, and the Arab minority, along with a clear and systematic demand that Israel become the state of Palestinian-Arab minority, such as the state of the Israeli Jewish majority.[6]

The failure of such a stream to emerge is no chance. It is delayed first and foremost by the fact that the state did not encourage and even officially opposed and hindered the emergence and activity in the field of such a stream. It would be an understatement to say that Israel does not encourage the Arabs to see it as their state, in the way that the Jews see it. Israel as a Jewish state that has enshrined this fact prevented the establishment of a political organization that could work on a country-wide basis and provide an organizational framework for the development of a binational ideology that would advocate the conversion of Israel into the state of both, Jews and Arabs.

Israeli domestic and foreign policy alike do not encourage the emergence of such a stream. They are unquestionably intended to keep the country as the state of the Jews (as stated by the Proclamation of Independence, in the election platforms of all the Jewish parties, including Meretz, in many speeches by national leaders, and in innumerable official documents). The Arabs are not an element weighing on the considerations for setting official policy in Israel; in many cases, such as of the Judaization of the Galilee or a strengthening the Jewish hold on their state, this policy is at their expense. These factors constitute a major obstacle to the emergence of an Israeli-Arab civil rights movement whose fundamental demands would center on a call for the country to be a state of equal rights and opportunities—the state of both, Arabs and Jews.

CIVIL SOCIETY AS AN ALTERNATIVE

The difficult situation of politics in general and political activity in particular among the Arab citizens of Israel has propelled many to look for an outlet for their energies. This has led to wide-scale activity to set up voluntary organizations of the sort typical of civil society. The main question is, whether such institutions can serve as a substitute for direct political activity? Can they provide an answer to the problems of the Arab minority in Israel?

The concept of "civil society" began to attract the attention of scholars as a way to describe the various types of organization by citizens opposed to the Communist regimes in Eastern Europe, such as Solidarity in Poland. Such organizations were thought to be providing an eventual substitute for the Communist regime, which "does not represent the citizens" (Muslih 1993, 258). Although the term was used by a number of scholars who described the emergence of civil society as an attempt to stand against the central government by citizens opposed to it, and it was explained and used in various ways by scholars and theoreticians representing sundry disciplines and streams (see Shils

1991), the stream use of the term refers to organization by citizens in a democratic state to build agencies that supplement the legitimate authorities and institutions. This usage is substantially different from that described earlier in this paragraph.

"Civil society" refers, then, to the organization of citizens in political parties, movements, voluntary associations, clubs, and every other sort of voluntary organization that falls between the institutionalized organization known as state and government, and the primordial organization known as family and clan. Thus organization in civil society is less than membership in a state and more than affiliation based on blood relations; it rests on the choice of individuals or groups to join forces with others in order to serve the members of the organization or the broader public in a way different that the state does and to some extent independently of it (for a discussion of the term and its meaning, see Keane 1988; Shils 1991; Walzer 1991; Seligman 1992).

Various factors have played a role in the emergence among the Arabs in Israel of organizations typical of civil society. The most important of these are the control exerted by the state over the Arab minority, the continuing discrimination, and the absence of any possibility of achieving equality thorough establishment paths. These were augmented by the enhanced self-confidence and politicization of the Arab minority, its increased strength and self-awareness, a greater willingness to contribute to the well-being of the community as a whole, and increased awareness of the distress that encompasses various aspects of the Arabs who live in Israel.

The chief manifestation of the emergence of an Arab civil society is the growth of institutions and organizations that assume responsibility for providing cultural, economic, social, and political services, either as a supplement to those provided by state institutions or as a substitute for them.

VOLUNTARY ASSOCIATIONS IN ARAB SOCIETY

The efforts to set up voluntary associations in Palestinian society began before the 1948 war and the establishment of Israel. During the Mandate period, various sectors began to organize to provide services to members and to the public at large. But these organizations involved only limited groups, had a religious-confessional basis, and were found mainly in the cities (Nakhleh 1990, 2–5). The results of the 1948 war, the establishment of Israel, and the dispersal of the Palestinians destroyed most of these organizations and put an end to the establishment of new ones.

After Israel became independent there were a few incipient attempts to establish voluntary associations among its Arab citizens, but the tight

Table 8.1. Voluntary Associations among the Arabs in Israel: by Year of Establishment

Year Founded	Percent of Organizations
Through 1948	5.4
1949–1959	2.2
1960–1969	0.5
1970–1979	16.7
1980–1990	75.2

NOTE: According to the Jaffa Institute, in 1990 there were 186 voluntary associations among the Arabs in Israel.
SOURCE: Jaffa 1990, 10.

control exerted by the state throughout the military government frustrated attempts to found voluntary organizations and deterred many from any serious attempt to establish them. As Table 8.1 shows, there was a quantum leap in the establishment of voluntary associations in the 1970s—that is, after the abolition of the military government, and the process accelerated in the 1980s.

Until 1990 there were according to two summations made by Nakhlih and the Yaffa Research Institute, about 180 public societies among the Palestinian Arab minority in Israel. In the last nine years since 1990 a new 656 Arab societies were established (Ziedan and Ghanem 2000), that means that the vast majoriey of Arab societies and Arabs who are involved in such activities started in the last decade. These societies strove to provide various services to their members or the general public, with a tendency to specialize in specific services according to the specific needs of the the society's neighborhood or the general Palestinian public in Israel.

Nakhlih had classified the societies into four main types. The first included societies established and organized on the basis of specific specializations, such as societies for health purposes, cultural subjects, art, and education. The second included societies with varied aims, whose activities were limited to a specific geographic area, such as the societies established to deal with the problems of urban inhabitants or certain communities. The third included societies dealing with definite and specific subjects throughout the country, such as societies to deal with the problems of a specific social sector or specific community. The fourth included countrywide societies estblished by organizations or political parties, such as the societies of the Islamic Movement or those belonging to political parties (Nakhlih 1990, 8).

These societies generally faced a number of key problems as well as some other less important ones. They suffered mainly from the lack of financial security, since they relied upon foreign sources to maintain their activities; they suffered from a lack of trained manpower prepared to initiate and participate in public activities, and, first and foremost, they suffered from the suspicious attitudes of the Israeli regime toward their activities and goals (Nakhlih 1990, 9–17).

Since 1990, the establishment of new associations has been hesitant and slow, for two main reasons. First, every Arab locality was on average already home to more than one such association. Since this type of organization guaranteed coverage of almost all Arab localities and their members, on the one hand, to block the establishment of new organizations with similar objectives, and, on the other hand, opened their ranks to all those who were interested in contributing. Second, in general the experience of these associations was not that successful. They were frequently accused of being "stores" set up by persons interested in gathering contributions and providing themselves with employment; but the declared objectives of the associations were not implemented and their efforts focused on providing services to particular persons and sometimes to the individual who stood at the head of the pyramid. The establishment of new voluntary associations, especially on a countrywide basis, required special effort, professional work, uncommon leadership, and an aspiration to provide adequate answers to critical problems that beset the entire Arab sector or particular subsectors thereof.

Despite the accelerated processes of the establishment and consolidation of organizations typical of civil society, such progress is not guaranteed and is in fact threatened by difficulties inherent in the structure and composition of Palestinian-Arab society itself, based largely on clan and confessional affiliations. People generally demonstrate their chief loyalty to these groups, which impede the development of civil society and the transfer of allegiance to its institutions. The bad economic situation among the Palestinians in Israel and the rampant poverty of broad sections forces the breadwinners (see Fares 1996; Haidar 1991a; 1991b), who should be the spearhead in the emergence of civil society, to devote most of their energy to feeding their families. This does not leave them time for efforts on behalf of the community, which could be translated into the construction of institutions of civil society.

The growth of civil society is further impeded by the Jewish-Zionist character of the state. The ethnic nature that preserves the primacy of the majority group, the Jews, does not allow Arabs full enjoyment of democracy. The development of civil society is limited by the restrictions that the majority places on the possibilities for the future development of the Arabs in Israel, of which the institutions of civil society are an integral part.

The principal problem that confronts the activity of these voluntary associations is their inability to work a serious change in the condition of the Arabs by means of such activity, given the structure of the Israeli political system. Israel is run by a centralized apparatus controlled by a parliamentary system in which decisions are made according to coalition considerations and agreements between Knesset factions and parties. Decisions by a Knesset majority require the implementation of the corresponding policy. Activity outside the political axis, such as that of voluntary associations, may further the interests of citizens in general and of Arab citizens in particular, but it cannot be a substitute for the chief tool of politics. That is the arena in which decisions are taken, compromises reached, and rewards divided. Only if the Arabs penetrate this arena on a sufficient scale to influence its agenda, can there be a fundamental change in their situation.

9

Toward Fulfilling the Right to Be Included: The Arabs' Future in a Binational Palestinian-Israeli State

The distress of the Arab citizens of Israel is epitomized in the fact that they are, at one and the same time, partial Israelis and partial Palestinians; that is, both their Israeli and Palestinian identities are incomplete. In the present circumstances, neither their Israeli identity nor their Palestinian identity can be full and comprehensive. This, in a nutshell, is the problem of the collective identity of the Arab citizens of Israel (Rouhana 1997).

On the one hand, the Arabs in Israel are officially citizens of the state. But their Israeli identity does not exist in the core of their collective identity, as a sense of psychological belonging and emotional sympathy. Israel was established with a Jewish-Zionist character to be the state of the Jewish people. Its objectives, symbols, and policy are built on that foundation and on denying the existence of a Palestinian national minority within its borders. This situation was made worse by the adoption of amendment 9 to the Basic Law: the Knesset, in 1985, whereby "a candidates' list shall not participate in elections to the Knesset if its objects or actions, expressly or by implication, include . . . negation of the existence of the State of Israel as the sate of the Jewish people."[1] Not only does this situation engender discrimination against the Arabs on the day-to-day level and undercut even the theoretical possibility of their attaining equality with the Jews, because of the need to give the Jews a feeling of primacy over others in their own state; in practice it leaves the Arabs in Israel, legally and officially, without a formal setting defined as their state and prevents the emergence of a liberal Israeli identity that could embrace the Arabs as well—analogous to the French, English, and American identities. The Israeli identity incorporates significant elements of Judaism and the Jewish heritage, so that only Jews can adopt it in full and become Israelis—a process experienced by most of the Jews who have immigrated to Israel since its independence. It is clear that the Arabs cannot be Israelis in the full sense of the word as defined as a stream. This relegates them to the margins of Israeli identity or leaves them only partial Israelis.

Until 1948, the Arabs in what became Israel were developing as part of the Palestinian and Arab national movement. The involuntary parting of ways engendered by the outcome of the 1948 war left the Arabs in Israel to develop in isolation, unable to draw directly on the vital streams of the Arab world and Palestinian national movement. The ongoing hostilities and security situation exacerbated this isolation. Even today there are still no signs of change in this domain. Even after the conclusion of peace agreements between Israel and some Arab countries and with the PLO, the situation continues to perpetuate the Arabs' isolation and inability to belong to the two circles, the Arab and the Palestinian. The Palestinian component of the identity of the Arabs in Israel cannot be complete when the Palestinian national movement is establishing the Palestinian homeland somewhere else.

The Arabs' quandary is not a contradiction between the two full identities, the Israeli and the Palestinian, but the incompleteness, in different ways, of each of these identities. This constitutes the most important evidence that the model of normal development (see Introduction) is fundamentally flawed with regard to the Arabs in Israel. The appropriate model is what the literature refers to as the "crisis development approach" (Ghanem 1996; 1998; Rouhana and Ghanem 1998), according to which the Palestinian-Arab community in Israel faces a crisis on two levels, the immediate and the strategic, which is likely to expand in the future. In the stream situation, the Arab community disposes of only limited options with regard to its relations with the state and with the Palestinian people, and cannot evolve normally. This situation restricts the development of the Arabs in Israel, especially their political development, and, as has been demonstrated throughout this book, creates a distress in this dimension that has implications for other dimensions as well, as we shall see below.

THE MULTI-FACETED DISTRESS IN THE INTERNAL DIMENSION OF THE PALESTINIAN-ARAB MINORITY DEVELOPMENT

Demographic Growth and Economic Deprivation

The change in the size of the Arab population and the physical structure of the village have not been accompanied by appropriate economic development. Arab towns still lack industrial zones (Hareven and Ghanem

1996). Arab localities are at the bottom of the socioeconomic scale of Israeli communities (Sikkuy 1996). According to official statistics, about 60% of the Arab citizens of Israel live below the poverty line (Hareven and Ghanem 1996a, 1996b; Fares 1996). As a result of government policy, the Arabs suffer a severe housing problem that has been getting worse over the years (Rosenhack 1996). Many Arab villages still lack official recognition, and accordingly do not receive basic services such as water and electricity (Ghanem 1992). The Bedouin Palestinians of Al-Naqab, who account for about 10 percent of all the Arabs in Israel, are the victims of ongoing persecution by the authorities. Their ownership of land is not recognized officially. The government is trying to concentrate them in settlements it has chosen for them, whereas the Jews in Al-Naqab can choose their own lifestyle and residential patterns (Fenster 1993). Economically, the Arabs suffer at all levels and equality with the Jews is still far away.

THE LACK OF A STRONG AND CONSOLIDATED LEADERSHIP

During the 1950s and 1960s, chiefly because of the military government, the Arabs were unable to develop a strong leadership to spearhead their struggle to improve their condition on the day-to-day and collective levels. The abolition of the military government and the gradual liberation from its shadow led to the first consolidation of a collective leadership, in the form of the committee of Arab local councils heads, established in 1974, and later the follow-up committee for Arab in Israel affairs, established in 1982. These groups have led the Arabs' struggle since the mid-1970s. The contest peaked in the late 1980s, in the proclamation of an Equality Day strike in June 1987 and of Peace Day in December of that year. These two strikes focused on the two centers of the Arabs' struggle: equality and peace. In the ensuing years there has been a gradual deterioration in the standing of the follow-up committee. In addition to the internal paralysis caused by power struggles among its various constituent groups, it is no longer viewed as a source of authority, neither by the general public nor even by its own members.

Significant political pluralism emerged among the Arabs in Israel during the 1980s, with the appearance and institutionalization of the Islamic Movement, the Progressive Movement, and the DAP, as well as various other countrywide and local organizations. Rather than strengthening the position of the leadership, which came to represent additional strata and sectors of the Arabs in Israel, the new pluralism actually weakened the leaders' power. The follow-up committee turned into a forum for incessant squabbling among the representatives of the various political groups; it was frequently deemed preferable to avoid convening it. As a result, by the early 1990s the follow-up committee was no longer playing a significant role, neither internally among the Arabs nor vis-à-vis the Israeli authorities, despite the fact that the goals it set for itself, peace and equality, still remain to be achieved—especially equality, which seems to be very far off.

THE ABSENCE OF A CLEAR CONCEPT OF THE FUTURE

On this level, the Arabs' distress is inherent in the fact that their leadership, whether represented on the follow-up committee or not, failed to crystalize a demand for a unique collective standing for the Arabs in Israel—as might be embodied by recognition as a national minority with its own specific national, linguistic, cultural, and ethical characteristics—even in general terms, or disseminated it to the general public. This stands in sharp contrast to the leadership of the Palestinian national movement in the West Bank, Gaza Strip, and Diaspora, who formulated a demand for Palestinian self-determination and gave it currency among the entire Palestinian people, and to leaders of the Jewish-Zionist national movement, who diffused a similar demand among the Jewish people. Even though the notion of a national minority and the demand that the Arabs be recognized as such have become a commonplace, the practical meaning of such recognition remains unclear. Even the Communist Party and DFPE, the original authors of the idea, have failed to clarify, in their literature or as individuals, how they understand this term.

SOCIAL STRUCTURE

The clan as a traditional primitive institution is still the potent basis of the social structure of the Arabs in Israel. The nuclear family, which has come to occupy a central economic role, has not yet done so in the social and political domains. This leads to many social and political complications and hinders the development of the Arab community in Israel (Rouhana and Ghanem 1993). It poses a question mark as to the ability of the Arabs in Israel to adapt to and adopt democratic norms of behavior.

The individual's situation, in the shadow of the functioning of the clan, is quite serious. Arab society discriminates against individuals and does not allow them a sufficient margin for normal development. The most significant manifestation of this discrimination affects the condition of Arab women, who are subject to an extensive network of forces and function as a minority among the Arab minority. Their situation is quite unsatisfactory, both in absolute terms and when compared to that of Jewish women in Israel (Bader-Aref 1995).

THE FAILURE TO INTERNALIZE DEMOCRATIC VALUES

As a result of internal developments associated with demographic growth and socioeconomic changes, in addition to the experience that the Arabs in Israel have had with its political system, they have taken on imperfect democratic pattern of life, behavior, and thought. The socioeconomic complications and selective policy of the Israeli authorities have produced significant contradictions that accompany the Arab democratization (Rouhana and Ghanem 1993, 163–180). The most important of these contradictions involve their active participation in Israeli politics at the national level, alongside their limited ability to influence decision-making acts at that level. Their vigorous struggle for equality and integration in the Israeli system, alongside the establishment of Palestinian-Arab national organizations; the increase in "violent" incidents by Arabs during the *intifada* period, alongside the emergence of a consensus that their struggle should be conducted within the bounds of Israeli law; the impossibility of choosing a countrywide leadership, even though the follow-up committee emerged and ostensibly functioned as such; giving maximum weight to national and ideological considerations when voting in Knesset elections, but voting largely on a clan basis in local elections—these contradictions reflect the practical difficulty of absorbing democracy and making it an integral part of the Arabs' milieu. Living in two worlds—the democratic and the traditional, nondemocratic—impedes their capacity for internal democratic development as well as the process of their absorption as an integral part of the Israeli political, social, and economic life. The practical outcome is the need to think about "special arrangements" appropriate to the Arabs, both as a group and as individuals, within the Israeli system.

CULTURAL CRISIS

The severe identity crisis is associated with the emerging dilemma of cultural and social values, at least among the Arab elite. After the 1948 war, the Palestinians found themselves involuntarily isolated from Palestinian culture and the Arab world. The war also devastated their urban centers, along with the middle-class and cultural elite who should have continued to nurture Palestinian-Arab culture. The Arabs in Israel were left without an infrastructure to create and nurture an Arab culture and without channels to the Arabic mother culture. The first window to the Arab world was opened after the Israeli victory in 1967. When additional channels were opened over the years, following the peace treaty with Egypt and later with Jordan, the Arab world itself was found to be experiencing an existential cultural crisis. Israel, on the other side, offered vibrant cultural institutions and activities. Because these are dominated by Jewish and Zionist slogans, however, the Arabs could only adopt the outer gloss of Israeli/Western culture, which lacks any connection to their own authentic roots.

In light of the persistence of the ethnic policy of Israel and its limited democratic accommodation of the Arabs, exacerbated by the Palestinian national movement's prolonged failure to pay attention to their problems, the problems surveyed earlier, as well as many others, at many levels and in many contexts (see Ghanem 1996; 1998; Rouhana and Ghanem 1998), may turn into a full-fledged crisis besetting the Arabs, their relations with the Jewish majority, and their relations with the Palestinian national movement (see Rouhana and Ghanem 1998). That crisis would affect the entire region, and not only the Arabs of Israel. Avoiding the crisis requires modifications in both the Israel and the Palestinian-Arab arenas. On the structural level these changes must guarantee the Arabs both the theoretical and practical ability of simultaneous affiliation on two levels, the national and the civic. Such dual affiliation is possible only in a liberal or egalitarian binational state.

TOWARD NORMALIZATION OF THE SITUATION OF THE ARABS IN ISRAEL

Conflict between groups is not insoluble. The solution lies in reasonable and appropriate response to the demands and needs of the various groups on both sides of the conflict. It can be guaranteed by the application of defined techniques for stability and preserving public order in societies that are deeply divided between different ethnic or national groups.

The guidelines for the resolution of intergroup problems result from a synthesis between the demands and needs of the minority group and the responses of the majority and of the state to these demands and needs. The theoretical literature on conflict resolution in pluralistic states that are deeply divided on an ethnic, religious, and national basis offers two main levels of principles for a just and democratic resolution of the status of the groups (Gurr 1993; Gurr and Harff 1994).

THE INDIVIDUAL LEVEL

This level deals with liberal rights—that is, the fundamental rights of the members of the groups, rights to which they are entitled by virtue of their equal citizenship, not by membership in a particular group. This includes the political, social, economic, and cultural rights to which each person is entitled as a citizen. The pure implementation of a system based exclusively on these rights is majoritarian liberal democracy, in which groups are not recognized as such and the state is not a party to any intergroup struggles that may exist and grants equal rights to individual citizens qua citizens (Lijphart 1977; Smooha 1990).

The Group Level

Throughout history, many groups have demanded group equality (see Horowitz 1985, 601–652; Kymlicka 1995). A group may advance a demand for expanded autonomy, in addition to the equal liberal rights enjoyed by its members and full partnership in directing the affairs of state. The ultimate outcome is the official and actual conversion of the state into a binational (or multinational, depending on the number of groups) state. The essence of a binational regime is recognition of groups as the key component of the public order and the division of power, rewards, and rights on a group basis, superadded to equality accorded to citizens on an individual basis. Conspicuous examples of this are the arrangement between the Flemings and Walloons in Belgium, and those in Switzerland and Canada (Lijphart 1977; 1999; Smooha 1990; Vos 1996). A binational accord for conflict resolution in divided societies depends on arrangements that rest on parity between the groups—that is, eliminating discrimination against minority groups and ending the institutionalized hegemony of the majority, while establishing equality between groups, either by negotiations involving all of them or between the state, which in practice is controlled by a particular group, and the groups that are discriminated against.

Some scholars favor a liberal solution to the problems of the Arab minority in Israel (see, for example, Rouhana 1997; Kook 1995)—that is, the emergence of a territorial Israeli identity that includes the Arab citizens on an equal footing with the Jewish citizens. But is this practicable in the foreseeable future? Do any forces favor movement in that direction or support such a solution?

I maintain that Israel as an ethnic state is a strong and stable system. The state practices a policy that overtly favors the Jewish majority over the Arab minority. Its commitment to this policy has not declined over the years and has even increased (Ghanem 1998). In addition, the Jewish majority, through its support for the ethnic state and dominance of majority, constitutes a key guarantor for the continuation of that regime. The overwhelming majority of the Jews want Israel to continue to be an ethnic state, with a Jewish-Zionist character and a commitment to favor the interests of the Jews over those of other citizens, including the Arabs, on all levels and in all spheres (Ghanem 1998a). Smooha (1995) summarized the main points of the dominant view among the Jewish majority with regard to the Arab citizens of Israel:

1. The Arabs are a hostile minority and must be watched.

2. The Arabs should be grateful for the progress they have made since 1948.

3. Israel is the state of the Jewish people and a Jewish-Zionist state. The Arabs must make do with limited individual rights and not demand recognition as a national minority.

4. The Arabs in Israel are a new minority with no connection to the Palestinian people.

5. The Arabs must accept the fact that they are excluded from the centers of power and decision-making in the state.

On the other side, neither do the Arabs support a liberal state or evince a willingness to adopt an Israeli civic identity shared with the Jews (Smooha 1997). Instead, they overwhelmingly support the establishment of a binational, Jewish-Arab state, within the borders of Israel inside the Green Line (Ghanem 1996a). The Arabs' position on this issue is important but insufficient to work any change in the structure of power and partnership between Jews and Arabs in the state. In fact, within Israel (inside the Green Line), the prospects for the establishment and development of a democratic and binational system, Jewish-Arab or Israeli-Palestinian, that would satisfy the aspirations and needs of the Arab citizens are practically nil. This is chiefly because of the Jews' dominance and their possession of a well-developed and solid ethnic nationality that is impervious to serious shocks. The ethnic reality of Israel, bolstered by other factors, causes the Arabs to develop as a minority in distress headed for a crisis. It prevents the minority from experiencing normal development (Rouhana and Ghanem 1998; Ghanem 1998a).

The Arabs will continue to suffer distress and crisis as long as there is no change in the ethnic system. A change of their distressed identity is possible if and only if they receive significant numerical reinforcement in the wake of unification with the Palestinians of the West Bank and Gaza Strip in a single political entity. This would expand their room for development and promote their liberation from the ethnic system and the pressures that impede their development as a normal community. The support of the Arab citizens of Israel for a binational regime is essential for the success of the idea. They will opt for such a solution only when they understand that their problems are insoluble in the present regime. Although this is certain, it could be hastened in conditions that augment the ethnic character of the state, a continuation of the process that gained momentum in 1996 after the return to power of the right, the strengthening of the Jewish-religious bloc, and the continued immigration from the former Soviet Union—all of which reinforce the marginal status of the Arabs within the Israeli system.

THE BINATIONAL REALITY IN MANDATORY PALESTINE/ ERETZ ISRAEL

About 4.6 million Jews and 3.8 million Palestinian Arabs are living as a stream within the borders of Mandatory Palestine, between the Jordan River and Mediterranean Sea. Most of the Jews arrived in the country in the various waves of immigration since 1881 and from the natural increase of these immigrants. The Palestinian Arabs are that portion of the Palestinian people who remained in the country after various waves of expulsion and emigration during the last century. On the formal legal level, the Palestinians in the country can be divided into three main groups with regard to their connection to Israel as the hegemonic power: the 900,000 Arab citizens of Israel; the 200,000 Palestinians in Jerusalem, most of whom are Israeli subjects rather than citizens; and the 2.8 million Palestinians in the West Bank and Gaza Strip, some of whom are citizens of the Palestinian authority and some of whom still live under direct Israeli control. There is also a fourth sector, the Palestinian Diaspora in the Arab world, Europe, and North America. This group accounts for about 50% of all Palestinians (Zuriek 1997, 21; Zakarya 1997, 176).

The state that controls the entire territory of Mandatory Palestine, Israel, is an ethnic state based on the marginalization of the Palestinians in the spheres of ideology, structure, and implementation, with regard to the distribution of power and physical resources, and the preservation of special privileges for the Jews. Arab citizens of Israel enjoy only limited democracy (Ghanem 1996a; 1998a); it does not exist in all for the Palestinians of the West Bank and Gaza Strip (Benvenisti 1988). This state of affairs harbors great potential for conflict, at various degrees of intensity, and is incompatible with long-term stability. Perpetuation of the present situation encourages dangerous incidents, both within the Green Line and outside it, including the possible involvement of the Arab states. Stability depends on the achievement of an arrangement that is more fair for the Palestinians (both Israeli citizens and residents of the West Bank and Gaza Strip).

Such an arrangement can be based on one of three approaches: partition; the establishment of a joint state with a liberal regime; or the establishment of a joint state based on group arrangements—that is, a binational state. My basic assumption is that separation between the Jews and the Palestinians, or at least between Israel and the West Bank and Gaza Strip, is impossible. A liberal state is also unfeasible. The only option left for normalizing relations between the Jews and the Palestinians is the establishment of a binational state in the entire territory of Mandatory Palestine, based on collective accords that bind the two peoples in a single political system. In a binational, Palestinian-Israeli state, the Palestinian/Israeli ethnic/national schism would remain a key structural feature of the political system, which would be based on the four principles of consociationalism: a broad coalition between the political representatives of the Jews and the Palestinians; mutual veto power regarding fundamental and substantive issues; proportional distribution of social goods, including political and public institutions; and a significant degree of personal autonomy for each group in the management of its internal affairs.

In practice, the initial conditions for the establishment of such a system already exist, though some basic changes are needed. Despite the Oslo process, the Palestinians in the West Bank and Gaza Strip still live under Israeli control, whether direct or indirect. In certain conditions, chiefly an inflexible Israeli rejection of the establishment of an egalitarian Palestinian state and the annexation of broad stretches of the West Bank and Gaza Strip to Israel, most of the Palestinians in these areas would, for various reasons (Ghanem 1998; Ghanem and Ozacky-Lazar 1997) give up the idea of the establishment of a Palestinian state; the Palestinian national authority would become no more than a way station on the road to the establishment of a binational system. Its citizens would form a joint front with the Arabs of Israel, constituting a single collective vis-à-vis the Jews. In the binational reality that would ensue, they would demand the conversion of the state, practically and formally, into a state that expresses both collectives. The Jews, most of whom reject a binational system, but at the same time do not want to surrender their hegemony, would have to deal with a variety of factors, including the Palestinians' demand for personal and group equality in a shared system.

HISTORICAL SOURCES FOR THE BINATIONAL IDEA

The debate about the fundamental possibility of a binational state as the expression of the reality of a binational society in Palestine is far from new. The first and to the large extent the only persons to entertain the idea were Jews. Its origins can be traced back to the beginning of Jewish immigration to and settlement in the country in the late nineteenth and early twentieth century. Some Jewish intellectuals expressed grave doubts about the possibility of achieving a Jewish majority in the country and setting up a Jewish state separate from the Arab world and the Arab majority in Palestine. They praised the positive characteristics of the Arabs, whom they viewed both as individuals and as members of a different national group whose right to the land that were not inferior to those of the Jews. They also believed that the Arabs would accept Jewish settlement in the country because of the progress and development it would bring to the region and would accordingly be prepared to think about the integration of the two groups in a single political framework.

These thinkers, such as Eliyahu Sapir (1869–1911), Izhac Epstein (1862–1943), Joseph Lurie, Nissim Mallul, Rabbi Binyamin (1880–1957), and even the Zionist leader Menachem Ussishkin, individually expressed their doubts about the establishment of a separate Jewish state in Palestine, because the Arab majority would not permit it. Accordingly they proposed integration with the Arabs and the creation of Jewish enclaves in regions not dominated by Arabs, thereby establishing the physical basis for the development of two societies, one alongside the other. This would then constitute the infrastructure for the establishment of a binational state. The idea that cooperation with the Arabs was essential was energized by the rise to power in Constantinople of the Young Turks, who were manifestly antagonistic to the Zionist project, in the first decade of the century. Most of these Jewish thinkers considered themselves to be Zionists in every respect. They believed that their approach would further the realization of Zionism, whose goal, as they saw it, was to revive and revitalize the Jewish people in the "Land of Israel," and not necessarily to found a separate Jewish state (Gorny 1985, 47–55).

These ideas first assumed an organized form with the appearance of the Breet Shalom movement, established in 1925 by Arthur Ruppin, and numbering among its other founders most of those who were on record as supporting the idea of a binational state or society. The organization favored the integration of the Jews into the Middle East and abandonment of the idea that they were a chosen people superior to the Arabs. Ruppin was the first who spoke explicitly about "the land of Israel as the state of the two nations." This is how he translated Epstein's idea about the dual right of the two peoples in the country, put forward at the start of the century, into a delineated operative idea (Gorny 1985, 150–151).

Breet-Shalom, though it clearly deviated from the official Zionist line, saw itself as a Zionist movement resting on Zionist ideology. Its first published pamphlet included passages to support its claim that the origins of the idea were rooted in Zionist thought. There were excerpts from people like Herzl, Ahad Ha'am, Rabbi Binyamin, A. D. Gordon, and Izhac Epstein. They advanced their aspiration for the establishment of a state of two nations, in which the two peoples would live with absolute parity of rights (Gorny 1985, 151). They proposed Switzerland and Finland as the models for their ideas and called for the establishment of institutions, such as a parliament, with equal representation of the two peoples, regardless of the relative numerical strength of Arabs and Jews. This proposal was meant to counter the idea, advanced by moderate Arabs of the period, of establishing institutions with proportional representation. Their opposition stemmed from the fear that the Arab majority would infringe upon the rights of the Jewish minority.

Ben-Gurion addressed the issue in the early 1930s, asserting that the state that would arise in Mandatory Palestine must preserve a balance between Jews and Arabs, with neither people ruling over the other. This position was adopted by the Mapai council in 1931 (Amitay 1988, 23). In the 1940s and 1950s the idea was promoted chiefly by the Po'alim–Hashomer Hatza'ir Party, founded in 1946 by the merger of Kibbutz Artzi/Hashomer Hatza'ir and the Socialist League. Because it rejected the state as a form of social organization, this party initially championed the establishment of a binational society; later it spoke of a binational state. The party considered this position to be legitimately Zionist and the objective of the entire Zionist enterprise. Its founding conference in 1946 passed a resolution about

> The urgent need for a change in the political path of the Zionist movement as defined by the Biltmore plan. We will intensify our war for the victory of the alternative political line, whose fundamentals are: unimpeded progress of the Zionist enterprise, meaningful international supervision, and political equality between the Jews and the Arabs in the framework of a binational regime in the land of Israel.

For Hashomer Hatza'ir, this objective underlay the very justification for the existence of the mandate, which should lead the country to independence as a binational state (Amitay 1988, 20–23).

Ahdut Ha'avoda–Po'alei Tziyyon, the future partner of Hashomer Hatza'ir in the establishment of the United Workers Party (Mapam) in 1948, opposed the binational idea from its inception in 1944. It favored the establishment of a national home for the Jews, aimed for a Jewish-socialist state in all parts of the land of Israel, and opposed partition. At the same time it took it for granted that the Hebrew state in the country would grant equal rights to all inhabitants, but rejected the idea that this equality take the form of sovereignty and territory (Amitay 1988, 20–21).

As a matter of principle, both wings of Mapam rejected the idea of partition under United Nations Resolution 181 of 29 November 1947.

After independence was declared, a debate broke out between the two groups over the binational idea. Ahdut Ha'avoda continued to believe in the possibility of uniting the country, even by means of a war initiated by Israel, and was accordingly opposed to the annexation of the West Bank by Jordan and Egyptian control of the Gaza Strip. It continued to believe in the possibility of establishing a Jewish socialist state that would grant equality to Arabs, but not sovereignty and territorial control. They asserted that there was no right to establish "another Arab state" in addition to the thirteen that already existed. By contrast, Hashomer Hatza'ir agreed to a partition as a tactical device, but supported the establishment of the Arab state in accordance with the partition plan and wanted to encourage "progressive" Arab forces to rule that state and establish an alliance, chiefly economic, with Israel, so that a binational, Arab and Jewish, state might eventually be founded (Amitay 1988, 115–129).

The internal debate within Mapam continued to rage, assuming the form of a debate about the idea of a "territorial party" and acceptance of Arabs as full members. This was meant to be a manifestation of binationalism in the party, an example of the type of relations that would exist in the future in a binational state. The discord led to a split in 1954. Hashomer Hatza'ir retained the name Mapam, while Ahdut Ha'avoda–Po'alei Ziyyon resumed its old name and began publishing the weekly *Lamerhav* (Amitay 1988, 159–161).

On the Arab side, the idea of a binational state was hardly mentioned. I do not believe that we can understand the call for the establishment of a secular democratic Palestinian state, put forward by circles within the Palestinian national movement since the late 1960s (al-Asmar, Davis, and Khader 1978; Gresh 1985) as incorporating the binational idea, because this democratic secular state would be based and expressed chiefly by privatization of the national, religious, and ethnic affiliation of the Jews and the Arabs. National affiliation would not be important and would be ignored by the state. This core idea here is that national affiliation would no longer be an element in the relations between the citizens of the future state. The individual and civic element would be the overarching goal that dictates positions and relations between the state and members of the groups and between members of the groups directly. By contrast, a binational state by definition recognizes two national collectives and considers membership in them to be a central element in the relationships in the future state. In practice, this arrangement would make it possible to expand national control over the entire territory of Mandatory Palestine, limited only by the need to take account of the desire of the members of the other collective that compete on a group basis (and of course its members individually) for the same resources that the country proposes to all its citizens.

The Palestinian national movement consistently rejected the possibility of a binational state and even gave it up as a tactical stage. Historically it is difficult to find any support for the idea on the Palestinian side, whether official or unofficial. Only recently have a number of Palestinians, both from the Diaspora and Israeli citizens, begun to put forward the binational idea as an alternative solution to separation between Palestinians and Israelis. Today, the option of an Israeli-Palestinian binational state is not on the political agenda of the political elites or the general public on either the Israeli or Palestinian side. Both groups currently speak chiefly of other solutions. When this option is mentioned at all, it is to serve as a catalyst to encourage adoption of a partition scheme.

On the Israeli side, one finds chiefly two antithetical positions. One supports the annexation of the West Bank to Israel, or at least the annexation of those parts of the West Bank and Gaza Strip that are not heavily populated by Palestinians. This in essence is the platform of the radical right in Israel. The Palestinians who live in these strips would not be granted full Israeli citizenship; some even speak of expelling the Arabs or of their voluntary transfer (Moledet and the remnants of Kach). Others speak about allowing the Palestinians to remain, but as noncitizens, under Israeli control.

The Zionists left in Israel, including Meretz and some supporters of the Labor party, favor separation. One of their central arguments for this solution is the fear that continued occupation or annexation of the West Bank and Gaza Strip would lead to the establishment of a binational state. In their opinion this would mark the end of the Zionist enterprise, which has found expression thus far in the establishment of Israel as a Jewish-Zionist state. This position attests to the fact that some Jews believe it would be possible to implement a binational system should Israel hold on to parts of the West Bank and Gaza Strip. Its use as a bugbear in election campaigns to win the support of Jewish voters is evidence that some political leaders are uncomfortable that continued Israeli control of the West Bank and Gaza Strip would lead to the establishment of a system that would ultimately develop into a binational regime.

Today there exists a consensus among a majority of the Jews in Israel concerning the need for separation, but without allowing the Palestinians to establish a sovereign state of their own. The Likud supports granting territorial and institutional autonomy to the Palestinians of the West Bank and Gaza Strip, while the Labor party supports "autonomy plus" or "a state minus." This would guarantee both long-term Israeli hegemony and control of the Palestinians, and a certain degree of Palestinian self-rule. In any case, such an arrangement would require significant territorial modifications in Israel's favor and would undercut any future possibility of the establishment of an independent Palestinian state in the West Bank and Gaza Strip with its capital in Jerusalem, as Palestinian moderates anticipate. In my opinion, any arrangement that involves continued direct Israeli control of the West Bank and Gaza Strip or some parts thereof, or that does not satisfy the Palestinian demand for independence, may lead to an Israeli annexation of parts of the West Bank and Gaza Strip as a first stage. But—if Palestinian leaders come to understand the essence of the arrangement proposed by Israel and its implications—it cannot stop the snowballing demand by the Palestinians in the West Bank and Gaza Strip for complete annexation to Israel or the establishment by agreement of a binational system.

On the other hand, the non-Zionist left, for all that it is a tiny minority, might in some conditions spur a renewed debate in the Israeli population about the price of separation and the need for new thinking about the idea of a binational state. This would be depicted both as a moral solution, as the only feasible solution in the conditions of continued Israeli occupation, whatever its form, and as a response to the possible emergence of a Palestinian dictatorship alongside Israel.

On the Palestinian side, there are also two main positions. The Rejectionist Front, which represents the radical left, Hamas, and the Islamic Jihad continue to insist that Mandatory Palestine is an indivisible geographic entity that should be the site of a Palestinian state. This position rejects the solution of separation and coincides with or inverts the position of the Israeli right.

On the other side we have the representatives of the mainstream, which supports the establishment of a Palestinian state alongside Israel. When Sari Nusseibeh, a lecturer at Bir Zeit University, revived the binational idea in the late 1980s, after the outbreak of the *intifada*, he was shunned and even beaten by activists of the Palestinian national movement, who saw it as a surrender of the movement's official demand for the establishment of a Palestinian state.

At the same time, we should remember that the Palestinian national movement is represented by Arafat and the Fatah movement. They led the change from support for a secular democratic state to support for separation in the mid-1970s and can now lead the reverse process, should it prove unrealistic to set up an independent Palestinian state. Recently some of Arafat's political opponents, apprehensive for the fate of democracy and human rights under the Palestinian national authority, joined by a number of the Palestinian minority, have been speaking about the binational idea as the only option that can guarantee the rights of the Palestinians and protect them against a dictatorial regime like those found elsewhere in the Arab world. Discussions of this have been gaining momentum. After the signing of the Oslo accords and the return to power of the Israeli right, it has drawn the support of several prominent Palestinians, such as Haidar Abd el-Shafi of Gaza and prominent intellectuals including Edward Said and Mahmud Darwish. They and others have voiced support for the idea and there has even been the beginnings of intellectual debate of the question.

In addition, the American Jewish intellectual Noam Chomsky has recently expressed support for a binational state as the future resolution to the Israeli-Palestinian problem. He did this while sharply castigating the Oslo agreement and the peace process, alleging that it cannot lead to peace but only serve as a fig leaf for continued Israeli control of the Palestinians.[2]

FACTORS DELAYING A SEPARATION BETWEEN ISRAEL AND THE WEST BANK AND GAZA STRIP: FACTORS RAISING THE LIKELIHOOD OF THE ESTABLISHMENT OF A JOINT STATE

A working premise justifying separation is based on the principle of reaching an agreement on the basis of the UN security council decision 242—that is, an Israeli withdrawal from the West Bank and Gaza Strip. I will list below the factors delaying such a separation, and perhaps even making it impossible as a political act requiring a physical, territorial, and national separation to be expressed in its implementation. These factors require, sooner or later, that we begin thinking of an entirely different strategy—namely, one of joint rule in all the country by representatives of both groups. This seems to be practically the only applicable way to advance toward a solution of the continuing conflict between the Jews and the Palestinians over the control of the land.

DIFFERENT EXPECTATIONS FROM THE SEPARATION

For most of the Palestinians, a separation should lead to the establishment of an independent Palestinian state in all the areas of the West Bank and Gaza, with East Jerusalem as its capital. This state should be able to cooperate on various issues, from a position of power and free choice, with the different states in the region, including Israel. This position is the guideline of the Palestinian leadership in negotiating with Israel on the solution for the conflict.

The Israeli public is more evenly divided in its position on this question. Most Israelis support a certain separation, and a great part of them also support the establishment of a Palestinian state, limited in its sovereignty and its territory (Arian 1997). The main political parties in Israel, including the Labor Party, which has removed from its constitution the objection to the establishment of an independent Palestinian state, are not willing to accept an independent Palestinian state, sovereign and equal to Israel in these respects. The perception of most Israelis and their representatives in the political parties can be summed up as a longing to "get out of the conflict" and to leave the Palestinians to deal with their problems, but to retain absolute control over security and foreign affairs, and an ability to threaten the Palestinians (and make good the threat) with closures or other punitive measures at any point in time. Of course, a significant portion of the Israeli public will not accept even a partial Palestinian independence or sovereignty. The current government, at the least, and any similar government in the future, depend upon the good will of this minority. These positions lead to the conclusion that Israel cannot offer the minimum which the Palestinians require to move from a conflict situation to a peaceable one. Furthermore, there is a high likelihood that this situation will not change rapidly, seeing that the processes of the change in the Israeli position are limited by other factors which prevent separation. These factors are as follows:

COMMON ISSUES

Between the two parties and between the two parts of the land to be divided, various common issues exist, and an appropriate use of them must indeed be common. Issues such as water sources, environment, employment, a product market, passage routes, ports, and so forth, cannot be separated. They are common and are currently a major factor hindering the separation process, as they will be a major obstacle to its implementation.

On a number of these issues, Israel, as the ruling power, insists that it remains the only ruler. According to various Israeli sources, Israel cannot share its absolute control over these areas with anyone. Even the government which signed the Oslo accords could not decide these issues in the agreement itself, and left them for the negotiations on the final settlement. In truth, every possible scenario of a final agreement would not allow these common issues to be in the exclusive control of one of the parties, even assuming both sides to be in favor. Therefore, they will continue to be factors opposing the separation and supporting the establishment of one common system throughout the country.

THE SETTLEMENTS

The Israeli-Jewish settlements in the West Bank and Gaza Strip are the sum total of the settling undertaken by Jews or by the government of Israel in these West Bank and Gaza Strip after 1967. These settlements comprise today 160,000 settlers (not taking into account East Jerusalem, which I will consider separately), 5,000 of those being in the Gaza Strip, and the rest (155,000) in the West Bank. These settlers are motivated by a variety of reasons, ideological and financial, and include both religious and secular settlers (JMCC 1997).

The settlements are spread over large areas and control many parts of the West Bank and the Gaza Strip. If we add the roads leading to the settlements, it becomes obvious that many parts of the West Bank and Gaza Strip are under the control of the settlers and used by them. This prevents the continuity of the areas ruled by the Palestinian authority and will be in the future a major impediment to the territorial consolidation of the Palestinian entity, which is the supposed outcome of the separation between the two peoples (Aronson 1996). Furthermore, the settlers, who are for the most part armed, are a major source of harassment for the Palestinian residents. They are the leaders of the process of expropriation of Palestinian lands, and they are the inflammatory influence behind the various steps taken against the Palestinian residents. In addition to this, several Palestinians in the occupied West Bank and Gaza Strip have been killed or injured by the settlers.[3]

Obviously the Palestinians cannot accept a situation where most of the settlements continue to exist. Their demand for the removal of the settlers must be unequivocal and inflexible, if they want the construction of the Palestinian entity to succeed. Of course, the main question is, Whether it is objectively possible for the government of Israel to uproot the settlers? The answer depends on several variables. Assuming that the current government will continue in power, and would even succeed in getting elected for another term of office, there is no reason to expect a change in its basic attitude. Obviously it will not agree nor be able to uproot the settlers. In its policy, it will make it much more difficult for any future government to realize such a step, which will become practically impossible to carry out. In such a case, the two sides would have to examine the possibilities of resolving the conflict while allowing the settlers, or at least most of them, to remain. Such an arrangement is practicable only within a common system, and not in a separation of the nations and the country. The settlers and their aspirations have been and will continue to be a major stumbling block to separation, and will force the leaderships of both peoples to consider other solutions, such as a binational state.

East Jerusalem

After the end of the 1948 war and the establishment of the state of Israel, Jerusalem was divided along the cease-fire line into West Jerusalem, in Israeli control, and East Jerusalem, administrationally a part of the West-Bank, ruled by Jordan and annexed by it with the rest of the West Bank in April 1950. Israel occupied Jerusalem with the rest of the West Bank in the June 1967 war, and annexed it with an amendment to the rule and justice regulations order, passed in the Knesset already by 27 June 1967. The following day the government of Israel published an announcement regarding the annexation of an area of about 70,000 *dunams* from the territory of East Jerusalem to West Jerusalem (B'tzelem 1995).

After the annexation, Israel granted the status of permanent resident to those Palestinians in East Jerusalem who participated in the census held following the annexation. Those receiving the status of a resident could apply for an Israeli citizenship and be granted it, provided they met the basic requirements of swearing of allegiance to Israel, renouncing any other nationality, and claiming a knowledge of Hebrew. Most Palestinian residents of Jerusalem still refuse the Israeli citizenship and still regard their future as similar to that of other Palestinians in the West Bank. They aspire to disengage themselves from Israeli control and be joined to the Palestinian entity ruling the other cities of the West Bank and Gaza Strip. This is also the position voiced by the political leadership of the Palestinians in Jerusalem.

As far as international law is concerned, East Jerusalem is occupied territory and therefore the conquering country may not change its status and may not annex it. Hence, in international gatherings Israel refuses to talk of "annexation" and prefers using the phrase "the integration of Jerusalem in the municipal administration area" (B'tzelem 1995). Naturally, when presenting East Jerusalem to the Israeli public opinion, the Israeli government presents it as an integral part of Israel, subject to all the regulations of Israeli law.

Side by side with the annexation, Israel pursues a policy of harsh enforcement of the law on the Palestinians in East Jerusalem, with the aim of bringing them to accept Israeli control. This policy includes steps such as expropriation of lands, a large presence of security forces, neglect in terms of the municipal services and the planning and building processes, and large-scale settlement in all the annexed parts of East Jerusalem and even beyond them (B'tzelem 1995). Today, about 140,000 Palestinians live in those parts of East Jerusalem which were annexed, whereas the number of Jews in those areas is 170,000. This is accompanied by a deep change in the physical scenery, in the geographical distribution, and in the control of the lands.

Israel has taken various steps, such as encircling East Jerusalem with Jewish neighborhoods, erecting Jewish neighborhoods within it, encircling it with roads, establishing the Israeli government institutions in the lands taken in June 1967, expropriating lands and strengthening the Israeli and Jewish control over them, among others. These steps are clearly and indisputably irrevocable. The international law, the position of most Palestinians in East Jerusalem, and even the specific section in the Oslo agreement dealing with the solution of the problem of control in East Jerusalem as a part of the final agreement, are all entirely irrelevant. Israel continues in its policy, designed to serve the national interests of the Jews, and is not willing to consider any gesture toward Palestinian control in East Jerusalem. In fact, even should the sides want a redistribution, it is now not possible to carry it out.

In the previously described reality, where the option of separation is not possible, along with a firm and determined position held by the Palestinians, the Arab world and the Muslim world, a position upheld by most of the states in the world and by international law, the only possible solution is one of partnership in a framework whose essence is a binational control of Jerusalem. Jerusalem could be an expression of a binational reality throughout the country.

REFUGEES

The Palestinian refugees are the sum total of Palestinians who lived in Palestine and were deported or forced to leave for other residences, whether in Palestine or outside it, in two major waves. The first wave arose immediately after the UN partition. 181 in 1947 and the outbreak of the 1948 war. During the war, 750,000 people left their homes as a result of deportation and intimidating tactics taken by the Jewish forces against the original population. The second wave occurred after the outbreak of the June 1967 war, and during the course of the war, 250,000 Palestinians were driven from their homes. Part of the refugees in the second wave are the same Palestinians driven out in 1948 (Jarrar 1997; Tamari 1996). In the negotiations between Israel and the PLO and in the major references to the issue, the term "refugees" designates mainly those Palestinians living outside the bounds of Israel, and in particular those still living in the countries of the region, including those Palestinians whose origin is in pre-1967 Israel and currently living in the West Bank and Gaza Strip.

According to various data, the percentage of refugees from the whole of the Palestinian people fluctuates between 50 percent and 60 percent, that is between 3.5 and 4 million, according to the latest survey taken by the UNRWA (the UN special agency for Palestinian refugees). Of that total, 17 percent still live in refugee camps and 8 percent still have no stable dwellings (Jarrar, 1997).

These refugees have not for the most part given up on their right to return to those communities they were exiled from in 1948 and 1967. A large part of them believe in their right and their intention to return in the future to the boundaries of Mandatory Palestine. The Arabs in Israel, the most moderate of all the Palestinian groups as

regards the settling of the conflict, including the refugee issue, still believe for the most part that the Palestinian refugees have a right to
return to their homes.

International decisions, chiefly Decision 194 of the UN general
council from 1948, support the right of the Palestinian refugees to
choose between returning to their homes and receiving appropriate
compensation for the houses and property left in the country. The
Palestinian leadership reiterates at every opportunity the same right.
Even the Oslo accords, the legal basis for the peace process between
Israel and the PLO, did not reject that right, but rather postponed the
settling of the question to the final agreement negotiations. This issue
is being hammered out in many joint forums and is one of the subjects
of the multilateral talks, theoretically still taking place between Israel
and the countries of the region, including the Palestinians.

Israel, on its side, has announced that it shall not under any circumstances agree to the return of refugees to its territory, and has even
expressed reservations about the return of refugees to the Palestinian
entity that will be established in the West Bank and the Gaza Strip.
Officially, Israel denies its responsibility for the creation of the refugee
problem, usually blaming the Palestinians themselves and the Arab
countries. These positions are upheld by the Israeli public, and there are
no signs of any weakening in the traditional Israeli position on this
issue. It is reasonable to assume that Israel will not agree to the Palestinian demands in the future, and that this issue will continue to trouble
the people of the area, both Israelis and Palestinians, for a long time.

Under the present circumstances it is obvious that even if Israel
were to allow the return of refugees to the Palestinian entity, this entity
is incapable financially of absorbing tens of thousands of refugees.
Moreover, probably most of the refugees will not wish to return to it,
but continue to believe in their right and ability to return in the future
to their homes within the Green Line. In short, any separation will not
be able to deal effectively with the refugee problem. My basic assumption is that only a resolution comprising a joint entity could creata
Palestinian-Israeli balance, relative to opening of the borders of the state
to the return of the refugees. This would be side by side with the
continuing absorption of Jews or as a compensation for the absorption
of ten thousands of Jews since 1948. Only a Palestinian Israeli cooperation on the issue, following the foundation of a binational system in the
country, can lead to the solution of the refugee problem.

THE IMAGE OF THE "HOMELAND" FOR THE JEWS AND THE PALESTINIANS

The Jews and the Palestinians see the whole of the country as their homeland, rather than a part of it. Even Palestinians and Jews proclaiming

their willingness for a territorial compromise, still believe for the most part that the entire country, Palestine to the Palestinians and the land of Israel to the Jews, is their unique and absolute homeland as far as pure justice goes. Their willingness to compromise comes from tactical and practical reasons. In a parallel development, the hard liners in both camps, such as the extreme right and the believers in the "complete land of Israel" among the Jews, and the radical Muslims and radical left among the Palestinians, are not willing to consider the compromise solutions and hold that pure justice compels them to fight the other side relentlessly.

A territorial compromise in the form of a separation which could be reached between the Jews and the Palestinians will not satisfy the hardliners, and cannot provide an ideological backing for the compromisers to allow them tactical and strategic acceptance of the compromise. The Jewish left, in the form of Hashomer Hatza'ir and Ahdut Ha'avoda–Poaley Zion, accepted painfully the idea of partition after the establishment of the state of Israel, and did not easily give up on the idea of the entire country as one political and territorial unit (Amitay 1988). The Palestinian national movement is beginning since the early seventies to come to terms, albeit slowly and painfully, with the idea of separation and territorial compromise. The reason for this pain is the difficulty of adjusting the faith in a right to the entire country with the reality of the partition. Only a situation in which both Palestinians and Jews live together in a framework allowing them access to all parts of the country could satisfy the belief in the full right over the entire country.

A BINATIONAL MODEL FOR ISRAELI-PALESTINIAN RELATIONS

The basic assumption that led me to the idea of a binational Palestinian-Israeli state is that separation is simply unworkable. The two peoples have no choice but to live together in a single state. It is true that as a first stage, given the balance of power in the region, the Jews will continue to dominate the Palestinians and even intensify the conditions of control, discrimination, and repression. Nevertheless, with the growing ferment among the Palestinians (in Israel and the West Bank and Gaza Strip) and a willingness to initiate violent actions against Jewish control, Jewish condemnation of the repression, and an awakening of world opinion about the situation, one can anticipate the development of local as well as international pressure to allow the Palestinians to participate, as individuals and as a political community, in managing the affairs in the country on an equal basis.

In a situation similar to those that pertained in South Africa before the change of regime in late 1980s, conditions are likely to ripen, in a time frame that depends on developments, in which the Jews and their leadership will be forced, for a number of reasons, to recognize the Palestinians as equal partners. They will have to hold discussions with their representatives and reach an agreement on power-sharing and control of resources. Separate and joint governmental institutions will be set up, including parliaments, cabinets, and judicial systems. Each national group will be recognized as autonomous with regard to its own affairs, while common matters will be worked out in joint forums where the two groups have equal representation. The military will represent both groups. The representatives of each group will have veto power over common decisions. Territorial control will be divided between members of the two groups. The country can be a single administrative strip or divided into federal units and cantons that are responsible for local affairs and subordinate to the central authorities in the capital, Jerusalem. There will also be special arrangements of division of power and control in Jerusalem.

These developments, which will lead to profound thinking about the possibility of the building of a binational state, will depend greatly on the maturing of the peace process and peace between Israel and the neighboring Arab countries. The peace with Egypt and Jordan, despite the problems, is stable and reflects the interests of all parties. It is reasonable to assume that in the short term Israel will sign agreements with Syria and Lebanon. In this situation Israel will be sensitive not only to Western pressures but also to relations with its Arab neighbors. Even if some of its leaders would prefer to get rid of the Palestinians by transfer, they would not be able to implement it, as in 1948 and 1967, because of the peaceful relations between Israel and its neighbors, and the Israeli desire to preserve them. The peace processes between Israel and its Arab neighbors thus have a positive influence on the emergence of an egalitarian binational regime in the country.

Recently a profound debate has been evolving, initiated chiefly by the supporters of the establishment of a secular democratic state. They hold that it is necessary to eradicate the national structures of both groups, the Jews and Palestinians, and to establish a secular democratic state, a liberal democracy that pays no attention to the national affiliation of its citizens. They oppose the binational idea (see, for example, Carmi 1997; Honig-Barnas 1997). In my opinion, the proponents of a liberal state have underestimated the strength of the national affiliation in the two movements. I think they are speaking of a utopia that cannot be realized. Any future accord must take account of the national structure of the two groups and the possibility of dividing control of resources on this basis.

Serious thinking about the possibility of the binational model I have described in general lines above as a solution for the pending problems between the two peoples requires a substantial change in nature of the relations between the two peoples; substantial changes in the two entities, the Palestinian and Israeli; substantial changes in the nature of the two national movements, the Zionist and the Palestinian, including the issue of the Jewish diaspora and the Palestinian diaspora, and question of the bond with the broader, Arab national movement; changes in how foreign countries relate to the region and its future; and changes in the nature of the relations between the superpowers and the countries of the region. The proposed model sketches intercommunal relations that would be substantially different from those postulated by any other option for Jewish-Arab relations in the country.

RELATIONS BETWEEN THE TWO PEOPLES

Today there is a dominant group—the Jews—and a dominated group—the Palestinians. This situation is the outcome of a struggle between the two peoples, which has been going on since the beginning of Jewish immigration in 1881 and continues to the present. In a binational state there is parity between members of the two groups, based on the division of power, resources, territory, and the like, on a proportional or equal basis, whatever the size of each group. A waiver by the hegemonic group of its dominance and the accommodation of the dominated group to equality in a binational state would entail great travail and perhaps much loss of life and property. Such a change would require the two communities to undergo a fundamental transformation in their educational, social, and political outlook, and their approach to the other group and its status.

CHANGES IN ISRAEL AND PALESTINE

Subsequent to the changes that the two societies would have to undergo, the two states, or Israel and the Palestinian entity, would also have to experience far-reaching changes. The two entities would have to reach a compromise, on both the substantive and symbolic levels, that would include changes in their laws, political structure, and security forces, as well as in political, economic, social, and strategic ideas concerning their place and standing, both domestically and toward the outside world. The changes would later be manifested in the replacement of the two existing entities by a new common polity.

CHANGES IN THE ORIENTATION OF THE TWO NATIONAL MOVEMENTS

The internal and external orientation of the two national movements would be significantly modified, from conflict and the impossibility of living together to acquiescence and compromise so that both can survive. The nature of the relations between the national movement of the

Jews in Israel and the Jews in the Diaspora, and the nature of the relations between the Palestinian national movement in Palestinian and elsewhere in the world, and with the Arab national movement, would be significantly different from the situation today. Because the supreme goal of both movements would be concentration on building a binational regime in the country, the growth and flourishing of separate national movements would be a means and not an end in itself.

In addition, the binational solution would require changes in the nature of the ties and relations between the state and other countries in the world, chiefly with regard to the clear orientation dictated by ties with superpowers such as the United States or the European Union or other countries in the Middle East. The binational state would have to manifest balance in its relations with these countries.

At more advanced stages in the development of the binational regime, similar to Belgium and Switzerland, which are described in the literature as leading examples (Lijphart 1977; 1984; 1999), it would be necessary to concentrate on implementing and developing the following elements as the basis for the future:

1. A broad coalition drawing on both groups: The stability of the binational state will depend on a strong coalition involving wide sectors of the elites of both groups and political leadership representing the majority of each group. Such a coalition will lead the state and be responsible for preserving order and managing its domestic and foreign affairs, while aspiring to achieve a consensus and compromise on controversial issues.

2. Mutual veto by each group: Sound administration of the binational system must be accompanied by the possibility that the representatives of one group can cast a veto in extreme cases, even on matters that are the internal affairs of the other group. The existence of such an arrangement requires the representatives of one group to take account of the interests of the other group.

3. Equal representation: The shared political and public institutions of the binational regime must comprise relative equal representation of each group. Each group will have a reserved quota for it representatives. With regard to certain posts, such as president of the state, premier, and ministers, the groups would have to agree to rotation or to dual officeholders, one from each group.

4. Internal autonomy for each group: The internal affairs of each group, such as education, culture, local government, and the like, will be handled separately. This autonomy can be territorial, personal, or mixed, as agreed upon by representatives of the two

groups. In areas where there is overlap, or in mixed population strips, the representatives of the two groups would have to cooperate to permit sound administration even of matters that, as a matter of principle, are considered to be separate.

THE PALESTINIAN-ARABS IN ISRAEL AND THE BINATIONAL SYSTEM

A binational regime is a democracy based on group arrangements that give the groups equal status, in addition to the equality extended to all citizens by virtue of their equal citizenship in the shared state.

On the level of the individual, in a binational Palestinian-Israeli state the Arabs of Israel will have equality by virtue of their being citizens equal to all other citizens. The special status that the stream Israeli system gives to Jews, because of the ethnic, Jewish-Zionist regime, will be altered. In a binational polity, the state will have to grant equality to all citizens and avoid any special status for some citizens, which constitutes a perpetual and serious threat to the stability of the system. The individual affairs of Arab citizens, including the Palestinians of the West Bank and Gaza Strip, will be dealt with by the state that grants equality in its relations with all citizens, Jews and Arabs alike. This will allow the Arabs in Israel to realize the civic dimensions of their identity in full.

On the group level, the Arabs of Israel will be part of the Palestinian collective, of which the lion's share lives in the West Bank and Gaza Strip. Collective matters such as leadership, representation, education, culture, and the like will be managed by a group in which each group, Jews and Palestinians, has institutional and cultural autonomy. This will extend even to the territorial dimension, permitting each group to manage its own spatial planning and development. The collective life of the Arabs in Israel will evolve as part of the overall Palestinian collective. A possible first step in this direction would be to subordinate the Arab citizens of Israel, living where they do today, to the Palestinian national authority, just as the Jews who live in the West Bank and Gaza Strip are subject to the Israeli system. This would make it possible to realize the full significance of the Palestinian collective affiliation of the Arabs in Israel.

The fulfillment of the civic and national affiliation of the Arabs in Israel in a binational regime would permit them to escape the distress that besets them today and open before them channels for future development that do not exist today. Only the development of such channels will make it possible for the Arab citizens of Israel to escape their distress and enjoy normal development.

Appendix

Distribution of the Arab Vote in Knesset Elections, 1949–1999

Knesset Year	Valid Votes	Partici- pants Percent	ICP and DFPE	PLP	NDA	DAP and Islamic Move- ment	Arab Lists	Labor Party	Other Zionist Parties	%
1949	26332	79	22				28	10	40	100
1951	58984	86	16				55	11	18	100
1955	77979	90	15				48	14	23	100
1959	81764	85	11				42	10	37	100
1961	86843	83	22				40	10	28	100
1965	106346	82	23				38	13	26	100
1969	117190	80	28				40	17	15	100
1973	133058	73	37				27	17	19	100
1977	145925	74	50				16	11	23	100
1981	164862	68	37				12	29	22	100
1984*	199968	72	32	18			−	26	24	100
1988*	241601	74	33	14		11	−	16	25	100
1992*	273920	70	23	9		15	−	20	33	100
1996**	307497	77	38			27	−	18	17	100
1999	321201	75	22		17	31		8	22	100

SOURCE: Ozacky and Ghanem 1996, and calculations of the author in 1999

*The Progressive List first appeared in 1984, when it won about 18 percent of the Arab vote; in the 1988 elections it won about 15 percent, and in the 1992 elections it won about 9 percent of the Arab vote.

**In 1996 the DFPE ran on a joint list with the NDA (National Democratic Alignment), and the DAP on a joint list with the Islamic Movement.

Notes

CHAPTER THREE

1. *Divrei Ha-knesset,* 17 March 1966, and by a speech by MK Obeid of the Mapai satellite, Cooperation and Fraternity, *Divrei Ha-knesset,* 17 July 1972.

2. See the address by MK Abd el-Aziz Zouabi of Mapam, *Divrei Ha-knesset,* 1 February 1967.

3. See, for instance, the remarks by George Sa'ad of Mapai, at the eleventh Histadrut Congress, held on 9–12 December 1969, *Proceedings of the Eleventh Congress 1969,* 155–156, and the remarks by Yussuf Hamis of Mapam (ibid., 186–187).

4. *Divrei Ha-knesset,* 15 November 1972.

5. See remarks by MK Obeid, *Divrei Ha-knesset,* 17 July 1972, and the remarks by MK Mu'adi, *Divrei Ha-knesset,* 3 June 1974.

6. *Divrei Ha-knesset,* 3 July 1974.

7. See, for example, the remarks by MK Obeid, *Divrei Ha-knesset,* 17 March 1969.

8. See the article by Muhammad Watad, Mapam activist and later MK, *al-Marsad,* 22 September 1967.

9. See, for example, the remarks by Ibrahim Saba, editor of the Arabic-language Mapam organ *al-Marsad,* 17 May 1992.

10. See the remarks by Sabri Khouri, a Mapam worker in the Arab sector, *Ba-Sha'ar,* May–June 1979.

11. See the remarks by Muhammad Watad, *Al-Biyader a-Siyasi,* 5 September 1978.

12. *Davar,* 4 June 1975.

13. Interview on 29 January 1987.

14. Interview on 4 August 1991.

15. See the remarks by MK Watad, *al-Biyader a-Siyassi,* 24 January 1987.

16. Interview with MK Darawshe at the University of Haifa, 29 January 1987.

17. MK Darawshe in an interview at the University of Haifa, 29 January 1987; see also the position of MK Watad, *al-Marsad,* 2 May 1987.

18. Walid Sadik, a leading Mapam activist in the Triangle and MK, in an interview with the author, 4 August 1989; Fahd Abboud in interview with the author, 18 August 1989.

19. Founding conference of the DAP, 9 April 1988.

20. DAP Platform 1988, p. 4.

21. Interview with As'ad Azaiza, 2 July 1989, and with Ahmad Abbas, 22 July 1989.

22. Interview with Ali Hasarma, former head of the Ba'ana local council and a member of the Likud central committee, 27 July 1989.

23. See the remarks by MK Abd el-Aziz Zouabi in a Knesset debate on the activities of the ministry of police, *Divrei Ha-knesset,* 14 June 1971.

24. See the remarks by MK Seif ed-din Zouabi, *al-Anba,* 25 November 1971.

25. See the remarks by Yussuf Hamis at a national conference on relations between Jews and Arabs in Israel, held on 3–5 May 1971, national conference 1971, 27–29.

26. *al-Marsad,* 13 August 1972.

27. Interview on 29 January 1987.

28. See interview with MK Darawshe in *Kol-Bo* [Haifa], 3 April 1987.

29. See interview with MK Darawshe, *Davar,* 2 August 1985.

30. Platform of the Democratic Arab Party, 1988.

31. *Histadrut Yearbook* 1968, 270.

32. See a letter sent by Mustafa Diab, principal of the school in the Galilee village of Tamra, to Yaakov Cohen, director of the department of Arab affairs in the Histadrut, ibid., 270.

33. *al Hamishmar,* 17 February 1962.

34. See the remarks by MK Mu'adi of the Mapai satellite Israeli Druze faction, *Divrei Ha-knesset,* 12 November 1968.

35. See the remarks by MK Seif ed-din Zouabi, Zouabi 1987, 121.

36. See the remarks by Ibrahim Shbat of Mapam, the editor of *al-Marsad,* 3 May 1975.

37. See the remarks by Zahi Iskander of Mapam, *al-Marsad*, 12 June 1975.

38. See the remarks by Nawaf Massalha, *Davar*, 4 June 1975.

39. *Ha-sha'ar*, June–July 1979.

40. See the remarks by Walid Sadik, *New Outlook*, September 1978.

41. See also the remarks by Mohammed Watad, *al-Ittihad*, 8 April 1985.

42. See remarks by MK Darawshe, *Kol-Bo*, 30 April 1987.

43. See the remarks by Sabri Khouri, an Arab member of Mapam, in *al-Marsad*, 1 January 1977, and the remarks by MK Darawshe, *Davar*, 2 August 1985.

44. *Ha'aretz*, 17 June 1988.

45. See the remarks by Ismail Abu Mokh, head of the Abu Mokh clan of Baqa el-Gharbiyya and a member of Labor, *Hadashot*, 23 May 1986.

46. Interview with Assad Aziza, 2 July 1989.

47. Interview on 29 January 1987.

48. *Al-Diyar*, 30 June 1988.

49. *Ha'aretz*, 24 January 1988.

50. See remarks by Mohammed Watad, *al-Marsad*, 22 September 1976.

51. *al-Marsad*, 2 May 1978.

52. *al Hamishmar*, 1 January 1985.

53. As expressed by Nili Karkabi of Labor, the deputy chair of the organization department of Na'amat, the Histadrut woman's organization, in interview conducted on 11 August 1989; and by MK Hussein Fares of Mapam, in an interview conducted on 28 July 1989.

54. *Al Hamishmar*, 15 April 1988.

55. MK Fares in an interview on 28 July 1989.

56. See remarks by MK Mu'adi, *Divrei Ha-knesset*, 10 March 1974.

57. *Maariv*, 29 October 1986.

58. Interview on 28 July 1989; also Nili Karkabi, 11 August 1989.

59. See remarks by MK Darawshe, *Kol al-Balad*, 9 September 1988.

60. Interview on 28 July 1989.

61. Interview with Karkabi, 11 August 1989.

62. See interview with MK Darawshe and Abu Asba, *Kol al-Balad*, 9 September 1988.

63. *Ha'aretz*, 17 June 1988.

CHAPTER FOUR

1. DFPE Platform 1993, 3–10.

2. Incidentally, it is still not clear why the Communist Party changed its position on that issue, other than its desire to win the votes of the residents of those areas, most of whom were, of course, Arabs.

3. See, for example, the article by the poet Samih al-Kassem, who was a member of the Communist Party for more than thirty years, in *al-Arabi,* 8 and 19 December 1989.

4. *Divrei Ha-knesset,* 17 July 1969.

5. See the discussion initiated by Assad Kanaana, a delegate to the sixteenth Party Congress, *Proceedings of the 16th Congress* 1969, 156–159.

6. Ibid., 498.

7. See the remarks by the Communist delegate to the Histadrut convention held on 9–12 December 1969, *Eleventh Histadrut Convention* 1968: 223–225.

8. See remarks by MK Toubi in the Knesset debate on passage of the law to abrogate Ottoman laws, *Divrei Ha-knesset,* 7 November 1972.

9. *al-Ittihad,* 22 July 1975.

10. See, for example, a selection of his remarks in a special publication put out by Rakah in the wake of the Land Day events, "A Commission of Inquiry Should be Established," 30 March 1976.

11. *al-Ittihad,* 10 March 1978.

12. *Proceedings of the 20th Congress* 1985, 185.

13. *al-Ittihad,* 28 April 1985.

14. See the resolutions of the 18th Communist Party Congress, *Proceedings of the 18th Congress* 1976, 193.

15. Remarks by MK Toubi at the opening session of the National Conference of the DFPE, 5 August 1983, reported in *al-Ittihad,* 1 August 1983.

16. *al Biyader a-Siyassi,* 20 January 1986.

17. See *al-Ittihad,* 21 August 1980; *Ha'aretz,* 30 November 1980.

18. *al-Ittihad,* 22 June 1987.

19. Rakah Platform for the eighth Knesset 1973.

20. *Proceedings of the 18th Congress* 1976, 187.

21. Interview on 17 August 1989.

22. Interview on 9 August 1989.

23. Interview with MK Muhammad Nafa of Rakah, 2 March 1990.

24. See the editorial by Emile Habibi, *al-Ittihad*, 2 September 1977.

25. *Proceedings of the 19th Congress* 1981, 65.

26. Interview on 2 October 1989.

27. Ibid.

28. See remarks by MK Toubi, *Divrei Ha-knesset*, 29 October 1969.

29. See remarks by Muhammad al-Has, a delegate to the 16th Communist Party congress, *Proceedings of the 16th Congress* 1969, 221–223.

30. *al-Ittihad*, 24 March 1972.

31. See article by Salim Jubran, *Ha'aretz*, 19 April 1982.

32. *Ha'aretz*, 25 October 1982.

33. *Journal of Palestine Studies* 49 [1983], 18.

34. *Ha'aretz*, 30 November 1980.

35. See the draft resolution submitted by Rakah MK Emile Habibi on the West Bank and Gaza Strip, *Divrei Ha-knesset*, 1 August 1967.

36. See resolutions of the 16th Communist Party congress, *Proceedings of the 16th Congress* 1969, 474.

37. Remarks by Emile Touma to the 17th Party congress, *Proceedings of the 17th Congress* 1972, 122.

38. See remarks by Rakah MK Tewfiq Zayyad, *Divrei ha-knesset*, 28 January 1974.

39. See remarks by Jamaal Musa, a Rakah member of the Histadrut central committee, at the twelfth Histadrut convention, *Proceedings of the Twelfth Histadrut Convention* 1974, 12.

40. *Divrei Ha-knesset*, 10 July 1974.

41. See remarks by MK Toubi in the Knesset, *al-Ittihad*, 20 January 1976.

42. *Proceedings of the 18th Congress* 1976, 122–123, 158.

43. See remarks by Ali A'ashour, a key figure in the Communist Party, *al-Ittihad*, 3 February 1978.

44. See remarks by MK Toubi in the Knesset, *al-Ittihad*, 20 January 1976.

45. Interview with Salim Jubran, 16 January 1989.

46. See article by Salim Jubran, *al-Ittihad*, 5 December 1984.

47. See interview with Emile Touma, *Journal of Palestine Studies* 94, (1983), 22.

48. See remarks by MK Toubi in the Knesset, *Divrei Ha-knesset*, 25 March 1968; remarks by MK Habibi in the Knesset, *Divrei Ha-knesset*, 19 February 1969; and remarks by Emile Touma at the 17th Party congress, *Proceedings of the 17th Congress* 1972, 124.

49. See interview with Amir Makhoul, chairman of the national committee of Arab students, *Kol ha'Emeq ve-ha-Galil,* 20 December 1985.

50. See Resolutions of the 17th Communist Party congress, *Proceedings of the 17th Congress* 1972, 291.

51. See remarks by MK Zayyad at a meeting of Arab local council heads in solidarity with the West Bank mayors, Bassam Shaq'a and Karim Khalef, after the assassination attempt against them, *Maariv,* 8 June 1980.

52. See remarks by Emile Touma at the 17th Party congress, *Proceedings of the 17th Congress* 1972, 122.

53. "Ten Answers to Ten Questions," 1977, 10.

54. See remarks by MK Toubi in his keynote address to the 19th Party congress, *Al Hamishmar,* 20 February 1981.

55. See the article by Zahi Karkabi, an important figure in the Communist Party, *al-Mahamaz,* 19 January 1988.

56. See article by Salim Jubran, *al-Ittihad,* 18 August 1989.

57. See resolutions of the 16th congress, 1969; resolutions of the 17th congress, 1972.

58. See resolutions of the 17th Party congress, *Proceedings of the 17th Congress* 1972, 347–351.

59. *al-Ittihad,* 19 January 1989.

60. See remarks by Emile Habibi, *al-Ittihad,* 28 August 1975.

61. Interview on 16 August 1989.

62. See article by Muhammad Masarwah, a DFPE activist in Kafr Kara in the Triangle, *al-Ittihad,* 30 October 1988.

63. See article by Marwan Dwairi, a DFPE activist in Nazareth, *Sawt al Nasira* 1988, 19; and remarks by MK Toubi, *al-Ittihad,* 29 August 1980.

64. Interview with Prof. Sammy Smooha of the University of Haifa, 8 January 1987; see also remarks by MK Zayyad on the plans for a strike the Arab sector on Equality Day, 26 June 1987, *al-Ittihad,* 22 June 1987.

CHAPTER FIVE

1. See special publications by the Front: *Sawt al-Jabha,* 17 October 1959; *Nadaa al-Jabha,* 30 June 1959.

2. *al-Ittihad,* 4 July 1958.

3. See special publication by the Front, *Sabil al-Jabha,* 10 December 1958.

4. *Ala al Darb* 1984.

5. See the pamphlet put out by the Arab students' committee at the Hebrew University in 1978, when it was controlled by the Sons of the Village, *al-Tahadi* 11/1978.

6. Student Committee poster, 13 October 1983.

7. See remarks by MK Muhammad Miari of the Progressive List, *Divrei Ha-knesset*, 10 March 1987, and remarks in a one-time publication of the Sons of the Village, *al-Hawiya we-al-Jamahir* 1989, 33.

8. Interview on 30 July 1989.

9. See the one-time publication by the Sons of the Village, *al-Hawiya we-al-Ard* 1987, 33.

10. See remarks by Awwad Abd el-Fatah, an activist in the Sons of the Village, *al-Raya*, 16 October 1987.

11. See *al-Raya*, 21 August 1987.

12. *Ha'aretz*, 4 February 1980.

13. See Platform of the National Progressive Movement, 1987, 9.

14. Interview on 27 August 1989.

15. Interview on 22 September 1989.

16. Guidelines 1996, 7.

17. Ibid., 8.

18. Platform of the National Progressive Movement–Jerusalem 1987.

19. See manifesto issued by the Arab students' committee at the University of Haifa, University of Haifa 1979; a one-time publication of the National Progressive Movement at the Technion, *Ala al-Darb* 1984.

20. *al Hamishmar*, 22 February 1980.

21. See Manifesto of the National Progressive Movement at the University of Haifa 1981.

22. *al-Mahamaz*, 19 October 1988.

23. Ibid.

24. *Journal of Palestine Studies* 38 [1984], 33.

25. *al-Tadamun*, 6 June 1984.

26. Interview with MK Miari by Prof. Sammy Smooha of the University Haifa, 22 January 1987.

27. *al-Raya*, 25 December 1987.

28. Interview on 13 July 1989.

29. Guidelines 1996, 8.

30. See *al-Hawaya we-al-antama*, July 1985; see also the remarks by Ibrahim Nasser, a key activist in the Sons of the Village, *al Hamishmar*, 22 February 1980.

31. See remarks by Raja Aghabaria, the general secretary of the Sons of the Village, *Ha'aretz*, 9 March 1989.

32. National Progressive Movement 1979; remarks by the founder of the Sons of the Village, Muhammad Kawan, *Bamerhav*, 6 January 1979.

33. See manifesto of the National Progressive Movement, Haifa, 1979.

34. *al-Hawaya al-Wataniya* 1985.

35. Platform of the Progressive List for Peace for the eleventh Knesset 1984.

36. See remarks by MK Miari, *Ha'aretz*, 8 June 1984.

37. *Yedioth Ahronoth*, 29 November 1974; see also the political platform of the Sons of the Village, 15 January 1979, and the student platform of the National Progressive Movement 1987.

38. See interview with Muhammad Kewan, *Ha'aretz*, 4 February 1980.

39. See remarks by Hassan Jabarin, the official spokesman of the Umm al-Fahm branch of the Sons of the Village, *Koteret Rashit*, 15 December 1988.

40. Platform of the Progressive List for Peace, elections for the eleventh Knesset 1984.

41. See editorial in *al-Raya*, the organ of the Sons of the Village, 27 November 1987.

42. *Hadashot*, 12 February 1985.

43. Guidelines 1996, 12.

44. See a one-time publication of the Sons of the Village, *al-Hawaya al-Wataniya* 1985, 39.

45. Interview with Raja Aghabaria, 31 July 1989.

46. Interview by Prof. Sammy Smooha with MK Miari, 22 January 1987.

47. 27 August 1989.

48. National Progressive Movement, 5 July 1981.

49. See a poster distributed by the Sons of the Village before the elections for the twelfth Knesset, 28 October 1988.

50. National Progressive Movement, 5 July 1981.

51. See interview with Muhammad Kewan, *Ha'aretz*, 4 February 1980.

52. Interview on 13 July 1989; similar statements were made by Waqim Waqim in an interview on 27 August 1989.

CHAPTER SIX

1. *Ha'ir,* (Tel Aviv), 27 July 1990.

2. *Maariv,* 29 July 1988.

3. *Maariv,* 17 February 1995.

4. *Ala-Falastin,* February 1990.

5. *Ha'aretz,* 29 July 1988.

6. *Ala Falastin,* February 1990.

7. Interview with Sheikh Aasi of Acre, *Ha'aretz,* 18 May 1990.

8. Interview with Sheikh Zakur of Acre, *Tzafon Ehad,* 18 May 1990.

9. *Ha'aretz,* 17 June 1988.

10. *Ala Falastin,* February 1990.

11. *Ha'aretz,* 19 April 1991.

12. *Koteret Rashit,* 23 August 1988.

13. *Qol Ha'emeq ve-ha-Galil,* 20 March 1992.

14. *Ha'aretz,* 19 October 1990.

15. The interviews were conducted in the summer of 1989 with a representative sample of the Arab leadership in Israel. The leaders of the Islamic Movement interviewed were Sheikh Abdallah Nimr Darwish, the head of the movement; Sheikh Amar Sharara, its representative on the Nazareth city council; Sheikh Hashem Abd el-Rahman, the deputy mayor of Umm al-Fahm; Sheikh Ra'ad Salah, the mayor of Umm al-Fahm; Sheikh Kamal Rian, the head of the Kafr Bara local council; Sheikh Kamal Khatib, a prominent leader of the movement; and Mohammed Rian, the head of the Kabul local council.

16. Interview in August 1989.

17. *Koteret Rashit,* 23 August 1988; see also his remarks in the organ of the Islamic Movement, *al-Serat,* 14–15 September 1987.

18. *Davar,* 29 July 1988.

19. *Jerusalem Post,* 16 October 1987.

20. *al-Serat,* September 1986.

21. See, for example, the opinion of Sheikh Darwish in the editorial of *al-Serat,* April 1989.

22. *Davar,* 6 November 1987.

23. *al-Serat,* February 1988.

24. *Jerusalem Post,* 16 May 1989.

25. *Koteret Rashit,* 23 August 1988.

26. *Ha'aretz,* 19 May 1989.

27. *Ha'aretz,* 29 July 1988.

28. *Maariv,* 29 July 1988.

29. *Davar,* 29 July 1990.

30. *Kol Ha'ir,* (Jerusalem), 19 January 1990.

31. *Kol Ha'ir,* 19 January 1990.

32. Ibid.

33. *Maariv,* 29 July 1988.

34. *Ala Falastin,* February 1990.

35. *Ha'aretz,* 19 May 1989.

36. See interview with Sheikh Darwish, *Koteret Rashit,* 23 August 1988, and his remarks in *al-Serat,* December 1987.

37. *Ha'ir,* (Tel Aviv), 27 July 1990.

38. *Petah Tiqva,* 7 April 1989.

39. *Jerusalem Post,* 16 October 1987.

40. *Al Hamishmar,* 26 September 1986.

41. *Kol-Bo,* (BeerAlsaba'), 17 March 1989.

42. *Kol Ha'ir,* (Jerusalem), 25 March 1988.

43. Ibid., 19 January 1990.

44. Islamic Movement, 10 October 1988.

45. *Kol Ha'ir,* (Jerusalem), 19 January 1990.

46. *Tzafon Ehad,* (Acre), 18 May 1990.

47. *Davar,* 19 January 1990.

48. *Nadaa Hara,* (Kabul), n.d.

49. *Tzafon Ehad,* (Acre), 18 May 1990.

50. *Ha'aretz,* 18 May 1990.

CHAPTER SEVEN

1. See *al Ittihad,* 22 and 25 June 1987.

CHAPTER EIGHT

1. Such as the annual reports of Sikkuy, the Association for the Advancement of Equal Opportunity in Israel.

2. The survey, conducted in September–October 1995 by Prof. Sammy Smooha of the department of sociology and anthropology of the University of Haifa, with my help, queried a representative population of 1,200 Israeli Jews above age eighteen. A parallel survey was conducted of Arabs in Israel, based on 1,202 respondents above the age of eighteen. The sampling error is 3 percent. Both surveys investigated Jewish-Arab relations.

3. See *al-Diar,* 3 July 1992.

4. *Kol al-Arab,* 22 October 1993.

5. See, for example, *al-Sinara,* 1 June 1999.

6. The demand raised by few intellectuals led by Azmi Bishara and the National Democratic Alliance for transferring Israel to become the state of all its citizens does not require transferring Israel to become a binational state of Arab and Jews.

CHAPTER NINE

1. *Dievri Ha-Knesset* 1985, 3951.

2. *On the Other Side* 10 (1997), 30–32.

3. B'tzelem, data published on December 26, 1996.

References

Abd Al-Jawad, Salah. 1990. "Development of Palestinian National Struggle from Beginning of Zionist Settlement Until Partition," *Palestinian Society.* Taibe, Center for Rival of Palestinian Heritage, pp. 479–494 (Arabic).

Abu-'Asba Khaled. 1996. "Education," in A. Hareven and A. Ghanem, eds., *Equality and Integration: Retrospect and Prospects.* Jerusalem: Sikkuy, pp. 3–26.

Aburaiya, Asam. 1989. "Developmental Leadership: The Case of the Islamic Movement in Um-Alfahim, Israel." MA thesis, Clark University, Clark.

ACCHRI (The Arab Coordination Committee on Housing Rights). 1996. *Housing for All? Implementation of the Right to Adequate Housing for the Arab Palestinian Minority in Israel.* Nazareth: Arab Coordination Committee on Housing Rights.

al-Asmar, Fawsi, Ori Davis, and N. Khader. 1978. *Towards a Socialist Republic of Palestine.* London: Ithaca Press.

al-Haj, Majid. 1986. "Adjustment Patterns of the Arab Internal Refugees in Israel." *International Migration* 24:651–674.

———. 1988a. ''The Arab Internal Refugees in Israel: The Emergence a Minority within the Minority." *Immigration and Minorities* 7:149–165.

———. 1988b. "The Sociopolitical Structure of the Arabs in Israel: External versus Internal Orientation," in John E. Hofman, ed., *Arab-Jewish Relations in Israel: A Quest of Human Understanding.* Bristol, Indiana: Wyndham Hall, pp. 92–123.

———. 1988c. "Social and Cultural Aspects in the Contacts between the Palestinians on the Two Sides of the Green Line," in Arnon Sofer, ed., *Twenty Years after the Six-Day War.* Haifa: Jewish-Arab Center, University of Haifa (Hebrew).

———. 1993. "The Impact of the Intifada on the Arabs in Israel: The Case of Double Periphery," in Akiba Cohen and Gadi Wolsfeld, eds., *Framing the Intifada: Media and People.* Stamford, CT: Albex Publishing Corporation.

————. 1995a. "The Changing Strategies of Mobilization among the Arabs in Israel: Parliamentary Politics, Local Politics, and National Organization," in Efraim Ben-Zadok, ed., *Local Communities and Israeli Politics.* Albany: State University of New York Press.

————. 1995b. *Education, Empowerment, and Control: The Case of the Arabs in Israel.* Albany: State University of New York Press.

————. 1996a. "Political Organization by the Arab Population in Israel: The Development of a Center within Margins," in Baruch Knei-Paz and Moshe Lissak, eds., *Israel Toward the Year 2000.* Jerusalem: Magnes Press (Hebrew).

————. 1996b. *Education among the Palestinian Minority.* Jerusalem: Magnes Press (Hebrew).

al-Haj, Majid, and Henry Rosenfeld. 1989. "The Emergence of an Indigenous Political Framework in Israel: The National Committee of Chairmen of Arab Local Authorities." *Asian and African Studies* 24 (2–3):75–115.

————. 1990a. *Arab Local Authorities in Israel.* Institute for Arab Studies, Givat Haviva (Hebrew).

————. 1990b. *Arab Local Government in Israel.* Boulder and London: Westview Press.

al-Haj, Majid, and Avner Yaniv. 1983. "Uniformity and Diversity: A Reappraisal of the Voting Behavior of the Arab Minority in Israel," in A. Arian, ed., *The Elections in Israel in 1981.* Jerusalem: Jerusalem Academic Press.

Alpher, Joseph. 1994. *Settlements and Borders.* Tel-Aviv: Jaffee Centre for Strategic Studies.

Amitay, Yossi. 1988. *Brotherhood of Nations Being Tested: Mapam 1948– 1954: Positions on the Issue of the Arabs of Israel.* Tel Aviv: Tcherikover (Hebrew).

Arian, Asher. 1990. *Politics and Government in Israel.* Tel Aviv: Zmora-Bitan (Hebrew).

————. 1997. *Public Opening on National Security Issues. 1997.* Tel Aviv: Yaffe Center (Hebrew).

Aronson, Geoffrey. 1996. *Settlements and the Israeli-Palestinian Negotiations.* Washington: Institute of Palestine Studies.

Association for Civil Rights in Israel (ACRI). 1996. *Human Rights in Israel: A Snapshot.* Jerusalem: ACRI (Hebrew).

Avineri, Shlomo. 1995. "The Hope Will Not Die." *Ha'aretz,* 20 October (Hebrew).

————. 1998. "National Minorities in Democratic Nation-States," in Elie Rekhess, ed., *The Arabs in Israeli Politics: Dilemmas of Identity.* Tel Aviv: Dayan Center, Tel Aviv University (Hebrew).

Bader-Aref, Camilia. 1995. "The Arab Woman in Israel at the Dawn of the Twenty-first Century," in Yakov Landau, As'ad Ghanem, and Alouph Hareven, eds., *The Arab Citizens of Israel as the Dawn of the Twenty-first Century: New Middle East* 37. Jerusalem: Oriental Society and Sikkuy, pp. 213–218 (Hebrew).

Barness S. and M. Kaase (Eds.) 1979. *Political Action.* London: Sage Publications.

Beit, Berl. 1992. *The Arab Sector and the Elections for the Knesset, 1992.* Beit Berl: Center for Israeli Arab Studies (Hebrew).

Ben Dor, Gabriel. 1979. *The Druze in Israel: A Political Study.* Jerusalem: Magnes Press.

———. 1981. "Change and Continuity in the Problems of Palestinian Nationalism," in Eitan Gilboa and Mordecai Naor, eds., *The Arab-Israeli Conflict.* Tel Aviv: Ministry of Defense Publishing House, pp. 161–172 (Hebrew).

Benvenisti, Meron. 1988. *Slingshot and Baton: West Bank and Gaza Strip, Jews and Arabs.* Jerusalem: Keter (Hebrew).

Benziman, Uzi, and Atallah Mansour. 1992. *Sub-Tenants, the Arabs of Israel: Their Status and the Policies towards Them.* Jerusalem: Keter (Hebrew).

Bishara, Azmi. 1995. "The Israeli Arab: Reading an Incomplete Discourse," *Majalat al-Dirasat al-Falastinia* 24:26-54 (Arabic).

B'tselem (Israel Information Center for Human Rights in the West Bank and Gaza Strip). 1995. *A Policy of Discrimination: Land Expropriation, Planning, and Construction in East Jerusalem.* Jerusalem: B'tselem (Hebrew).

Burton, John. 1990. *Conflict: Human Needs Theory.* New York: St. Martin's Press.

Carmi, Ghada. 1997. "One Land and Two Peoples." *Ha'aretz* 9 (7) (Hebrew).

Cayman, Charles. 1984. "After the Catastrophe: The Arabs in the State of Israel 1948–1950." *Notebooks for Research and Criticism* 10 (Hebrew).

Central Bureau of Statistics. 1994. *Statistical Abstract of Israel, No. 39.* Jerusalem: Central Bureau of Statistics (Hebrew).

———. 1997. *Statistical Abstract of Israel, No. 42.* Jerusalem: Central Bureau of Statistics (Hebrew).

Cohen, Raanan. 1985. "Process of Political Organization and Voting Patterns of the Palestinian Minority." M.A. thesis, Faculty of Humanities, Tel Aviv University (Hebrew).

———. 1989. "Political Development of the Palestinian Minority as Reflected in Their Voting in Eleven Knesset Elections, 1948–1984." Ph.D. dissertation. Tel Aviv University (Hebrew).

———. 1990. *In the Thicket of Loyalties: Society and Politics in the Arab Sector.* Tel Aviv: Am Oved (Hebrew).

EEP, Frante. 1976. *The Palestinians: Portrait of a People in Conflict*. Scottdale, PA: Herald Press.

Elazar, Daniel. 1987. "The Local Dimension of Government and Politics in Israel," in Daniel Elazar and Haim Kalcheim, eds., *Local Government in Israel*. Jerusalem (Hebrew).

Falah, Ghazi. 1990. "Arabs versus Jews in Galilee Competition for Regional Resources." *Geojournal* 21 (4):325–336.

Fares, Amin. 1996. *Poverty in Arab Society in Israel*. Beit Berl: Institute for Israeli Arab Studies (Hebrew).

Fenster, Toby. 1993. *The Bedouin in Israel*. Sikkuy: Jerusalem (Hebrew).

Fien, H. 1993. *Genocide: A Sociological Perspective*. London: Sage Publications.

Friedrich, C. J. 1963. *Man and His Government: An Empirical Theory of Politics*. New York: McGraw-Hill.

Ghanem, As'ad. 1990. "Ideological Trends on Question of Jewish-Arab Co-existence among Arabs in Israel: 1967–1989." M.A. thesis, Department of Political Science, University of Haifa (Hebrew).

———. 1991. "The Popular Arab Front and the Struggle against Land Expropriation." *Qadaya* 3: 50–58 (Arabic).

———. 1992a. "How the Islamic Movement in Israel Views Peace in the Region," in I. Pappe, ed., *Islam and Peace: Islamic Approaches to Peace in the Contemporary Arab World*. Givat Haviva: Institute for Peace Research, pp. 83–99 (Hebrew).

———. 1992b. "The Arabs in Israel in Advance of the Elections for the Thirteenth Knesset." *Surveys of the Arabs in Israel* 8. Givat Haviva: Institute for Peace Research (Hebrew).

———. 1993. *The Arabs in Israel on the Dawn of the Twenty-first Century: Base-Position Survey*. Givat Haviva: Institute for Peace Research (Hebrew).

———. 1994. "The Rise and Fall of the Israel Communist Party (Maki), a Discussion of the Causes," *Studies in the Rebirth of Israel* 4:549–555. Beer Sheva: Ben-Gurion Heritage Center, Ben-Gurion University of the Negev (Hebrew).

———. 1996a. "Political Participation among Arabs in Israel." Doctoral dissertation, Department of Political Science, University of Haifa (Hebrew).

———. 1996b. "Palestinians in Israel, Part of the Problem and Not of the Solution: Their Status in Peace Era." *State, Government and International Relations* 41/42:123–154 (Hebrew).

———. 1996c. *Comparative Statistics on Arabs and Jews in Israel*. Jerusalem: Sikkuy (Hebrew).

————. 1996d. "Limits of the Arabs' Influence on the Political System In Israel." *al-Siyasa al-Falastinia* 9:20–38 (Arabic).

————. 1998a. "State and Minority in Israel: The Case of the Ethnic State and the Predicament of Its Minority." *Ethnic and Racial Studies* 21 (3):428–448.

————. 1998b. "The Limits of Parliamentary Politics: The Arab Minority in Israel and the 1992 and 1996 Elections." *Israeli Affairs* 4 (2):72–93.

————. 1998c. "One Problem, One Solution." *al-Ahram Weekly* 23–29 July.

Ghanem, As'ad, and Sara Ozacky-Lazar. 1990. "The Green Line—Red Lines, the Arabs in Israel in View of the Intifada." *Skirot* 2, Institute for Peace Research: Giv'at Haviva (Hebrew).

————. 1993. "The Perception of Peace by Arabs in Israel." *Skirot* 11, Institute for Peace Research: Giv'at Haviva (Hebrew).

————. 1994. "The Arab Local Authority Elections of November 1993: Results and Analysis." *Skirot* 13. Givat Haviva: Institute for Peace Research (Hebrew).

————. 1997. "The Arab Vote in the Elections to the 14th Knesset, 29 May 1996." Tel Aviv University, Moshe Dayan Center for Middle East and African Studies, Program on Arab Politics in Israel: Tel Aviv.

————. 1999. "The Arab Vote to the Fifthteenth Knesset." *Skirot* 24, Institute for Peace Research: Giv'at Haviva (Hebrew).

Ghanem, As'ad, Nadim Rouhana, and Oren Yiftachel. 1998. "Questioning 'Ethnic Democracy.'" *Israel Studies* 3 (2).

Giffner (Kubersky), Ellen. 1974. "An Israeli-Arab View of Israel." *Jewish Social Studies* 36:134–141.

Gorny, Yosef. 1985. *The Arab Question and the Jewish Problem.* Tel Aviv: Am Oved (Hebrew).

Gresh, Alan. 1985. *The PLO: The Struggle Within.* London: Zed Books.

Gurr, Ted Robert. 1993. *Minorities at Risk: A Global View of Ethnopolitical Conflict.* Washington: U.S. Institute of Peace Press.

Gurr, Ted Robert, and Barbara Harff. 1994. *Ethnic Conflict in World Politics.* Boulder and San Francisco: Westview Press.

Haider, Aziz. 1985. *Technical Education in the Arab Sector in Israel.* Tel Aviv. International Center for Middle East Peace (Hebrew).

Haider, Aziz. 1988. "The Different Levels of Palestinian Ethnicity," in Milton Esman and Itamar Rabinovich, eds., *Ethnicity: Pluralism and the State in the Middle East.* Ithaca and London: Cornell University Press, pp. 95–120.

————. 1991a. *The Arab Population in the Israeli Economy.* Tel Aviv: International Center for Middle East Peace (Hebrew).

————. 1991b. *Needs and Welfare Services in Arab Sector in Israel*. Tel Aviv: International Center for Middle East Peace (Hebrew).

Hareven, Alouph, ed. 1993. *Equality and Integration: Annual Report on Progress*. Jerusalem: Sikkuy (Hebrew).

————, ed. 1994. *Equality and Integration: Annual Report on Progress*. Jerusalem: Sikkuy (Hebrew).

————, ed. 1995. *Equality and Integration: Annual Report on Progress for 1994–1995*. Jerusalem: Sikkuy (Hebrew).

Hareven, Alouph, and As'ad Ghanem, eds. 1996a. *Equality and Integration: Annual Report on Progress, 1994–1995*. Jerusalem: Sikkuy (Hebrew).

————, eds. 1996b. *Equality and Integration: Retrospect and Prospects*. Jerusalem: Sikkuy.

Harkaby, Yehoshafat, ed. 1975, "Decisions of the Palestinian National Council," in *The Arabs and Israel* (3–4). Jerusalem: Am Oved and Hebrew University (Hebrew).

Honig-Barnas, Tikva. 1997. "Bi-Nationalism versus the Secular-Democratic State." *News Within*, 13 (3): 26–29.

Horowitz, Donald. 1985. *Ethnic Groups in Conflict*. Berkeley: University of California Press.

Israeli, Raphael. 1990. *The Charter of Allah: The Platform of the Islamic Resistance Movement (Hamas)*. Jerusalem: Truman Institute.

Jaffa. 1990. *Catalogue of Arab Voluntary Organizations in Israel*. Jaffa: Jaffa Research Institute (Arabic).

Jarar, Najah. 1994. *The Palestinian Refugees*. Jerusalem: Palestinian Academy for International Affairs (Arabic).

Jeryis, Sabri. 1966. *The Arabs in Israel*. Haifa, Al-Ittihad (Arabic).

————. 1973. *The Arabs in Israel*. Beirut: Institute for Palestinian Studies (Arabic).

JMCC (Jerusalem Media and Communication Centre). 1997. *Signed, Sealed, Delivered: Israeli Settlements and the Peace Process*. Jerusalem: JMCC.

Jonassohn, K., and F. Chalk. 1987. "A Typology of Genocide and Some Implications for the Human Rights Agenda," in I. Wallimann and M. Dubkowski, eds., *Genocide and the Modern Age*. New York: Greenwood Press, pp. 3–20.

Kanaana, Sharif. 1976. *Channels of Communication and Mutual Images between the West Bank and Areas in Israel*. Bir Zeit: Bir Zeit University.

Kendrick, Frank, Theodore Fleming, James Eisenstein, and James Burkhart. 1974. *Strategies for Political Participation*. Cambridge: Winthrop Publishers.

Keane, John. 1988. *Civil Society and the State*. New York: Verso.

Khalidi, Raja. 1988. *The Arab Economy in Israel*. London: Cromm Helm.

Khamaissi, Rassem. 1990. *Planning and Housing among Arabs in Israel*. Tel Aviv: International Center for Middle East Peace (Hebrew).

Klein, Claude. 1987. "Israel as a Nation-State and the Problem of the Arab Minority: In Search of a Status" (mimeographed). Tel Aviv: International Center for Peace in the Middle East.

Kook, R. 1995. "Dilemmas of Ethnic Minorities in Democracies: The Effect of Peace on the Palestinians in Israel." *Politics and Society* 23 (3):309–33.

Kretzmer, D. 1990. *The Legal Status of the Arabs in Israel*. Boulder: Westview Press.

———. 1992. "Israel as Jewish State and State Security and Its Influence upon the Status of Israel's Arabs," in T. Ben-Gal et al., eds., *Human and Civil Rights in Israel: Readings*, pp. 174–180. Jerusalem: Association for Civil Rights in Israel (Hebrew).

Kuper, Leo. 1971. *Race, Class, and Power: Ideology and Revolutionary Change*. London: Duckworth.

———. 1977. *The Pity of It All: Polarization of Racial and Ethnic Relations*. Minneapolis: University of Minnesota Press.

Kymlicka Will. 1995. *Multicultural Citizenship*. New York: Oxford University Press.

Landau, Yaakov. 1971. *The Arabs in Israel: Political Studies*. Tel Aviv: Maarachot (Hebrew).

———. 1981. "Estrangement and Tensions in Political Behavior," in Aharon Lish, ed., *The Arabs in Israel: Continuity and Change*. Jerusalem: Magnes Press, pp. 197–212 (Hebrew).

———, ed. 1989. *The Arab Sector in Israel and the Knesset Elections, 1988*. Jerusalem: Jerusalem Institute for Israel Studies (Hebrew).

———. 1993. *The Arab Minority in Israel: Political Aspects*. Tel Aviv: Maarachot (Hebrew).

Lijphart, Arend. 1977. *Democracy in Plural Societies*. New Haven: Yale University Press.

———. 1984. *Democracies*. New Haven: Yale University Press.

———. 1999. Patterns of *Democracy*. New Haven and London: Yale University Press.

Lustick, Ian. 1979. "Stability in Deeply Divided Societies: Consociationalism versus Control." *World Politics* 31:325–344.

————. 1980. *Arabs in the Jewish State: Israel's Control of a National Minority.* Austin: University of Texas Press.

————. 1985. *Arabs in the Jewish State: Israel's Rule over a National Minority.* Haifa: Mifras (Hebrew).

————. 1987a. "Israeli State-Building in the West Bank and the Gaza Strip: Theory and Practice." *International Organization* 41 (I):151–171.

————. 1987b. "The Political Road to Binationalism: Arabs in Jewish Politics," in Ofira Selictar and Ian Peleg, eds., *The Emergence of a Binational Israel: The Second Republic in the Making.* London and Boulder: Westview Press, pp. 97–123.

————. 1988. "Creeping Binationalism within the Green Line." *New Outlook* 31 (7): 14–19.

Malik, Abrahem. 1990. "The Islamic Movement in Israel." *Skirot* 4. Givat Haviva: Institute for Peace Research (Hebrew).

Mansour, Attalah. 1993. *Arab Personalities in Israel.* Jerusalem: Sikkuy (Hebrew).

Maynes, C. 1993. "Containing Ethnic Conflict." *Foreign Policy* 90:3–21.

Meir, Thomas. 1989. "Young Muslims in Israel." *The New East: Special Issue on the Arabs in Israel, between Religion and National Awakening.* Jerusalem: Magnes Press, pp. 10–21 (Hebrew).

Morris, Benny. 1989. *The Birth of the Palestinian Refugee Problem, 1947–1949.* Tel Aviv: Am Oved (Hebrew).

Mourkous, Nimr, ed. n.d. *Yanni Qustandi Yanni, 1895–1962.* Kafr Yassif: Local Authority (Arabic).

Muslih, Muhammad. 1993. "Palestinian Civil Society." *Middle East Journal* 47 (2):258–274.

Nakhlih, Khalil. 1975a. "The Direction of Local-level Conflict in Two Arab Villages in Israel." *American Ethnologist* 23:497–516.

————. 1975b. "Cultural Determinants of Palestinian Collective Identity: The Case of the Arabs in Israel." *New Outlook* 18 (7):31-40.

————. 1977. "The Goals of Education for Arabs in Israel." *New Outlook* (April-May):29–35.

————. 1979. *Palestinian Dilemma: National Consciousness and University Education in Israel.* Belmont, MA: Association of Arab-American University Graduates.

————. 1982. "The Two Galilees." *Arab World Issues, Occasional Papers* 7 (September).

———. 1990. *The Voluntary Organizations in Palestine*. Jerusalem: Arab Thought Center (Arabic).

Ozacky-Lazar, Sarah. 1990. "Positions of the Palestinian Minority towards the State, 1949–1967." M.A. thesis, Department of Middle Eastern History, University of Haifa (Hebrew).

———. 1992. "The Elections for the Thirteenth Knesset among the Arabs in Israel." *Skirot 9*. Givat Haviva: Institute for Peace Research (Hebrew).

Ozacky-Lazar, Sarah, and As'ad Ghanem. 1990. "Autonomy for Arabs in Israel: A Preliminary Discussion," *Skirot 4*, Institute for Peace Research, Giv'at Haviva (Hebrew).

———. 1995. "Between Peace and Equality: The Arabs in Israel under the Labor-Meretz Government." *Skirot 16*. Givat Haviva: Institute for Peace Research (Hebrew).

———. 1996. "The Arab Vote in the Elections for the Fourteenth Knesset." *Skirot 16*. Givat Haviva: Institute for Peace Research (Hebrew).

Paz, Reuven. 1989. *The Islamic Movement in Israel in the Wake of the Local Elections*. Tel Aviv: Dayan Center (Hebrew).

———. 1990. "The Islamic Movement in Israel and the Municipal Elections of 1989." *Jerusalem Quarterly*, 53.

Peled, Yoav. 1992. "Ethnic Democracy and the Legal Construction of Citizenship: Arab Citizens of the Jewish State." *American Political Science Review* 86 (2):432-443.

———. 1993. "Strangers in Utopia: The Civil Status of the Palestinians in Israel." *Theory and Criticism* 3 (winter):21–38 (Hebrew).

Peres, Yochanan. 1970. "Modernization and Nationalism in the Identity of the Palestinian Minority." *Middle East Journal* 24:479–492.

Peres, Yochanan, and Nira Yuval-Davis. 1968. "On the National Identity of the Palestinian Minority." *New East* 18 (1–2):106–111 (Hebrew).

———. 1969. "Some Observations on the National Identity of the Palestinian Minority." *Human Relations* 22:219–233.

Porat, Yehoshua. 1976. *The Growth of the Palestinian Arab Nationalist Movement, 1918–1929*. Tel Aviv: Am Oved.

———. 1978. *From Resistance to Revolt, the Palestinian National Movement, 1929–1939*. Tel Aviv: Am Oved (Hebrew).

Qahwaji, Habib. 1972. *The Arabs in the Shadow of the Israeli Occupation since 1948*. Beirut: Research Center of the Palestine Liberation Organization (Arabic).

Reiss, Nerra. 1991. *The Health Care of the Arabs in Israel.* Boulder: Westview Press.

Reiter, Yitzhak. 1989. "The Ideological and Political Structure," in Rami Hochman, ed., *Jews and Arabs in Israel.* Jerusalem: Hebrew University (Hebrew).

Reiter, Yitzhak, and Reuven Aharoni. 1992. *The Political World of the Palestinian Minority.* Beit Berl: Institute for Israeli Arab Studies (Hebrew).

Rekhess, Elie. 1976. "The Palestinian Minority after 1967: The Development of the Problem of Orientation." *Surveys* 1. Tel Aviv: Shiloah Institute (Hebrew).

————. 1977. "The Palestinian Minority and Land Expropriation in the Galilee: Background, Incidents, and Implications, 1975–1977." *Surveys* 53. Tel Aviv: Shiloah Institute (Hebrew).

————. 1985. *The Arab Village in Israel: A Renewing National and Political Center.* Tel Aviv: Dayan Center (Hebrew).

————. 1986. "Between Communism and Arab Nationalism: Rakah and the Arab Minority in Israel, 1965–1973." Ph.D. dissertation, Tel Aviv University (Hebrew).

————. 1988. "First Steps in the Crystallization of Israeli Policy toward the Palestinian Minority." *Monthly Review* 34 (11):33–36 (Hebrew).

————. 1989a. "The Palestinian Minority and the Arabs of the West Bank and Gaza: Political Affinity and National Solidarity." *Asian and African Studies* 23:119–154.

————. 1989b. "The Arabs in Israel and the Arabs in the West Bank and Gaza Strip: Political Affinity and National Solidarity, 1967–1988," in Aharon Lish, ed., *The New East: Special Issue on the Arabs in Israel, between Religion and National Awakening.* Jerusalem: Magnes Press, pp. 165–191 (Hebrew).

————. 1993. *The Arab Minority in Israel between Communism and Arab Nationalism.* Tel Aviv: Hakibbutz Hameuchad (Hebrew).

Rosenhak, Zeev. 1996. *Housing Policies and Arabs in Israel, 1948–1977.* Jerusalem: Floersheimer Institute for Political Research (Hebrew).

Rouhana, Nadim. 1986. "Collective Identity and Arab Voting Patterns," in Asher Arian and Michal Shamir, eds., *The Elections in Israel 1984.* Tel-Aviv: Ramot Publishing, pp. 121–145.

————. 1988. "The Civic and National Subidentities of the Arabs in Israel: A Psycho-Political Approach," in John E. Hofman, ed., *Arab-Jewish Relations in Israel: A Quest of Human Understanding.* Bristol, Indiana: Wyndham Hall, pp. 123–154.

————. 1989. "The Political Transformation of the Palestinians in Israel: From Acquiescence to Challenge." *Journal of Palestine Studies* 18 (3):35–59.

————. 1993. "Accentuated Identities in Protracted Conflicts: The Collective Identity of the Palestinian Citizens in Israel." *Asian and African Studies* 27:97–127.

————. 1997. *Identities in Conflict: Palestinian Citizens in an Ethnic Jewish State.* New Haven: Yale University Press.

Rouhana, Nadim, and As'ad Ghanem. 1993. "The Democratization of a Traditional Minority in an Ethnic Democracy: The Palestinians in Israel," in Edy Kaufman, S. Abed, and R. Rothstein, eds., *Democracy, Peace, and the Israeli-Palestinian Conflict.* Boulder and London: Lynne Rienner, pp. 163–188.

————. 1998. "The Crisis of Minorities in an Ethnic State: The Case of the Palestinian Citizens in Israel." *IJMES* 30 (3): 321–346.

Seliger, H. 1976. *Ideology and Politics.* New York: Free Press.

Seligman, Adam. 1992. *The Idea of Civil Society.* New York: Macmillan.

Shabi, Aviva, and Roni Shaked. 1994. *Hamas: From Faith in Allah to the Path of Terrorism.* Jerusalem: Keter (Hebrew).

Sharabi, Hisham. 1981. *Salih Baransi: The Silent Struggle.* Bierut: Dar Al-Talea (Arabic).

Shils, Edward. 1991. "The Virtue of Civil Society." *Government and Opposition* 26 (2):3–20.

Sikkuy (the association for advancement of equal opportunity). 1996. *The Socioeconomic Level of Jewish and Arab Communities in Israel: A Comparative Data.* Sikkuy: Jerusalem (Hebrew).

Smith, Pamela Ann. 1984. *Palestine and the Palestinians, 1876–1983.* New York: St. Martin's Press.

Smooha, Sammy. 1975. "Pluralism and Conflict: A Theoretical Exploration." *Plural Societies* 6:69–89.

————. 1980a. "Control of Minorities in Israel and Northern Ireland." *Comparative Studies in Society and History* 22:256–280.

————. 1980b. "Existing Policy and Alternatives towards the Arabs in Israel." *Megamot* 1 (Hebrew).

————. 1983. "Minority Responses in a Plural Society: A Typology of the Arabs in Israel." *Sociology and Social Research* 67 (4): 436–456.

————. 1984a. *The Orientation and Politicization of the Arab Minority in Israel.* Haifa: University of Haifa.

————. 1984b. *Social Research on Arabs in Israel, 1977–1982: A Bibliography.* Haifa: Jewish-Arab Center, University of Haifa.

————. 1987. "Four Models and One More." *Politika,* 61–63 (Hebrew).

————. 1988. "Comparison of the Palestinians in the West Bank and Gaza Strip and in Israel as a Test of the Thesis of Irreversible Creeping Annexation," in Arnon Sofer, ed., *Twenty Years after the Six-Day War.* Haifa: Jewish-Arab Center, University of Haifa (Hebrew).

————. 1989a. *Arabs and Jews in Israel: Vol. 1.* Boulder and London: Westview Press.

————. 1989b. "The Arab Minority in Israel: Radicalization or Politicization," in Peter Medding, ed., *Israel: State and Society.* Oxford: Oxford University Press, pp. 59–88.

————. 1990a. "Minority Status in an Ethnic Democracy: The Status of the Arab Minority in Israel." *Ethnic and Racial Studies* 13 (3):389–413.

————. 1990b. "Israeli Options for Handing the Palestinians in the West Bank and Gaza Strip," in Pierre Van Den Berghe, ed., *State, Violence, and Ethnicity.* Niwot: University of Colorado, pp. 143–186.

————. 1991. "The Divergent Fate of the Palestinians on Both Sides of the Green Line: The Intifada as a Test." Paper presented to the conference, "The Arab Minority in Israel: Dilemmas of Political Orientation and Social Change." Tel-Aviv University, June 3–4.

————. 1992. *Jews and Arabs in Israel: Vol. 2.* Boulder and London: Westview Press.

————. 1993. "Class, Ethnic, and National Schisms and Democracy in Israel," in Uri Ram, ed., *Israeli Society: Critical Aspects.* Tel Aviv: Berirot (Hebrew).

————. 1996. "Ethnic Democracy: Israel as an Archetype." *Studies in the Rebirth of Israel* 6:277–311 (Hebrew).

————. 1997. *Coexistence between Arabs and Jews in Israel: Attitude Change during the Transition to Peace. Research Report.* Haifa: University of Haifa, Department of Sociology and Anthropology.

————. 1998. "Ethnic Democracy: Israel as an Archetype." *Israel Studies* 3 (2):198–241.

Smooha, Sammy, and Ora Cibulski. 1987. *Social Research on Arabs in Israel, 1948–1976: Trends and Annotated Bibliography.* Haifa: Jewish-Arab Center, University of Haifa.

Smooha, Sammy, and Theodor Hanf. 1992. "The Diverse Modes of Conflict-Regulation in Deeply Divided Societies." *International Journal of Comparative Sociology* 33 (1–2):26–47.

Smooha, Sammy, and Don Peretz. 1993. "Israel's 1992 Elections: Are They Critical?" *Middle East Journal* 47 (3):444–463.

Tamari, Salem. 1996. "Palestinian Refugee Negotiations from Madrid to Oslo II." Washington: Institute for Palestine Studies.

Touma, Emile. 1982. *The Path of Struggle of the Arab Masses in Israel.* Acre: al-Aswar (Arabic).

Vos, Louis. 1996. "Nationalism, Democracy, and the Belgian State," in Richard Caplan and John Fefer, eds., *Europe's New Nationalism.* Oxford: Oxford University Press, pp. 55–100.

Walzer, Michael. 1991. "The Idea of Civil Society." *Dissent* 38 (2):293–304.

Yiftachel, Oren. 1992. "Debate: The Concept of 'Ethnic Democracy' and Its Application to the Case of Israel." *Ethnic and Racial Studies* 15 (1):125–136.

————. 1993a. "Model of 'Ethnic Democracy' and Jewish-Arab Relations in Israel: Geographical, Historical and Political Aspects." *Horizons in Geography* 37–38: 51–59 (Hebrew).

————. 1993b. "Research on the Arab Minority in Israel and Its Relations with the Jewish Majority: Survey and Analysis." *Skirot* 12. Givat Haviva: Institute for Peace Research (Hebrew).

————. 1994a. "Spatial Planning, Land Control, and Jewish Arab Relations in Galilee." *City and Region* 23: 55–98 (Hebrew).

————. 1994b. "The Evolution of Ethnic Regional Protest: Palestinian-Arabs in the Galilee, Israel" (mimeographed). Beer Sheva: Department of Geography, Ben-Gurion University of the Negev.

————. 1996. "The Internal Frontier: Territorial Control and Ethnic Relations in Israel." *Regional Studies* 36 (5): 493–508.

————. 1997a. "Israeli Society and Jewish-Palestinian Reconciliation: 'Ethnocracy' and Its Contradictions." *Middle East Journal* 51 (4):505–519.

————. 1997b. *Guarding the Vineyard, Majd Al-Kurum as a Parable.* Beit Berl: Institute for Israeli Arab Studies (Hebrew).

Zakarya, Christina. 1997. "The Palestinian Authority in Numbers. A Call for a Census of the Palestinian People." *Palestinian Studies* 3. Givat Haviva: Institute for Peace Research (Hebrew).

Zaretsky-Toledano, Edna. 1989. "Positions of the Jewish Leadership in Israel vis-à-vis the Arab Citizen." M.A. thesis, Faculty of Social Sciences and Mathematics, University of Haifa (Hebrew).

Ziedan, Elias, and As'ad Ghanem. 2000. *Charity and Voluntarism among the Arab-Palestinian Society in Israel.* BeerSheba: Israel Center for Third Sector Research.

Zouabi, Anaam, ed. 1987. *Seaf Al-Dean Al-Zouabi: Personal Witness and Memories.* Shefa'amre: Dar Al-Mashreq (Arabic).

Zureik, Elia. 1979. *The Palestinians in Israel: A Study in Internal Colonialism.* London: Routledge and Kegan Paul.

———. 1997. *The Palestinian Refugees and the Peace Process.* Beirut: Institute for Palestinian Studies (Arabic).

Index